300

BEST SELLING
HOME PLANS

$3 \frac{98}{8/96}$

One-Level Living with a Twist

No. 20083

Here's an inviting home with a distinctive difference. Active living areas are wide-open and centrally located. From the foyer, you'll enjoy a full
view of the spacious dining, living, and kitchen
areas in one sweeping glance. You can even see the
deck adjoining the breakfast room. The difference
in this house lies in the bedrooms. Each is a private
retreat, away from active areas. The master suite
at the rear of the house features a full bath with
double sinks. Two additional bedrooms, off in their
own wing, share a full bath and the quiet atmosphere that results from intelligent design.

First floor — 1,575 sq. ft.
Basement — 1,575 sq. ft.
Garage — 475 sq. ft.

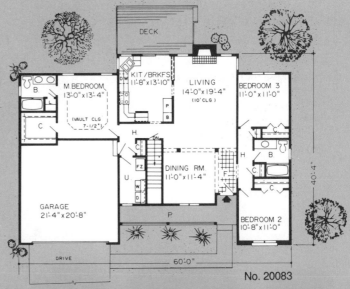

No. 20083

Contemporary Floor Plan Nicely Blended With Distinctive Exterior

No. 10500

Lots of living is packed into this well organized design with its first floor great room which is accented by a massive fireplace and beamed, cathedral ceiling. A doubly inviting kitchen and breakfast room are divided by an angled cooking center. The formal dining room is readily accessible for gracious entertaining. The first floor master bedroom suite includes a luxurious five-piece bath complete with tile shower enclosure and a raised tile tub. Three more bedrooms and a loft, which overlooks the foyer, are located on the second floor. Each bedroom has its own walk-in closet and direct access to a full bath.

First floor - 2188 sq. ft.
Second floor - 1083 sq. ft.
Garage - 576 sq. ft.
Basement - 2188 sq. ft.

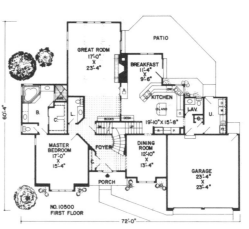

Unique Floor Plan Accommodates Larger Family

No. 10545

This four-bedroom beauty offers all you could want in a larger house and more. Three of the bedrooms and the dining areas are located on the upper floor, with the primary living areas on the lower floor. The family room has a fireplace and sloped ceiling. A bedroom and full bath on the lower floor provide privacy for guests.

Main level - 2162 sq. ft.
Dormer level - 722 sq. ft.
Basement - 1385 sq. ft.
Garage - 858 sq. ft.

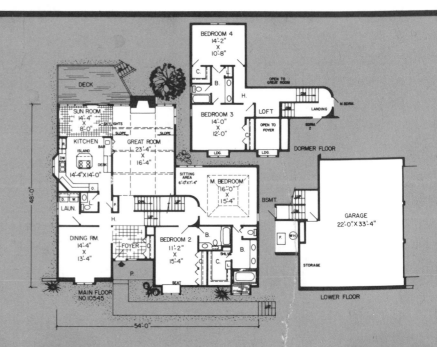

Covered Drive and Entrance Add Touch of Elegance to Spanish Ranch

No. 10536

An impressive covered entry leading to the tiled foyer highlights the luxury of this four-bedroom home. Two patios offer ample space for outdoor entertaining. Adjacent to a roomy kitchen with the convenience of an island and plenty of cabinet space, is the hearth room which doubles as an informal dining area and family room. Additional family living spaces are incorporated into the large great room and the formal dining room with its built-in hutch and corner china cabinet. Each of the four bedrooms has a private bath. A scenic garden court divides bedrooms three and four.

First floor-3972 sq. ft.
Basement-3972 sq. ft.
Garage-924 sq. ft.

HEARTH ROOM 15'-4" X 13'-0"

KITCHEN 14'-6" X 16'-0"

GREAT ROOM 19'-0" X 27'-4"

PATIO

LIBRARY 13'-10" X 13'-4"

CLO. BATH CLO.

3-CAR GARAGE 25'-4" X 33'-4"

LAUND.

FORMAL DINING 13'-0" X 17'-4"

FOYER

MASTER BEDROOM 16'-6" X 17'-4"

BEDROOM #4 13'-0" X 13'-2"

BEDROOM #3 13'-0" X 13'-2"

COVERED ENTRY

GARDEN COURT

BEDROOM #2 15'-0" X 13'-4"

108'-8"

COVERED DRIVEWAY

NO. 10536

FLOOR PLAN

Lots Of Living Space In Compact Plans

No. 10502

This three bedroom home, with its interesting exterior roof lines, opens to a well designed family
floor plan. Two bedrooms are separated on the
second level while the master suite is secluded on
the first floor. The master suite includes a five-
piece bath with double vanity plus a full-wall
closet. The remainder of the first floor encompasses a spacious living room complete with
sloped ceiling, a hearthed fireplace and double
windows. The dining room enlarges the living
room and adjoins the U-shaped kitchen which is
separated from the sunny breakfast room by a
bar. The deck area provides a lovely area for
outdoor family gatherings.

First floor-1,172 sq. ft.
Second floor-482 sq. ft.
Garage-483 sq. ft.

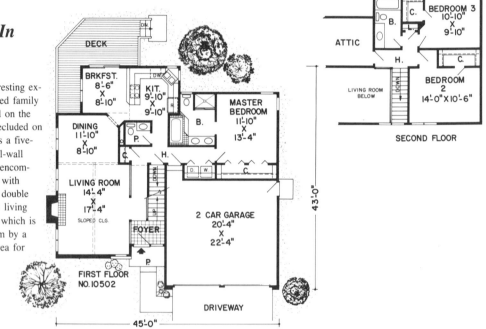

Four-Bedroom Has Luxury Master Suite Plus Guest Room

No. 10510

Three of this home's four bedrooms are located on
the second floor with the fourth on the first floor
with its own private bath. Its an ideal arrangement
for the multi-generation family. The second floor
master suite is large and luxurious with a private
deck, double vanity in the dressing area that includes a walk-in closet, plus a master bath which
has both a shower and a round tub. Two more bedrooms and a bath complete the upper story. The
large, first floor family room has a fully appointed
bar area, a fireplace, and access to the patio. The
breakfast nook overlooks the family room and adjoins the efficiently designed kitchen.

First floor — 1485 sq. ft.
Second floor — 958 sq. ft.
Garage — 723 sq. ft.

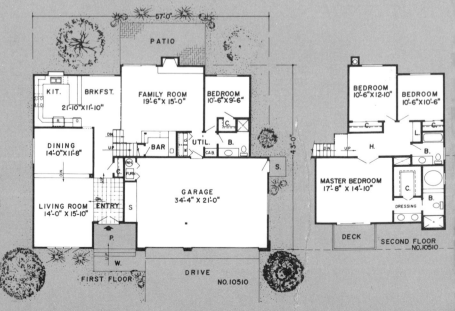

4

Compact Two-Story Design
Ideal for Small Lot

No. 10517

On the second floor of this well-arranged home are two bedrooms which flank a bath that is illuminated by a skylight. Adjacent to the bath are individual dressing areas each with its own basin and large walk-in closet. The interesting angles incorporated into the plan of the first floor create extra space in the master suite. The living room has a sloped ceiling and a fireplace with tile hearth. The angular kitchen includes a pantry, space for a dinette set and direct access to the rear deck. Other features include a half bath on the first floor, a conveniently located laundry, and an inviting two-story foyer.

First floor — 1171 sq. ft.
Second floor — 561 sq. ft.
Basement — 1171 sq. ft.
Garage 484 sq. ft.

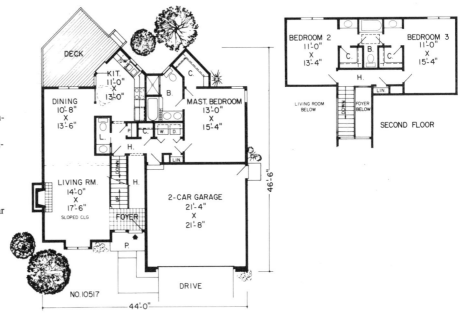

Bump-Out Windows Add Light and Space

No. 20108

Shutters, round-cut shingles, and an attractive railed porch lend classic charm to this three-bedroom home. But this traditional exterior houses an open, updated interior designed for privacy and convenience. A central entry leads three ways: into the formal living room, past the open stairs to a huge, sunny family room crowned by a fireplace, and down an L-shaped hall to the bedroom wing, which includes two full baths. Notice the elegant ceiling treatment and room-size walk-in closet in the master suite. The kitchen is a gourmet's dream, with its range-top island, bump-out window perfect for an indoor herb garden, and strategic location between family and dining rooms.

Main living area — 2,120 sq. ft.
Basement — 2,120 sq. ft.
Garage — 576 sq. ft.

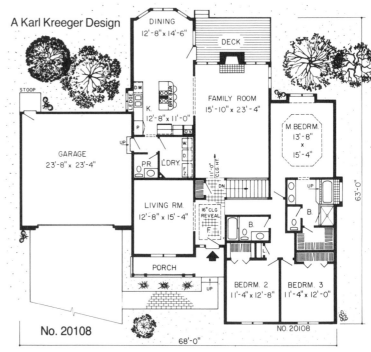

A Karl Kreeger Design

No. 20108

Elegant Design Offers Special Living

No. 10521

This well-crafted design features four bedrooms, three baths and a balcony overlooking the two-story foyer. The master suite includes a five-piece bath, an oversized walk-in closet and a separate linen closet. The kitchen has a breakfast nook and includes both a desk and pantry. The formal living room with fireplace has direct access to the rear deck.

First floor — 1,191 sq. ft.
Second floor — 699 sq. ft.
Basement — 1,191 sq.ft.
Garage — 454 sq. ft.

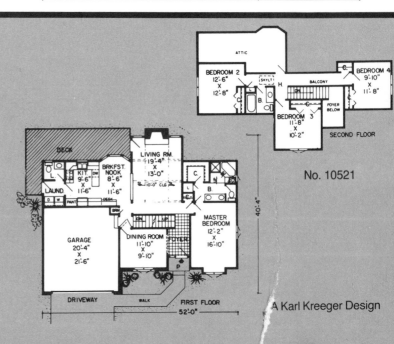

No. 10521

A Karl Kreeger Design

Open Plan Accented by Loft, Windows and Decks

No. 10515

The first floor living space of this inviting home blends the family room and dining room for comfortable family living. The large kitchen shares a preparation/eating bar with the dining room. The ample utility room is designed with a pantry plus room for a freezer, washer and dryer plus the furnace and hot water heater. Also on the first floor is the master suite with its two closets and five-piece bath which opens onto the greenhouse. The second floor is highlighted by a loft which overlooks the first floor living area. The two upstairs bedrooms each have double closets and share a four-piece, compartmentalized bath.

First floor — 1,280 sq. ft.
Second floor — 735 sq. ft.
Greenhouse — 80 sq. ft.
Playhouse — 80 sq. ft.

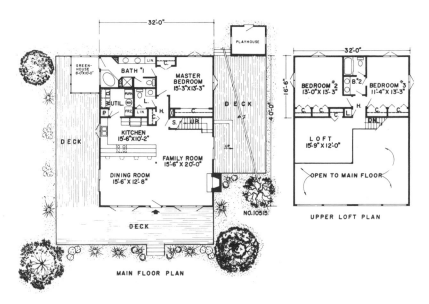

MAIN FLOOR PLAN

UPPER LOFT PLAN

Master Suite Crowns Outstanding Plan

No. 10334

Incorporating a study, walk-in closet and lavish bath with whirlpool, shower, and skylight, the master suite adds a finishing touch to this exceptional home. The deck-edged main level details an eye-catching 25-ft. oak-floored great room with bow window. Also outlined are two bedrooms, a slate floored dining room, and kitchen with pantry and snack island. On the basement level, the family room joins the patio via sliding glass doors, and a fourth bedroom and extra bath are included.

Main level-1,742 sq. ft.
Upper floor-809 sq. ft.
Lower level-443 sq. ft.
Basement-1,270 sq. ft.
Garage-558 sq. ft.

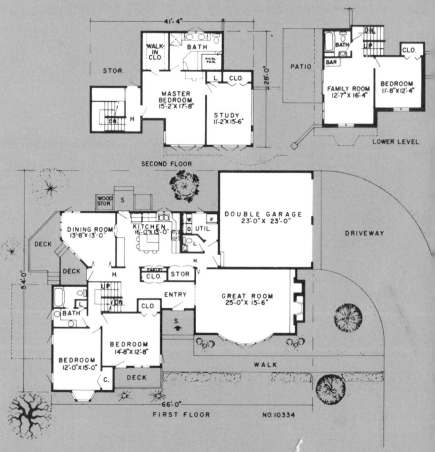

Living Room Focus Of Spacious Home

No. 10328

Equipped with fireplace and sliding glass doors to the bordering deck, the two story living room creates a sizable and airy center for family activity. A well planned traffic pattern connects dining area, kitchen, laundry niche and bath. Closets are plentiful and a total of three 15 foot bedrooms are shown.

First floor – 1,024 sq. ft.
Second floor – 576 sq. ft.
Basement – 1,024 sq. ft.

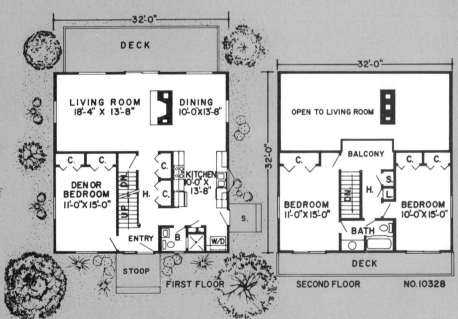

FIRST FLOOR

- 32'-0"
- DECK
- LIVING ROOM 18'-4" X 13'-8"
- DINING 10'-0"X13'-8"
- C. C.
- C.
- KITCHEN 10'-0" X 13'-8"
- C.
- DEN OR BEDROOM 11'-0"X15'-0"
- UP / DN.
- H.
- S.
- ENTRY
- B.
- W/D
- STOOP

SECOND FLOOR   NO. 10328

- 32'-0"
- 32'-0"
- OPEN TO LIVING ROOM
- C.
- BALCONY
- C. C.
- DN.
- H.
- S.
- L.
- BEDROOM 11'-0"X15'-0"
- BEDROOM 10'-0"X15'-0"
- BATH
- DECK

Lots of Living in Four-bedroom Starter

No. 10520

This traditional exterior, with its charming dormers, provides four bedrooms and lots of style even on a small lot. The very large master suite on the second floor includes the luxury of a jacuzzi. The other second floor bedroom also has a private bath and a walk-in closet. On the first floor are two more bedrooms which share a bath. The living room is reminiscent of the old-fashioned parlor. The dining area and U-shaped kitchen are located toward the back of the house overlooking the lawn and provide an ideal setting for family meals.

First floor — 960 sq. ft.
Second floor — 660 sq. ft.
Basement — 960 sq. ft.

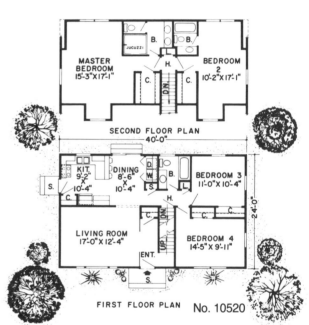

Sunny and Warm

No. 10734

Let the kids invite their friends in. You can send them upstairs to the spacious loft and never worry about your guests seeing the playroom of this lovely Tudor home. And, it's just a couple of steps up to the childrens' bedrooms, equipped with their own baths and a double vanity. Save the downstairs for family fun and entertaining. There's a formal dining room off the entry, right across from the study, which would make an ideal home office. Enjoy informal meals in the sunroom or on the deck. The adjacent kitchen, designed for efficiency, features an island cooktop and loads of counter space. When the sun goes down, sit by the fire in the beamed living room or master suite.

First floor — 2,887 sq. ft.
Second floor — 1,488 sq. ft.
Basement — 2,888 sq. ft.
Garage — 843 sq. ft.

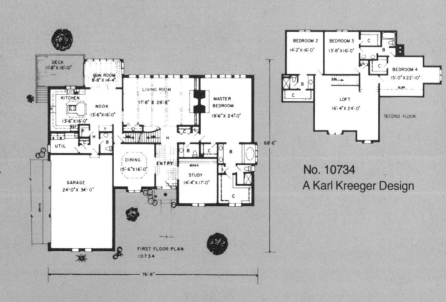

No. 10734
A Karl Kreeger Design

Compact Design Promotes Leisure

No. 10518

Built to be efficient, this home still has lots of living space in a three bedroom, two bath design. The trim on the deck suggests a chalet, but this modern home would be welcome anywhere. Tucked into the peak of the roof is the master bedroom with its own private bath. Two more bedrooms plus a four-piece bath are located on the first floor. The combined living-dining room opens onto the deck which extends the full width of the house. The front kitchen is easily accessible from the entry and is designed for efficient meal preparation.

First floor — 864 sq. ft.
Second floor — 307 sq. ft.

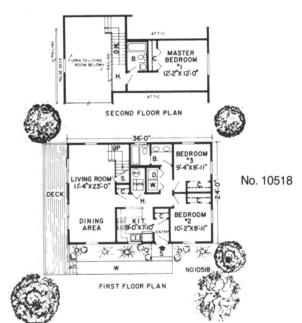

No. 10518

SECOND FLOOR PLAN

FIRST FLOOR PLAN

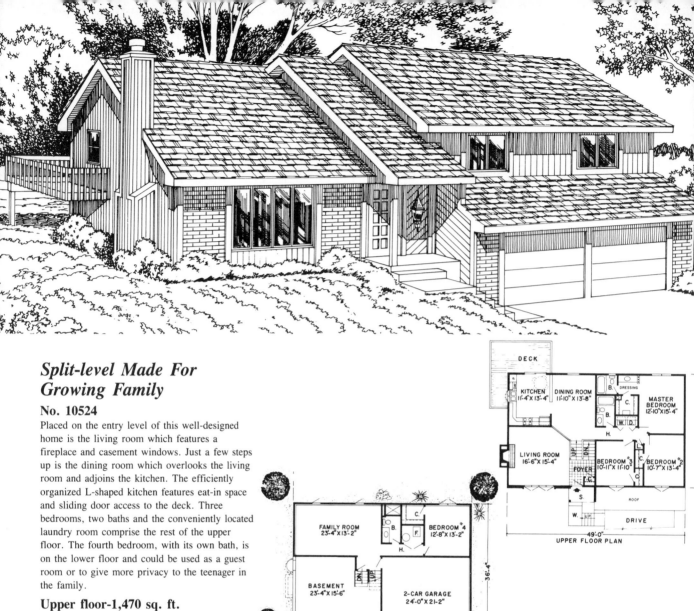

Split-level Made For Growing Family

No. 10524

Placed on the entry level of this well-designed home is the living room which features a fireplace and casement windows. Just a few steps up is the dining room which overlooks the living room and adjoins the kitchen. The efficiently organized L-shaped kitchen features eat-in space and sliding door access to the deck. Three bedrooms, two baths and the conveniently located laundry room comprise the rest of the upper floor. The fourth bedroom, with its own bath, is on the lower floor and could be used as a guest room or to give more privacy to the teenager in the family.

Upper floor-1,470 sq. ft.
Lower level-711 sq. ft.
Basement-392 sq. ft.
Garage-563 sq. ft.

Master Suite Dominates Second Floor

No. 10533

The luxurious master suite is a relaxing haven for the adults of the family. A sitting room with bay window and built-ins is adjacent to the bedroom area and leads to the double, walk-in closets and roomy bath. The two other bedrooms on the second floor share a four-piece bath. The living spaces on the first floor include a charming parlor and dining room flanking a formal foyer accented by tile. An expansive great room with bar, a U-shaped kitchen, a sunlit dining nook, an oversized laundry room and a three-car garage complete this family home.

First floor-1669 sq. ft.
Second floor-1450 sq. ft.
Basement-1653 sq. ft.
Garage-823 sq. ft.

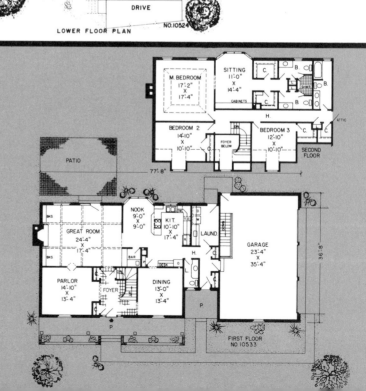

Four-bedroom Design
Combines Multiple Features

No. 10522

All four bedrooms, including the well appointed
master suite, are located on the second floor of
this tastefully simple home. The first floor living
areas are well zoned into formal and informal
areas. The living room features a traditional picture window, a built-in bookcase and a fireplace.
The dining room opens onto the deck through
French doors and is located conveniently near the
U-shaped kitchen. Additional first floor features
include a guest bath, a laundry room and a sunny
dining nook.

First floor — 873 sq. ft.
Second floor — 844 sq. ft.
Basement — 873 sq. ft.
Garage — 544 sq. ft.

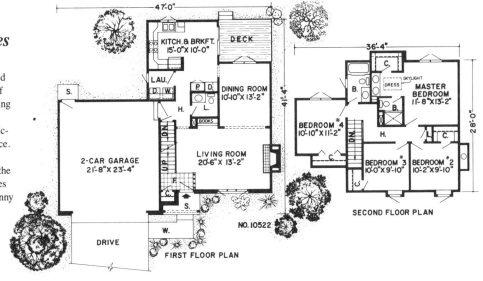

FIRST FLOOR PLAN

No. 10522

47'-0"

KITCH. & BRKFT.
15'-0" X 10'-0"

DECK

LAU.

DINING ROOM
10'-10" X 13'-2"

2-CAR GARAGE
21'-8" X 23'-4"

LIVING ROOM
20'-6" X 13'-2"

41'-4"

DRIVE

SECOND FLOOR PLAN

36'-4"

MASTER BEDROOM
11'-8" X 13'-2"

BEDROOM #4
10'-10" X 11'-2"

BEDROOM #3
10'-0" X 9'-10"

BEDROOM #2
10'-2" X 9'-10"

28'-0"

Elegant Two-story Features Expansive Great Room

No. 10526

The central corridor of this lovely home features both a two-story foyer overlooked by the second floor balcony and the expansive great room graced by a beamed, cathedral ceiling. Also on the first floor are a library-den and a fourth bedroom with private bath that is ideal for guests. The unusual window treatment in the dining room is echoed in the breakfast room. Centrally located between these two rooms is the spacious kitchen. Each of the three second-floor bedrooms feature a walk-in closet and an individual dressing area.

First floor — 1,890 sq. ft.
Second floor — 1,399 sq. ft.
Basement — 1,890 sq. ft.
Garage — 529 sq. ft.

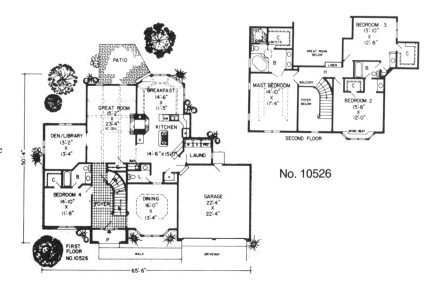

No. 10526

Room for Active Families

No. 10649

With two covered porches and a brick patio, this traditional Cape is an inviting abode for your out-door-loving family. The central entry leads down a hallway to the family room. Warmed by a fireplace and boasting a wetbar, lots of windows and French doors, this enormous room is a great gathering place. Serve meals in the bay-windowed breakfast nook or the formal dining room located on either side of the kitchen. Window seats adorning the front bedrooms upstairs provide a pleasant retreat for quiet moments.

First floor — 1,285 sq. ft.
Second floor — 930 sq. ft.
Garage — 492 sq. ft.

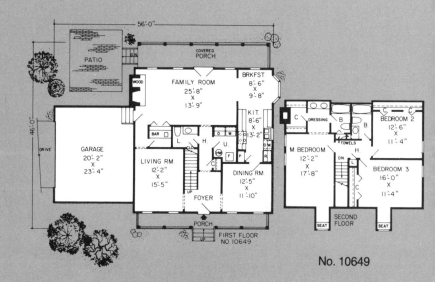

No. 10649

French Charmer Features Two-story Foyer and Great Room

No. 10529

The second floor incorporates three bedrooms and two baths, with the hall overlooking both the great room and the foyer. The master bedroom and bath are on the first floor. The expansive great room includes a bar, a fireplace and opens onto the patio. The kitchen is convenient to the dining room, breakfast room and walk-in pantry.

First floor — 1,634 sq. ft.
Second floor — 879 sq. ft.
Basement — 1,634 sq. ft.
Garage — 491 sq. ft.

SECOND FLOOR PLAN

No. 10529

MAIN FLOOR PLAN

Upper Deck Affords Roadside View

No. 10768

You'll never outgrow this fabulous five-bedroom Victorian. And, you'll never stop appreciating all its amenities: a wet-bar in the family room, built-in seating in the breakfast room, an island kitchen with a planning desk and room-sized pantry, and a handy laundry chute. The staircase dominating the entry foyer wraps around a planter that basks in the light of a skylight far overhead. Flanked by the library and living room, the foyer leads back to the kitchen, which easily serves both breakfast and formal dining rooms. There's even a handy bar for quick snacks. Warm up your informal gatherings at the family room fireplace. Or, if you want a quiet spot to relax, escape to the magnificent master suite, which features a private deck. Four more bedrooms share two adjoining baths.

First floor — 2,573 sq. ft.
Second floor — 2,390 sq. ft.
Basement — 1,844 sq. ft.
Crawl space — 793 sq. ft.
Garage — 1,080 sq. ft.

Balcony Affords Splendid View

No. 20097

Standing in the central foyer, you can see active areas and the rear deck off this sunny classic in one glance. Straight ahead, the living room ceiling, pierced by a skylight, soars to a two-story height. Living and dining rooms flow together in one spacious unit. And, both are easily served by the handy kitchen with a breakfast bar peninsula. Down a hallway off the living room, you'll find a quiet sleeping wing behind the garage. Two bedrooms feature access to an adjoining bath with double vanities. The second floor is all yours. Imagine stealing away for a luxurious soak in your private tub, or a relaxing afternoon with your favorite book.

First floor — 1,752 sq. ft.
Second floor — 897 sq. ft.
Basement — 1,752 sq. ft.
Garage — 531 sq. ft.

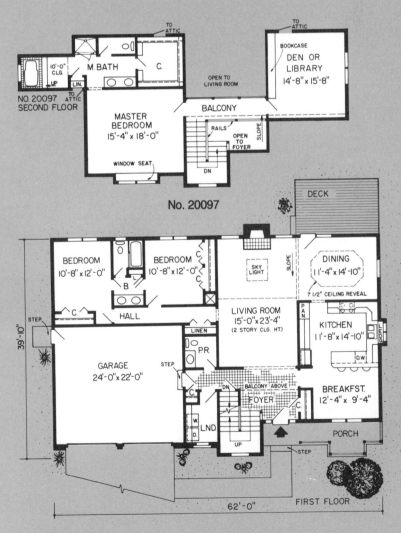

No. 20097

A Karl Kreeger Design

Stone Facade Accents Five-bedroom Home

No. 10530

The tiled entry foyer rises to the second floor and leads to the upper story via the curved staircase, or to the first floor living areas. The central hearth room features a window seat overlooking the deck and a wood stove. The U-shaped kitchen is designed for convenience and opens to both the hearth room and the laundry. Other living spaces include a cozy library, a formal dining room and a massive great room. The first floor master bedroom features a fireplace, five-piece bath and a private entrance to the greenhouse. Four bedrooms, two baths, a cedar closet and a study are comfortably arranged on the second floor.

First floor-2,344 sq. ft.
Second floor-1,384 sq. ft.
Basement-2,344 sq. ft.
Garage-792 sq. ft.

Split Level Incorporates Diagonal Wood Siding Exterior

No. 10546

This beautiful split level's exterior consists of diagonal wood siding with natural rock enhancing a window area plus a wood railing that leads to an outdoor concrete patio. The interior's lower level has one bedroom with a full bath. The living room is made formal by the sloping ceiling, wood-burning fireplace and a sun room. Also in the lower level is a space for a washer and dryer. The rest of the basement may be finished to individual taste. A two-car garage is also located on the lower level. The upper level has a U-shaped kitchen with a breakfast area and a formal dining room. Inside the entrance, a large air-tight foyer has plenty of closet space for hanging outdoor garments and/or other household items.

Upper floor-1,504 sq. ft.
Lower floor-268 sq. ft.
Basement-396 sq. ft.
Garage-440 sq. ft.

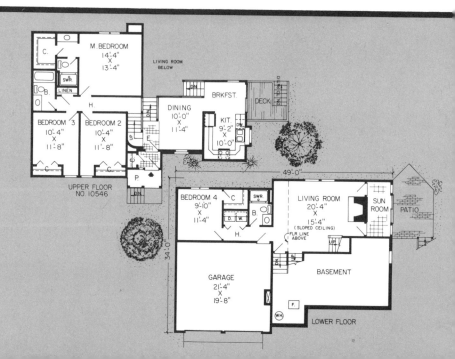

Attractive Rock Fireplace Exhibited In Split Level

No. 10579

This split level design is built with superb architecture throughout which incorporates diagonal and vertical siding, a clerestory window and a beautiful bold rock fireplace. The lower level only houses a spacious two-car garage. The main floor has an expansive open formal dining/great room area. The open-beamed, sloping ceiling and a fireplace add gracious living features to this design. This plan comes equipped with an L-shaped kitchen with eating space. The foyer has closet space and the hallway comes with its own skylight that adds lots of natural lighting to this design. Three bedrooms are on the main floor. Two bedrooms have plenty of closet space and share one full bath. The master bedroom has a walk-in closet, a full bath area and a large square bay window area for more room.

Main level-1,400 sq. ft.
Loft-152 sq. ft.
Basement-663 sq. ft.
Garage-680 sq. ft.

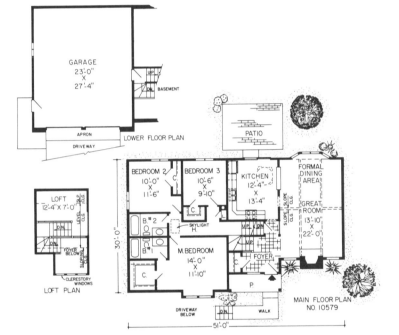

GARAGE
23'-0"
X
27'-4"

UP
DN
BASEMENT

APRON   LOWER FLOOR PLAN
DRIVEWAY

PATIO

LOFT
12'-4" X 7'-0"

FOYER
BELOW

CLERESTORY
WINDOWS

LOFT PLAN

BEDROOM 2
10'-0"
X
11'-6"

BEDROOM 3
10'-6"
X
9'-10"

KITCHEN
12'-4"
X
13'-4"

FORMAL
DINING
AREA

GREAT
ROOM
13'-10"
X
22'-0"

B.# 2

SKYLIGHT
H.

B.# 1

M. BEDROOM
14'-0"
X
11'-10"

FOYER

30'-0"

DRIVEWAY
BELOW

DN   WALK

P

MAIN FLOOR PLAN
NO. 10579

51'-0"

Balcony and Spiral Staircase Accent Traditional Four-bedroom

No. 10537

This roomy kitchen comes complete with a pantry and lots of cabinet space. The unique morning room is complemented with a large fireplace and an entry onto the patio for year 'round enjoyment. All four bedrooms are complete with full baths and walk-in closets.

First floor — 3,114 sq. ft.
Second floor — 924 sq. ft.
Basement — 3,092 sq. ft.
Garage — 917 sq. ft.

No. 10537

A Karl Kreeger Design

Compact and Appealing

No. 20075

Here's an L-shaped country charmer with a porch that demands a rocking chair or two. You'll appreciate the convenient one-level design that separates active and sleeping areas. Right off the foyer, the formal dining and living rooms have a wide-open feeling, thanks to extra wide doorways and a recessed ceiling. The kitchen is centrally located for maximum convenience. For informal family meals, you'll delight in the sunny breakfast nook that links the fireplaced living room and outdoor deck. Enjoy those quiet hours in the three bedrooms separated from family living spaces. With its own double-sink full bath and walk-in closet, the master suite will be your favorite retreat.

First floor — 1,682 sq. ft.
Basement — 1,682 sq. ft.
Garage — 484 sq. ft.

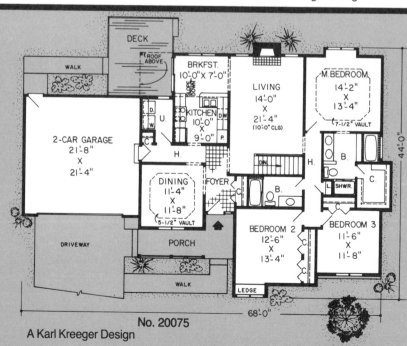

No. 20075

A Karl Kreeger Design

Elegant Home Provides Formal and Informal Areas

No. 10532

A courtyard entry sets the tone for a blend of informal living and formal accents. The library and formal dining room are complemented by an open great room, large kitchen and dining nook, plus a sun porch, covered porch and patio. The fully appointed master bedroom with a dressing room and private bath plus two half baths and a utility room complete first floor. Three bedrooms and two more baths comprise the second floor.

First floor — 2,618 sq. ft.
Second floor — 1,195 sq. ft.
Basement — 2,396 sq. ft.
Garage — 559 sq. ft.

A Karl Kreeger Design

No. 10532

Brick Design Has Striking Exterior

No. 10549

This ranch has a circlehead window that sets off a striking exterior view. Inside this single-story design, three bedrooms are located in one part of the plan with all of the bedrooms having separate full baths. The master bedroom features a sloping ceiling, large closet space plus a private bath with both a tub and a shower. Another striking design feature is the great room with its impressive open beams that crisscross down a sloping ceiling. It also has a wood-burning fireplace. The great room also has easy access through sliding glass doors onto an elevated wooden deck. The kitchen leads readily to both the dining and/or the breakfast rooms. Both of these rooms have decorative ceilings. A half bath lies just off of the kitchen as does the utility room.

First floor-2,280 sq. ft.
Basement-2,280 sq. ft.
Garage-528 sq. ft.

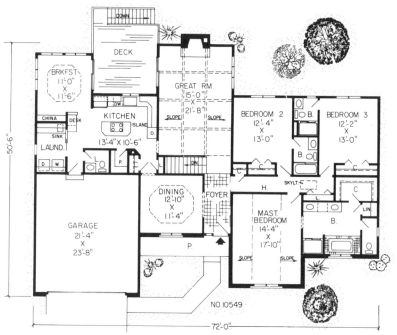

Oversized Picture Windows Reveal Beautiful Design

No. 10566

This traditional style two-story design's exterior features a brick front, two impressive oversized picture windows, and formal double doors at the front entrance. Inside on the first level, the living room is located next to the foyer and has beamed ceilings and a fireplace. The dining room is located next to the living room and the kitchen. The kitchen has an eating area, and for added convenience, a full bath area and the utility room lie right next to it. The family room has a sloping ceiling with two impressive open beamed cross members plus another fireplace that adds presence to the design of the room. The master bedroom is spacious in floor area with a full bath and walk-in closet.

First floor-2,184 sq. ft.
Second floor-956 sq. ft.
Garage-487 sq. ft.

Sturdy Stucco Boasts Sunny Atmosphere

No. 20355

If you enjoy entertaining, don't overlook this sky-lit, brick and stucco masterpiece. The sunken, bay-windowed dining room and parlor flank the gracious entry foyer. At the rear of the house, you'll find a soaring, well-appointed island kitchen that serves active areas with ease. Step down to the toasty, book-lined family room for informal gatherings. Or retire to the adjoining four-season porch with windows on three sides. Tucked behind the garage, there's a full bath, a fourth bedroom, and an elegant master suite complete with a skylit bath featuring a garden tub and double vanities. Walk up the central staircase to two more bedrooms with walk-in closets, another full bath, and your own cedar closet for summertime storage.

First floor — 2,207 sq. ft.
Second floor — 630 sq. ft.
Basement — 2,207 sq. ft.
Garage — 768 sq. ft.

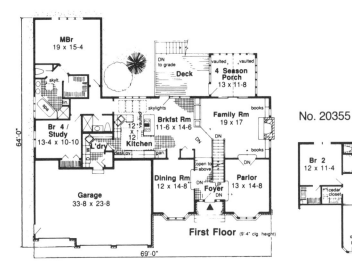

No. 20355

First Floor (9'-4" clg. height)

Second Floor

Classic Farmhouse

No. 10362

This house says "home" to everyone who remembers a bygone era but thinks ahead for comfort and values. The big wrap porch follows tradition. Imagine the cool summer evenings spent there. A split landing stairway leads to the 4 bedrooms on the upper level, complete with two bathrooms and lots of closets, perfect for the growing family. On the main level a woodburning built-in fireplace in the living room adds to the nostalgic charm of this home. Sliding glass doors open onto the porch. The main level also boasts a den, lavatory, utility room, kitchen and separate dining room overlooking the porch.

Main floor – 1,104 sq. ft.
Upper level – 1,124 sq. ft.
Basement – 1,080 sq. ft.
Garage – 528 sq. ft.

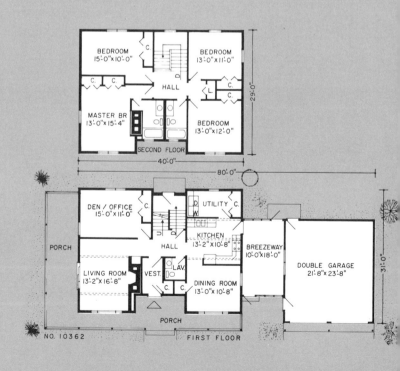

Sheltered Porch Graces Family Dwelling

No. 20067

Consider an easy-to-care-for home if you have a growing family. An all wood exterior that relieves you of yearly maintenance is just one of the features. The compact floor plan minimizes housekeeping yet arranges the play area so that an eye can be kept on young children, whether inside or in the backyard. Note touches like the tiled foyer that stops muddy traffic entering from either the front door or garage. Three bedrooms are located near to one another on the same level for nighttime security. The basement provides room for expansion as the children get older.

Living area — 1,459 sq. ft.
Basement — 697 sq. ft.
Garage — 694 sq. ft.

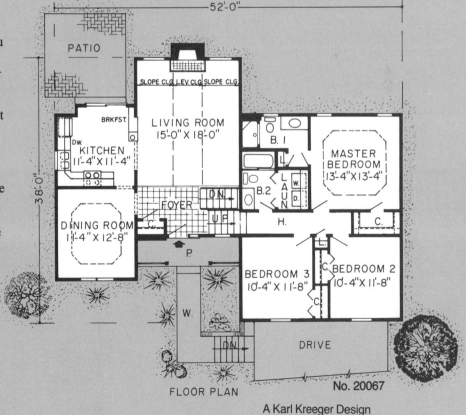

FLOOR PLAN   No. 20067

A Karl Kreeger Design

Enjoy the Backyard Views

No. 10550

There's lots of room for your growing family in this four bedroom Tudor beauty. Recessed ceilings in the dining room and master bedroom suite, a vaulted front office, and a beamed great room give first floor living areas distinctive angles. And, the sunporch off the breakfast nook is a warm place to curl up even on the coldest day. You'll never have to worry about traffic jams on busy weekday mornings. With two full baths upstairs and two convenient lavatories on the first floor, everyone can get out on time.

First floor — 2,069 sq. ft.
Second floor — 821 sq. ft.
Basement — 2,045 sq. ft.
Garage — 562 sq. ft.

A Karl Kreeger Design

Stucco and Stone Reveal Outstanding Tudor Design

No. 10555

This beautiful stucco and stone masonry Tudor design opens to a formal foyer that leads through double doors into a well-designed library which is also conveniently accessible from the master bedroom. The master bedroom offers a vaulted ceiling and a huge bath area. Other features are an oversized living room with a fireplace, an open kitchen and a connecting dining room. A utility room and half bath are located next to a two-car garage. One other select option in this design is the separate cedar closet to use for off-season clothes storage.

First floor — 1,671 sq. ft.
Second floor — 505 sq. ft.
Basement — 1,661 sq. ft.
Garage — 604 sq. ft.
Screened porch — 114 sq. ft.

A Karl Kreeger Design

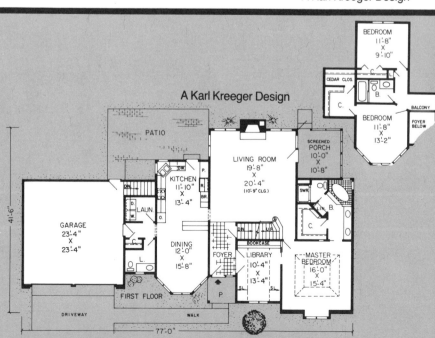

Family-preferred Features In Tudor Design

No. 10568

Many family-preferred features are offered in this deluxe Tudor design. An energy efficient foyer leads into a great room that has its own wood-burning fireplace. Off of the great room lies the master bedroom, the only bedroom on the first level. The master bedroom has its own private wood deck, and the bath area has a two-way shower and a his/her bathroom space with separate facilities. Also on the first level is an efficient kitchen with a large breakfast nook, and just off of the kitchen is a utility room. The second level includes a cedar closet, a loft area that overlooks the great room below and two bedrooms that share a full bath.

First floor-2,167 sq. ft.
Second floor-755 sq. ft.
Basement-2,224 sq. ft.
Garage-1,020 sq. ft.

Stacked Windows Create Exciting Exterior

No. 20009

Here's a three-bedroom beauty that unites interior living spaces with the great outdoors. A generous supply of huge windows, easy access to a deck and patio off the dining and family rooms, and a plan that eliminates unnecessary walls all add up to a wide-open atmosphere you'll love. The kitchen features a convenient pass-through to the sunny break-fast bay. And, thanks to the open plan, the cook can enjoy the cozy warmth of the family room fireplace. Upstairs, the two rear bedrooms share a full bath with double vanities. The master suite, dominated by a stacked window arrangement, features cathedral ceilings and a private bath with a raised tub and walk-in shower.

First floor — 982 sq. ft.
Second floor — 815 sq. ft.
Basement — 978 sq. ft.

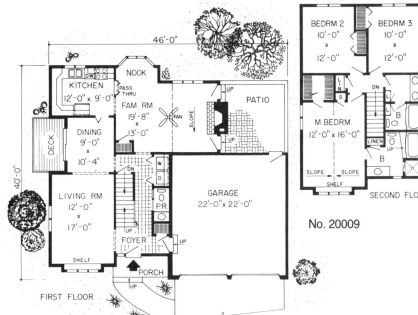

Compact and Efficient

No. 10751

Building this cozy cottage won't break the bank. Slab construction, elimination of extra hallway space, and stacked plumbing will keep your budget under control. But, efficiency doesn't mean you have to sacrifice beauty. The spacious, fireplaced living room seems even larger with its soaring ceilings. A galley kitchen, full bath, and roomy bedroom complete the first floor. View the scene below from the balcony, which leads to a second bedroom, full bath, and a sewing room that could double as a home office or den.

First floor — 660 sq. ft.
Second floor — 330 sq. ft.

Lunch by the Pool

No. 10696

After a day of sun and swimming, you'll enjoy retreating to the master wing with skylit bath, room-sized closets, and quiet, book-lined study. But when you're in the mood to entertain, this convenient floor plan guarantees success. Greet your guests in the foyer and lead them into the formal living room or family room with adjoining bar and patio. The island kitchen, with its huge pantry and breakfast nook overlooking the pool, has plenty of room for more than one cook. A cozy library at the top of the stairs leads to three more bedrooms and two full baths.

First floor — 3,252 sq. ft.
Second floor — 873 sq. ft.
Garage — 746 sq. ft.

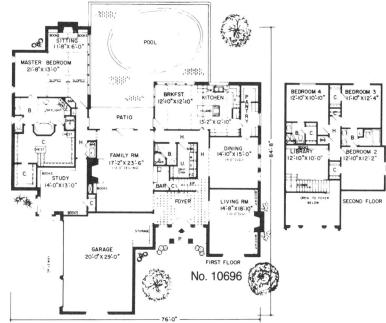

Expansive Two-Story Foyer Creates Dramatic Impression

No. 10588

French doors in the breakfast nook give this traditional colonial home a touch of romance. Divided from the kitchen by a peninsula with a counter for informal meals, the breakfast nook is adjacent to the fireplaced family room. Right across the hall, the foyer links living and dining rooms and harbors the angular staircase to four bedrooms and two baths on the second floor.

First floor — 1,450 sq. ft.
Second floor — 1,082 sq. ft.
Basement — 1,340 sq. ft.
Garage — 572 sq. ft.

Perfect for a Hillside

No. 10595

From the road, the appearance of this two level home is deceiving. A central staircase directs traffic from the front entry to the den and master bedroom suite, to the living room, with its sloping ceiling and fireplace, or to the half bath, laundry and garage. Enter the island kitchen and formal dining room from either the breakfast or the living rooms. Two screened porches make outdoor living easy, rain or shine. Downstairs, the huge recreation room features a kitchenette and fireplace for entertaining. Two more bedrooms and a full bath complete this level, which could even be used for in-law quarters.

Upper floor — 1,643 sq. ft.
Lower floor — 1,297 sq. ft.
Garage — 528 sq. ft.

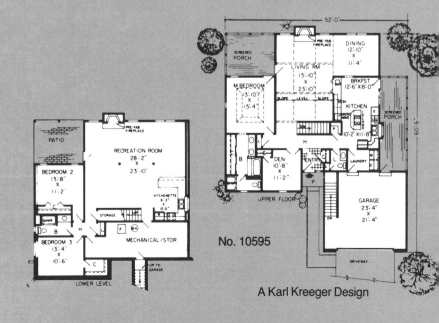

No. 10595

A Karl Kreeger Design

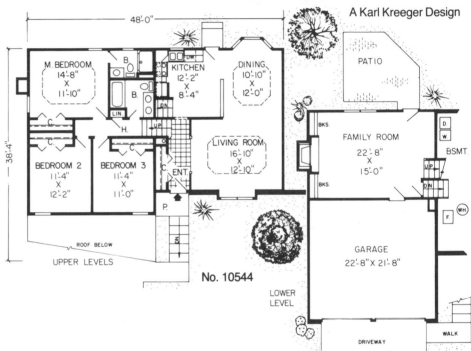

Split-Level Tudor Offers Comfort and Versatility

No. 10544

This contemporary Tudor-style design boasts features that make a house a home, including a master bedroom with a full bath, a spacious kitchen adjoining the formal dining room, and a fireplace in the large family room on the lower level. Steps up to the three bedrooms from the rest of the living areas gives the sense of privacy for family or guests. The bay window in the dining room provides a bit of elegance for entertaining.

Upper levels — 1,366 sq. ft.
Lower level — 384 sq. ft.
Basement — 631 sq. ft.
Garage — 528 sq. ft.

A Karl Kreeger Design

UPPER LEVELS

M. BEDROOM 14'-8" X 11'-10"
KITCHEN 12'-2" X 8'-4"
DINING 10'-10" X 12'-0"
BEDROOM 2 11'-4" X 12'-2"
BEDROOM 3 11'-4" X 11'-0"
LIVING ROOM 16'-10" X 12'-10"

48'-0"
38'-4"

ROOF BELOW
ENT.

No. 10544

LOWER LEVEL

PATIO
FAMILY ROOM 22'-8" X 15'-0"
GARAGE 22'-8" X 21'-8"
BSMT.
DRIVEWAY
WALK

The Perfect Combination of Grace and Convenience

No. 20352

Here's a sprawling Tudor masterpiece that will house your family in comfort and elegance. An airlock vestibule combines with a back-to-back fireplace in the formal living room and expansive family room to protect main floor common areas from winter chills. When mealtime arrives, choose the luxurious atmosphere of the bayed dining room, or the cheerful ambience of the breakfast room surrounded by a huge, rear deck. Built-ins add convenience and lots of extra storage, from the family room planning desk and bookshelves, to the walk-in pantry off the service hall and the handy bench in the vestibule. Two well-appointed baths serve the bedrooms upstairs, which include the vaulted master suite with its own, private deck.

First floor — 1,647 sq. ft.
Second floor — 1,191 sq. ft.
Basement — 1,647 sq. ft.
Garage — 576 sq. ft.

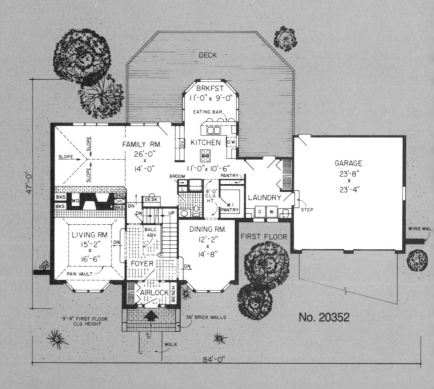

Entertaining is No Problem

No. 10610

Start picking out the porch furniture. You won't be able to resist sitting on this magnificent veranda on a lazy summer day. Walking through the front door, you'll encounter a large planter that divides the entry from active areas at the rear of the house. You'll find a sunny bay with built-in seating in the formal dining room, which shares a massive, two-way fireplace with the vaulted, sunken living room. If the living room bar doesn't fill all your entertaining needs, the nearby island kitchen certainly will. And, if the crowd gets too large, the full-length deck, accessible from the living room or breakfast room, can handle the overflow. There are two bedrooms and a full bath on the first floor, but the master suite enjoys a private location at the top of the stairs.

First floor — 1,818 sq. ft.
Second floor — 528 sq. ft.
Basement — 1,818 sq. ft.
Garage — 576 sq. ft.

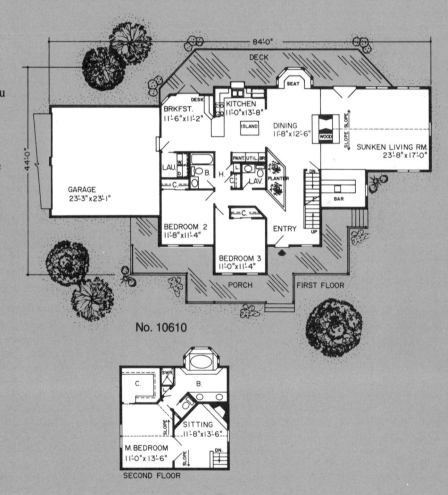

No. 10610

Veranda Mirrors Two-Story Bay

No. 10780

This elegant Victorian with a modern twist celebrates the classic beauty of turn-of-the-century architecture. The huge foyer, flanked by the formal parlor and dining room, leads to the island kitchen with adjoining pantry, the breakfast bay, and sunken gathering room at the rear of the house. Walk upstairs two ways: from the expansive great hall or the sunny alcove with wrap-around rear deck. Double doors open to the master suite and the book-lined master retreat with dormer sitting area. Look at the elegant master bath, which features a raised tub and an adjoining cedar closet. Other upstairs bedrooms boast distinctive shapes, huge closets, and access to the full bath with double vanities.

First floor — 1,946 sq. ft.
Second floor — 1,733 sq. ft.
Basement — 1,946 sq. ft.
Garage — 764 sq. ft.

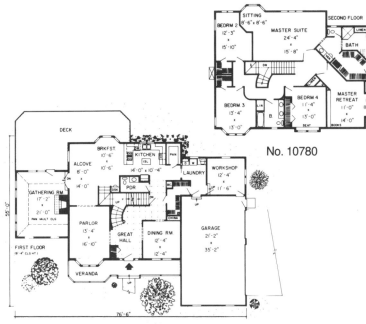

No. 10780

Storage Space Galore in Garage

No. 20065

This simple design's exterior features a large picture window and rock front. On the first floor from the foyer is a spacious living room with its own wood-burning fireplace. The dining room lies in front of the living room and next to the kitchen. From the kitchen to the right is the breakfast room with access to a large outdoor wooden deck. A half bath and laundry facilities are other rooms on the first floor. On the second floor are three bedrooms. Two bedrooms share a full bath with its own skylight, while the master bedroom has its own private bath and walk-in closet. One final feature of this plan is the large amount of storage space available in the two-car garage.

First floor — 936 sq. ft.
Second floor — 777 sq. ft.
Garage-storage — 624 sq. ft.

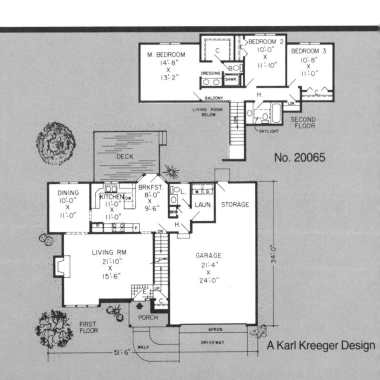

No. 20065

A Karl Kreeger Design

Build Now, Plan for Tomorrow

No. 10612

Here's a rambling country farmhouse that will house your family in casual comfort, and allow for future expansion. The staircase dominating the central foyer not only leads to an 1,100 square foot attic, it provides a noise buffer for the three bedrooms down the hall to the left. Designed to accommodate a crowd, this plan allows easy access to every room from the foyer. Formal living and dining rooms at the front of the house are nice for entertaining, but the massive family room with its twin sliders to the outdoor patio is a cozy spot to gather around a crackling fire. Enjoy family suppers in the sunny nook adjoining the kitchen, which serves both dining rooms with ease.

Main living area — 2,730 sq. ft.
Basement — 2,730 sq. ft.
Garage — 653 sq. ft.

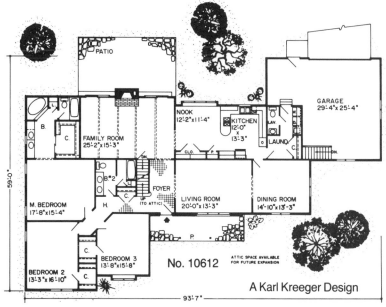

No. 10612

A Karl Kreeger Design

Contemporary Height

No. 10675

Vertical siding and stacked windows combine to
create a soaring facade for this three-bedroom contemporary. Inside, sloping ceilings, bump-out windows, and an open staircase unite the foyer, living
room and formal dining room into one bright, airy
space. The fireplaced family room and breakfast
nook flanking the kitchen both open to an outdoor
deck at the rear of the house. You'll find a full bath
that serves two ample bedrooms right at the top of
the stairs. And to the right, behind double doors,
lies a luxurious master suite with skylit bath, walk-
in closet, and double vanities.

First floor — 969 sq. ft.
Second floor — 714 sq. ft.
Basement — 969 sq. ft.
Garage — 484 sq. ft.

Comfortable Contemporary Design

No. 10567

This simple but well designed contemporary
expresses comfort and offers a lot of options normally found in larger designs. On the first level, a
front kitchen is offered with an open, non-parti-
tioned dining area. Two bedrooms are located on
the first floor. The living room sports a skylight,
adding more natural lighting to the room, and has a
prefabricated wood-burning fireplace. The second
floor has a secluded master bedroom with a sitting
room, walk-in closets, and a full bath. Other features include a two-car garage and a brick patio.

First floor — 1,046 sq. ft.
Second floor — 375 sq. ft.
Basement — 1,046 sq. ft.
Garage — 472 sq. ft.

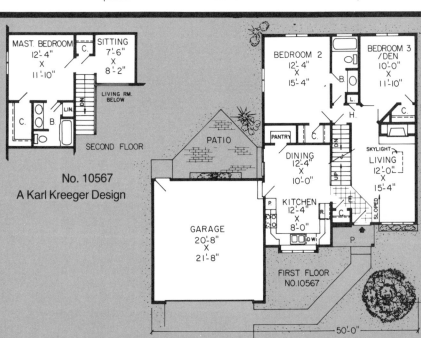

No. 10567
A Karl Kreeger Design

36

Ranch Design Utilizes Skylights

No. 10570

A partial stone veneer front makes this large ranch design very inviting. Inside, a vestibule entry serves as an airtight airlock. A large library-den next to the foyer shares a two-way fireplace with the living room and has a sloped ceiling, as does the living room. The living room leads to a deck or screened porch. A very large kitchen has a hexagonal island with a connecting dining room. The dining room also has skylights adding warmth and additional lighting to the room. Also in the dining room, sliding glass doors lead out to the veranda. This spacious design has four bedrooms and ample closet space.

Main floor — 2,450 sq. ft.
Basement — 2,450 sq. ft.
Garage — 739 sq. ft.

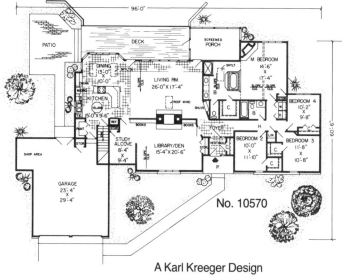

No. 10570

A Karl Kreeger Design

Eye-appealing Brick Exterior

No. 10559

This elegant Tudor-style home offers an eye-appealing exterior of brick, stone and stucco masonry. Its airlock foyer leads into a spacious great room with open beam ceilings. Many conveniences are offered in this plan, beginning with all three bedrooms on one floor. Additionally, the master bedroom has a vaulted ceiling plus its own private, very large bath, which comes equipped with both a shower and an oversized tub. Other conveniences include the tasteful connection of the dining, kitchen and pantry rooms. The dining room also has sliding glass doors that lead onto a screened porch for outdoor pleasures. A utility room is located near the two-car garage.

First floor — 1,809 sq. ft.
Basement — 1,809 sq. ft.
Garage — 585 sq. ft.

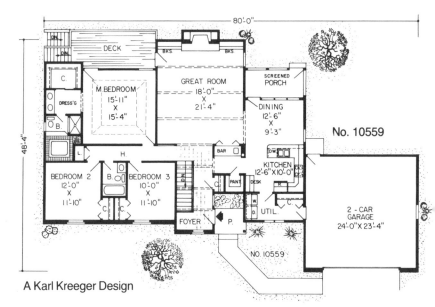

A Karl Kreeger Design

High Impact on a Low Budget

No. 10742

Build this Spanish-style, three bedroom gem on a slab to keep costs down and interest high. A trio of arches graces the porch of this one-level home, and provides a warm welcome to entering guests. Inside, dramatic cathedral ceilings bring an exciting atmosphere to the open living room, separated from the foyer by a half-wall, and warmed by a fireplace that dominates one wall. Soaring ceilings at the rear of the house are pierced by a skylight, bathing the dining room and island kitchen in warmth and light. The adjoining patio, accessible from the dining room and master suite, is a perfect spot to enjoy your first cup of coffee on a beautiful summer morning.

Main living area — 1,617 sq. ft.
Garage — 528 sq. ft.

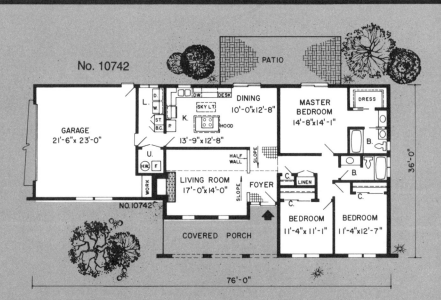

Porch Recalls a Romantic Era

No. 20098

Arched windows and a two-story bay lend an air of elegance to this exceptional four-bedroom beauty. Interior spaces are characterized by distinctive ceiling treatments, sloping ceilings pierced by skylights, and efficient room placements. Notice how easily the kitchen serves the hexagonal breakfast room, the formal dining room, and the adjoining deck. Even the fireplaced living room is only steps away. And, when the alarm rings early in the morning, you'll be grateful for the master suite's proximity to the coffee pot. The staircase off the foyer leads to three more bedrooms and a full, skylit bath with double vanities. Be sure to notice the wonderful angles and generous closet space in each room.

First floor — 1,843 sq. ft.
Second floor — 1,039 sq. ft.
Basement — 1,843 sq. ft.
Garage — 484 sq. ft.

No. 20098

A Karl Kreeger Design

Floor-to-Ceiling Window Graces Formal Parlor

No. 20080

There's a taste of Tudor elegance in this three-bedroom family home. You'll see it in the brick and stucco facade with rustic wood trim, in the tiled foyer, and in the fireplaced family room with ten foot ceilings. But, it's easy to see how convenient this plan is, too. The island kitchen and breakfast nook are adjacent to a gracious formal dining room and outdoor deck, perfect for a summer supper. The first-floor master suite means you won't have to trek down the stairs for your morning coffee. The kids will love their upstairs bath. A skylight assures privacy and a sunny atmosphere.

First floor — 1,859 sq. ft.
Second floor — 556 sq. ft.
Basement — 1,844 sq. ft.
Garage — 598 sq. ft.

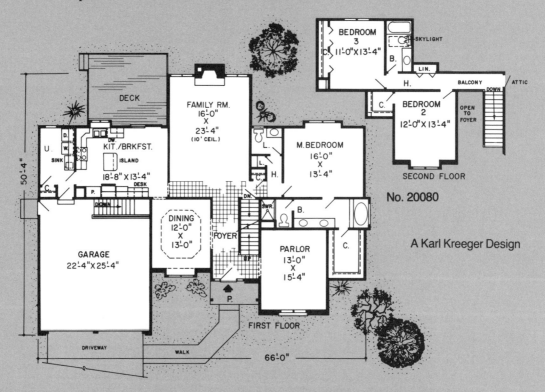

No. 20080

A Karl Kreeger Design

Surrounded with Sunshine

No. 20092

Here's a cheerful one-level, character-ized by lots of oversized windows and an airy plan. Garage and front entries open to the central foyer, which leads right into a huge, fireplaced living room and a view of the back yard. Bask in the sun as you sip your morning coffee in the skylit dining room with sliders to the deck. And, look at that adjoining, U-shaped kitchen. You can't ask for a more convenient arrangement! Down a short hall off the living room, three bedrooms share a corner of the house away from active areas. Notice the walk-in closets in the master suite and front bedroom, the skylit second bath, and the luxurious master bath with its vaulted ceilings, double vanities and raised tub.

**Main living area —
1,693 sq. ft.
Basement — 1,693 sq. ft.
Garage — 484 sq. ft.**

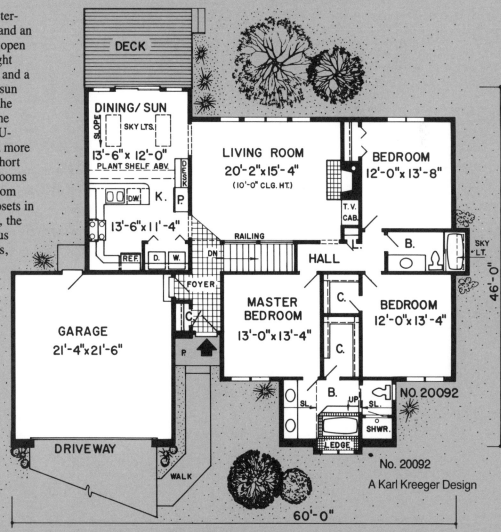

Contemporary Ranch Has Courtyard Entrance

No. 10560

This spacious design's most prominent inside feature is the great room. It has a beamed ceiling, a wet bar, a wood-burning fireplace complete with built-in bookshelves, and utilizes plenty of natural lighting from the clever introduction of twin skylights. Other options are a well-designed kitchen with the laundry room connected to it. This plan also has a sitting room with a half-bath, plus easy access through sliding glass doors leading outdoors onto a large wooden deck. The sitting room is also conveniently located next to the master bedroom. The master bedroom has a vaulted ceiling, a dressing area, a large walk-in closet and a full bath. The dining room also has a vaulted ceiling which adds more formality to the room.

First floor-1,970 sq. ft.
Second floor-829 sq. ft.
Basement-1,970 sq. ft.
Garage-549 sq. ft.

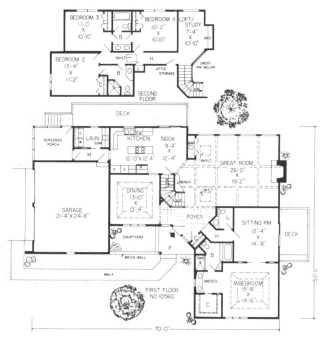

Ranch Offers Modern Kitchen Facilities

No. 10548

Inside this ranch, a modern kitchen with built-in facilities enjoys great attention. The kitchen is L-shaped in design and has a built-in microwave counter next to the range inset. A desk is conveniently built in for planning needs concerning the whole household budget. Sliding glass doors provide easy access from the kitchen to the screened porch. Next to the kitchen, a spacious living room has a sloping ceiling, a wood-burning fireplace and built-in bookshelves. The living room has access to a large outdoor brick patio. The dining room is formal in design, revealing a vaulted ceiling, while the laundry room area is concealed by sliding wood doors. Two bedrooms share a full bath, while the master bedroom has its own dressing area and full bath.

First floor-1,688 sq. ft.
Basement-1,688 sq. ft.
Garage-489 sq. ft.
Screened porch-120 sq. ft.

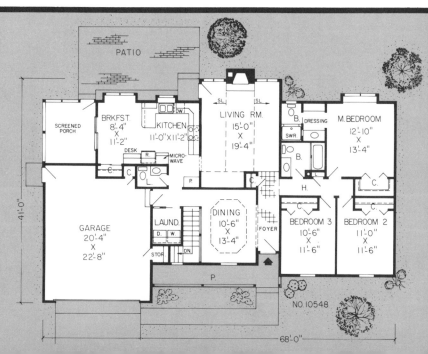

Carefree Living on One Level

No. 20089

Here's an inviting little charmer that will keep housework to a minimum and give you plenty of room for hobbies. A full basement and oversized two-car garage is large enough to store your cars and boat, with space left for a workshop. Upstairs, one-level living is a breeze in this plan that keeps active and quiet areas separate. Three bedrooms and two full baths tucked down a hallway include the spacious master suite with double vanities. The fireplaced living room, dining room, and kitchen are wide open and conveniently arranged for easy mealtimes. Take it easy after dinner, and enjoy dessert and coffee outside on the deck off the dining room.

Main living area — 1,588 sq. ft.
Basement — 780 sq. ft.
Garage — 808 sq. ft.

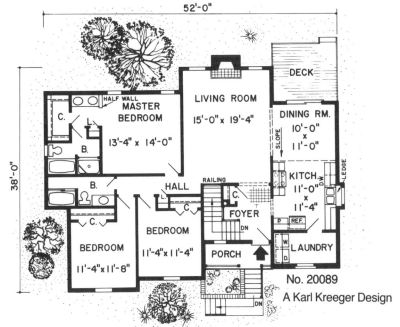

52'-0"

38'-0"

DECK

HALF WALL
MASTER BEDROOM
13'-4" x 14'-0"

LIVING ROOM
15'-0" x 19'-4"

DINING RM.
10'-0" x 11'-0"

SLOPE

C.
B.
B.
C.

HALL

RAILING

C.

KITCH.
11'-0" x 11'-4"

LEDGE

FOYER
DN

BEDROOM
11'-4" x 11'-4"

BEDROOM
11'-4" x 11'-8"

P.
REF.

W
D

LAUNDRY

PORCH

DN

No. 20089
A Karl Kreeger Design

Secret Room Incorporated into this Luxury Home Plan

No. 10458

Hidden in the recesses of the master bedroom's walk-in closet is a secret room for valuables. The remainder of the master closet has built-in dressers, and a skylight illuminates the adjoining five-piece bath. The centrally located living room is accented by beamed, 10-foot ceilings plus bookcases and a fireplace. The large, yet efficient kitchen conveniently divides the formal dining room from the more informal nook which looks onto the patio. The family room, complete with wetbar and its own fireplace is located at the rear of the house and has a wall of windows overlooking the lawn.

First floor — 2,925 sq. ft.
Garage — 490 sq. ft.

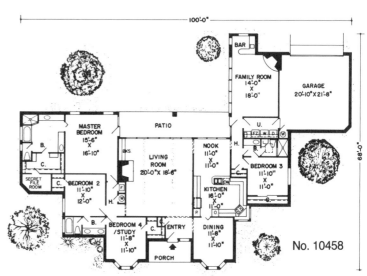

No. 10458

Touched with Tudor

No. 20088

With four upstairs bedrooms, each featuring a walk-in closet, there's plenty of room for everyone. And, three full baths insure the morning rush won't be a problem. Down the U-shaped stairway, a central hallway links family areas at the rear of the house with the two-story foyer and formal areas. Living and dining rooms, featuring a bump-out window and recessed ceiling, form one open space. With the island kitchen right next door, entertaining will be easy. Enjoy family meals in the breakfast room with adjoining pantry, or out on the deck. Window walls and sliders in the breakfast room and fireplaced family room unite outdoor and interior spaces for an airy feeling your family will cherish.

First floor — 1,404 sq. ft.
Second floor — 1,346 sq. ft.
Basement — 1,404 sq. ft.
Garage — 521 sq. ft.

A Karl Kreeger Design

No. 20088

Ranch Offers Attractive Windows

No. 10569

This four bedroom ranch offers two full baths with plenty of closet space. Also in this design, the living room has a sloping, open-beamed ceiling with a fireplace and built-in bookshelves. The dining room is connected to the foyer and has a vaulted ceiling, adding to an already spacious room. The kitchen has an ample amount of dining space available and has sliding glass doors that lead out onto a brick patio. A half-bath with shower is located next to the kitchen as well as a pantry and washer-dryer space for more convenience. A two-car garage is included in this plan.

First floor — 1,840 sq. ft.
Basement — 1,803 sq. ft.
Garage — 445 sq. ft.

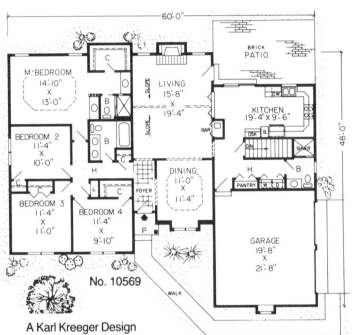

No. 10569

A Karl Kreeger Design

Dormer Windows Accent Bedroom Zone

No. 5035

Dormer windows, shutters and a faithfully detailed traditional entry combine to create a unique appeal in this Cape Cod offering. Perhaps the easiest way to zone sleeping areas is to place bedrooms on a another floor, and, in this case, the result is a substantial master bedroom and two smaller bedrooms, all provided with adequate closet space. Below, the living room reaches a full 22 feet to allow plenty of room for entertaining and borders a handy half bath. Swinging doors separate kitchen and dining room.

First floor — 725 sq. ft.
Second floor — 651 sq. ft.
Basement — 725 sq. ft.
Garage — 265 sq. ft.

No. 5035

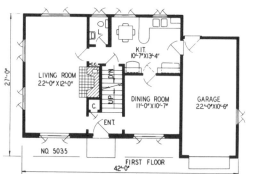

Compact, but Elegant

No. 20077

You'll never get bored with the rooms in this charming, three-bedroom Victorian. The angular plan gives every room an interesting shape. From the wrap-around veranda, the entry foyer leads through the living room and parlor, breaking them up without confining them, and giving each room an airy atmosphere. In the dining room, with its hexagonal recessed ceiling, you can enjoy your after-dinner coffee and watch the kids playing on the deck. Or eat in the sunny breakfast room off the island kitchen, where every wall has a window, and every window has a different view. You'll love the master suite's bump-out windows, walk-in closets, and double sinks.

First floor — 1,393 sq. ft.
Second floor — 1,096 sq. ft.
Basement — 1,393 sq. ft.
Garage — 491 sq. ft.

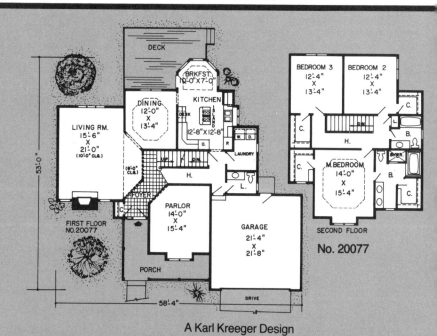

No. 20077

46

A Karl Kreeger Design

ow Window Creates
triking Living Room

o. 9310

e popularity of split foyer designs continues to
ow. One reason is that they not only maintain
ir resale value but usually the value appreciates
nsiderably. This one has a very attractive facade
ich includes a large bow window in the living
om and two square bay windows in the front bed-
ms. The living-dining room area is quite large
d offers a large amount of furniture arrangement
ssibilities. The lower level recreation room pro-
des plenty of space for parties and family
tivities.

pper level — 1,461 sq. ft.
ower level — 740 sq. ft.
arage and shop — 651 sq. ft.

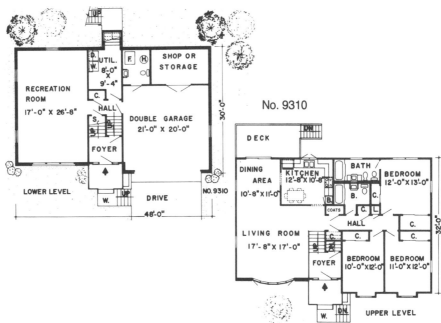

No. 9310

Arches Dominate Stately Facade

No. 10666

Gracious living is the rule in this brick masterpiece designed with an eye toward elegant entertaining. Window walls and French doors link the in-ground pool and surrounding brick patio with interior living spaces. The wet-bar with wine storage provides a convenient space for a large buffet in the family room. Built-in bookcases in the living room, family room, and skylit second-floor library can house even the largest collection. Separated from living areas by halls or a bridge, every bedroom is a quiet retreat, with its own dressing room and adjoining bath.

First floor — 3,625 sq. ft.
Second floor — 937 sq. ft.
Garage — 636 sq. ft.

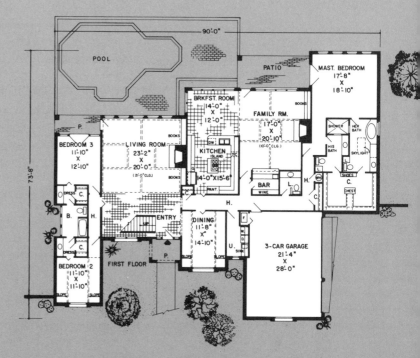

No. 10666

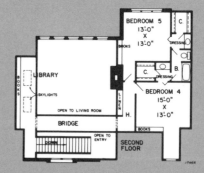

Traditional Warmth

No. 10806

With its abundant windows and covered porch, this traditional Tudor masterpiece boasts an atmosphere that says "welcome." Show your guests into the sunken living room just off the entry, or the adjoining dining room at the rear of the house. With the efficient island kitchen just steps away, the cook's job will be easy. When the gathering's informal, the adjoining fireplaced great room, which features access to both a screened porch and outdoor deck, is a comfortable alternative. Guests will appreciate the first-floor powder room just around the corner. A graceful staircase leads to three ample bedrooms, each with a walk-in closet, one optional sitting room-bedroom, and two full baths.

First floor — 1,469 sq. ft.
Second floor — 1,241 sq. ft.
Garage — 3-car

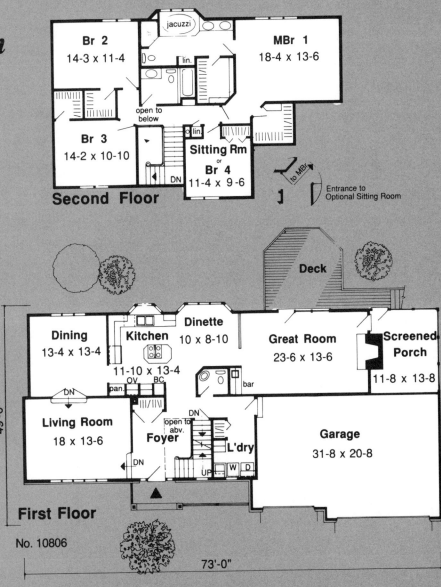

Second Floor

- Br 2 14-3 x 11-4
- jacuzzi
- lin.
- MBr 1 18-4 x 13-6
- open to below
- Br 3 14-2 x 10-10
- lin.
- Sitting Rm or Br 4 11-4 x 9-6
- DN
- to MBr
- Entrance to Optional Sitting Room

First Floor

- Deck
- Dining 13-4 x 13-4
- Kitchen 11-10 x 13-4
- Dinette 10 x 8-10
- Great Room 23-6 x 13-6
- Screened Porch 11-8 x 13-8
- pan. OV BC
- bar
- Living Room 18 x 13-6
- Foyer
- open to abv.
- DN
- L'dry W D
- UP
- Garage 31-8 x 20-8
- DN
- 49'-6"
- 73'-0"

No. 10806

Screened Porch Designed For Dining

No. 8262

Opening to dining room and convenient to kitchen, the screened porch extends this stone veneer plan and offers sheltered open air dining. Placing the fireplace in the corner of the living room succeeds in spreading the atmosphere over the entire living-dining area, and unique expanses of windows flood the areas with light. Master bedroom merits full bath with shower.

First floor-1,406 sq. ft.
Basement-1,394 sq. ft.
Garage-444 sq. ft.

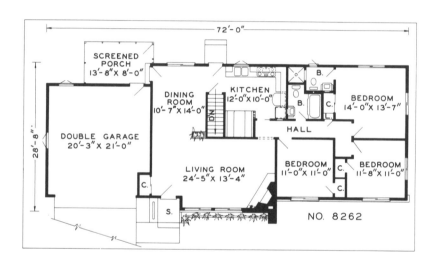

Glass Walls Seem to Enlarge Front Living Areas

No. 10482

The second floor of this original design contains two bedrooms plus a shared walk-through bath. Fronting the second floor are the stairway and a balcony which overlooks the glass-walled living room. The dining room also boasts a front glass wall and opens onto the efficient U-shaped kitchen. The full bath on the first floor may be accessed privately through the master bedroom or off the central hall. The laundry room, which also includes the utility area, is conveniently located between the kitchen and the master bedroom.

First floor - 966 sq. ft.
Second floor - 455 sq. ft.
Garage - 353 sq. ft.

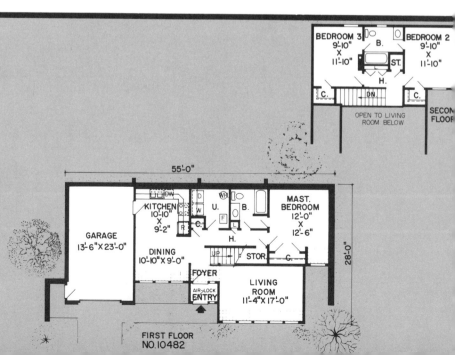

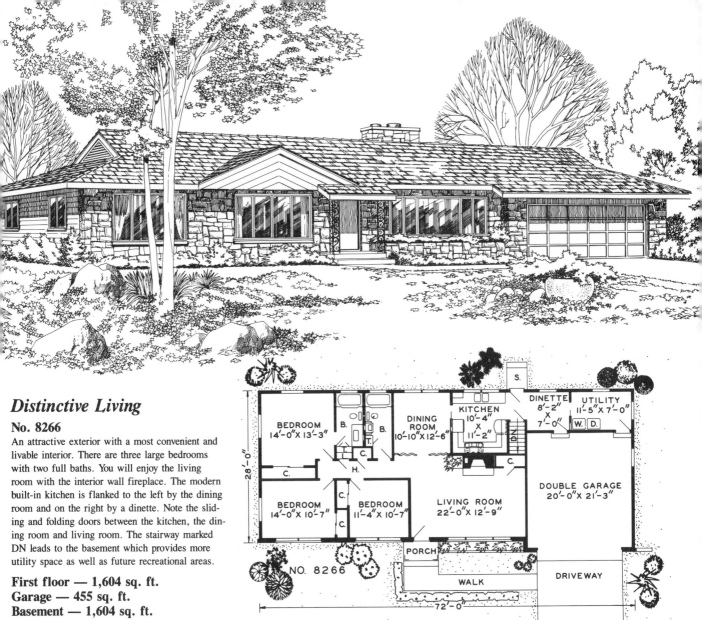

Distinctive Living

No. 8266

An attractive exterior with a most convenient and livable interior. There are three large bedrooms with two full baths. You will enjoy the living room with the interior wall fireplace. The modern built-in kitchen is flanked to the left by the dining room and on the right by a dinette. Note the sliding and folding doors between the kitchen, the dining room and living room. The stairway marked DN leads to the basement which provides more utility space as well as future recreational areas.

First floor — 1,604 sq. ft.
Garage — 455 sq. ft.
Basement — 1,604 sq. ft.

BEDROOM 14'-0"X13'-3"

DINING ROOM 10'-10"X12'-6"

KITCHEN 10'-4" X 11'-2"

DINETTE 8'-2" X 7'-0"

UTILITY 11'-5"X7'-0"

BEDROOM 14'-0"X10'-7"

BEDROOM 11'-4"X10'-7"

LIVING ROOM 22'-0"X12'-9"

DOUBLE GARAGE 20'-0"X21'-3"

PORCH

NO. 8266

WALK

DRIVEWAY

28'-0"

72'-0"

SOLAR HOME

Porch Adorns Elegant Bay

No. 20093

Here's a compact Victorian charmer that unites tradition with today in a perfect combination. Imagine
waking up in the roomy master suite with its
romantic bay and full bath with double sinks. Two
additional bedrooms, which feature huge closets,
share the hall bath. The romance continues in the
sunny breakfast room off the island kitchen, in the
recessed ceilings of the formal dining room, and in
the living room's cozy fireplace. Sun lovers will
appreciate the sloping, skylit ceilings in the living
room, and the rear deck accessible from both the
kitchen and living room.

First floor — 978 sq. ft.
Second floor — 812 sq. ft.
Basement — 978 sq. ft.

A Karl Kreeger Design

Cape Cod Passive Solar Design

No. 10386

A solar greenhouse on the south employs energy
storage rods and water to capture the sun's warmth,
thereby providing a sanctuary for plants and supplying a good percentage of the house's heat. Other
southern windows are large and triple glazed for
energy efficiency. From one of the bedrooms, on
the second floor, you can look out through louvered
shutters to the living room below, accented by a
heat circulating fireplace and a cathedral ceiling
with three dormer windows which flood the room
with light. On the lower level, sliding glass doors
lead from the sitting area of the master bedroom
suite to a private patio. Also on this level are a dining room, kitchen, mud room, double garage with a
large storage area, and another larger patio.

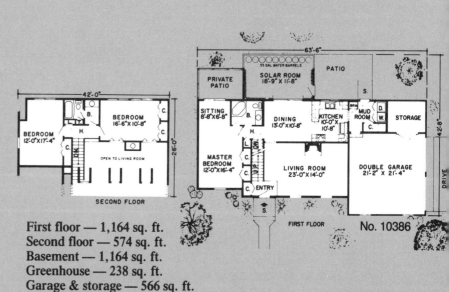

First floor — 1,164 sq. ft.
Second floor — 574 sq. ft.
Basement — 1,164 sq. ft.
Greenhouse — 238 sq. ft.
Garage & storage — 566 sq. ft.

Comfortable Cottage Suits Narrow Lot

No. 8082

Adaptable to a 50-foot lot, this small cottage boasts an exterior of horizontal siding, brick, and shutters, as well as a cozy interior. Entry is directly into the living room, splashed with light from the plentiful windows. Large enough to entertain a group of people, the living room is shut off from sleeping quarters by a door, which encourages maximum privacy and quiet. Two adequate bedrooms and full bath are set opposite an extra storage closet.

First floor – 936 sq. ft.
Basement – 936 sq. ft.

BEDROOM
12'-10" x 11'-7"

BEDROOM
11'-4" x 11'-0"

C B C

L

H

C

DN

LIVING ROOM
17'-0" x 13'-0"

DINING ROOM
8'-0" x 10'-0"

KITCHEN
9'-2" x 10'-0"

36'-0"

26'-0"

NO. 8082

SOLAR HOME

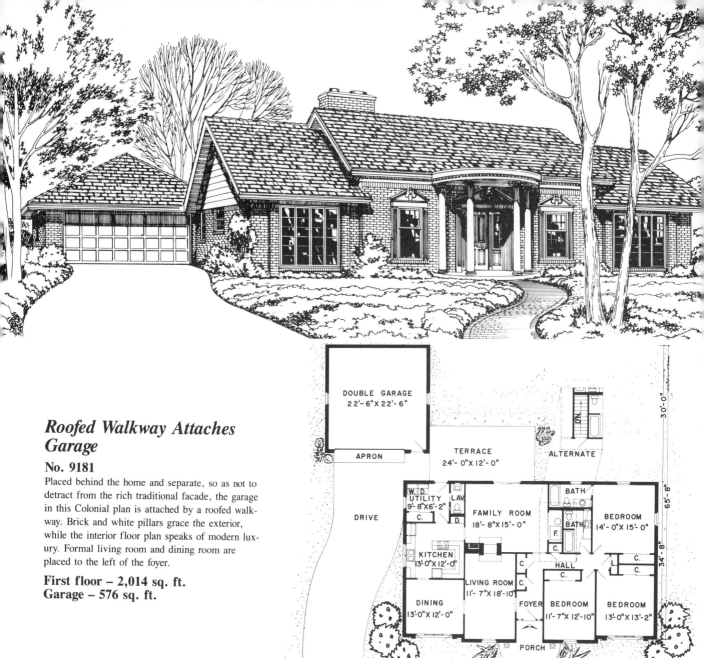

Roofed Walkway Attaches Garage

No. 9181

Placed behind the home and separate, so as not to detract from the rich traditional facade, the garage in this Colonial plan is attached by a roofed walkway. Brick and white pillars grace the exterior, while the interior floor plan speaks of modern luxury. Formal living room and dining room are placed to the left of the foyer.

First floor – 2,014 sq. ft.
Garage – 576 sq. ft.

Charming Traditional Emphasizes Living Areas

No. 22014

Besides its 20-ft. family room with fireplace, this one story traditional calls for a dining room, breakfast nook, and sizable gameroom that can function as a formal living room if preferred. Each of the three bedrooms adjoins a full bath, with the master bedroom meriting a luxurious "his and hers" bath with two walk-in closets.

House-2,157 sq. ft.
Garage-485 sq. ft.

Exterior Exposed Beams

No. 10437

40 inch high bookshelves line several of the family and living room walls, giving the reader or family collector plentious space to display his treasures. Patio access, fireplace and bar are also featured in these two adjacent rooms. The central portion of the home is very functional and work oriented. Utility area here not only houses the laundry facilities, but also the furnace and water heater. Hallways and stairway allow for smooth traffic patterns for both levels. Kitchen and casual eating nook to the rear share a view of the patio, patio access and abundant cabinet space. Pleasing eye appeal and variety describe the exterior facade. Interesting details include bay windows, false dormers, brick quions and exposed beams near the dining room and entry.

First floor – 1,954 sq. ft.
Second Floor – 685 sq. ft.
Garage – 556 sq. ft.

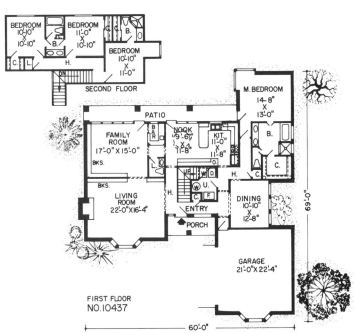

Balcony Offers Sweeping Views

No. 10778

Do you like entertaining? This sturdy brick and stucco beauty will accommodate the largest crowd! Show your guests into the living room or formal dining room off the foyer, or gather around the fireplace in the great room. And, the convenient island kitchen, just steps away from both dining rooms and the three-season porch, is large enough for an army of cooks. If you're in the mood to relax, retreat to the quiet study, or upstairs to the cozy master suite. A fireplace and a private deck make this an ideal escape in any season. And, the raised spa is sure to bring pleasant endings to your hectic days. Three additional bedrooms feature a built-in window seat or desk and loads of closet space.

First floor — 1,978 sq. ft.
Second floor — 1,768 sq. ft.
Basement — 1,978 sq. ft.
Garage — 3-car

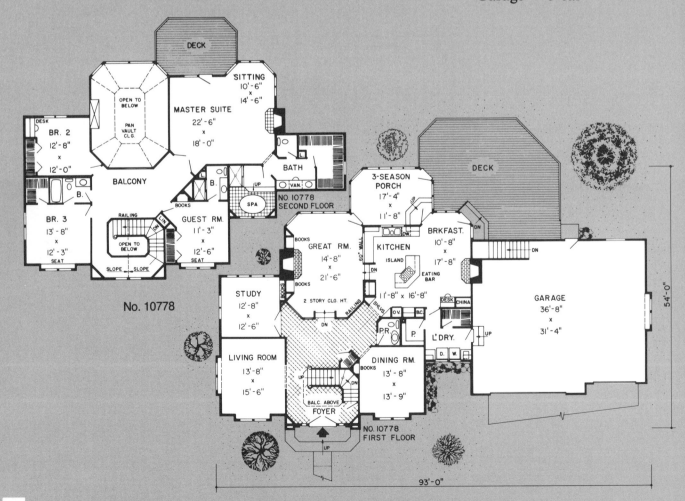

No. 10778

Skylit Loft Crowns
Updated Traditional

No. 10754

Touches of old and new unite to make this a perfect home for the modern family. Rough-hewn beams adorn 11-foot ceilings in the fireplaced living room, mirroring the classic Tudor exterior. Elegant, recessed ceilings grace the master suite and formal dining room. Energy-saving fans lend an old-fashioned air to these lovely rooms. But, the modern plan brings efficiency to the huge island kitchen, which serves the dining room, breakfast nook, and adjacent deck with ease. And, the first-floor master suite, with its double vanities, walk-in closets, and luxurious whirlpool tub, is a convenient feature you're sure to appreciate. Tucked upstairs, two additional bedrooms adjoin a full bath.

First floor — 1,962 sq. ft.
Second floor — 870 sq. ft.
Garage — 611 sq. ft.

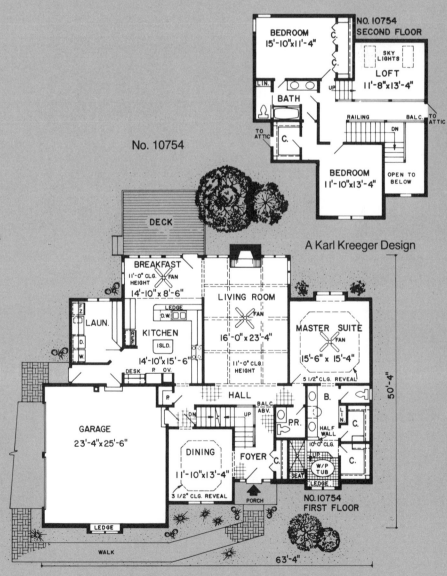

No. 10754

A Karl Kreeger Design

Fireplace In Living and Family Room

No. 9263

This beautiful ranch design features an extra large living room with plenty of formal dining space at the opposite end. Large wood-burning fireplaces are found in both the living and family rooms. A mud room, located off the kitchen, features a laundry area, half bath, and storage closet. The charming master bedroom has a full bath and plenty of closet space.

First floor — 1,878 sq. ft.
Garage — 538 sq. ft.

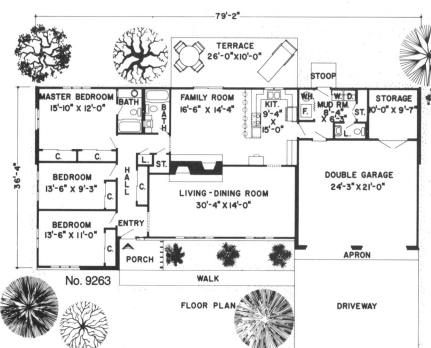

No. 9263 FLOOR PLAN

Wide-open and Convenient

No. 20100

Stacked windows fill the wall in the front bedroom of this one-level home, creating an attractive facade, and a sunny atmosphere inside. Around the corner, two more bedrooms and two full baths complete the bedroom wing, set apart for bedtime quiet. Notice the elegant vaulted ceiling in the master bedroom, the master tub and shower illuminated by a skylight, and the double vanities in both baths. Active areas enjoy a spacious feeling. Look at the high, sloping ceilings in the fireplaced living room, the sliders that unite the breakfast room and kitchen with an adjoining deck, and the vaulted ceilings in the formal dining room off the foyer.

Main floor — 1,727 sq. ft.
Basement — 1,727 sq. ft.
Garage — 484 sq. ft.

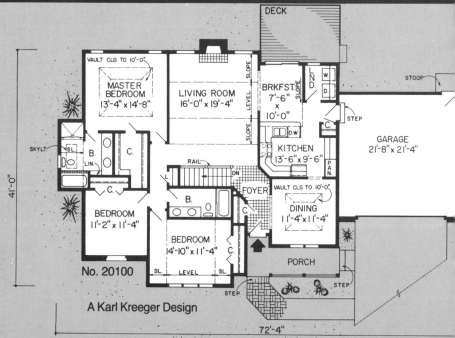

No. 20100

A Karl Kreeger Design

Stylish and Practical Plan

No. 20069

Make the most of daily life with a stylish and practical plan. The garage and seldom-used formal dining room separate the main areas of the house from traffic noise, while the rear of the home maximizes comfort and livability. The kitchen contains a breakfast area large enough for most informal meals and serves snacks to the living room or deck equally well. The spacious living room is a joy in either summer or winter thanks to the fireplace and broad views of deck and back yard. All bedrooms have plenty of closet space, and you'll especially appreciate the attic storage.

First floor — 1,313 sq. ft.
Second floor — 588 sq. ft.
Basement — 1,299 sq. ft.

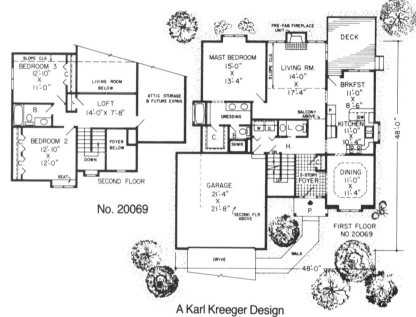

No. 20069

A Karl Kreeger Design

Sheltered Porch is an Inviting Entrance

No. 20070

Enjoy the beauty and tradition of a two-story home. From the spacious, tiled entry with coat closet to the seclusion of second floor bedrooms, you'll appreciate the classic features that distinguish a two-story home. And you'll delight in the modern touches that make this plan sparkle: the handsome window treatment in the living room; the oversized master bedroom with walk-in closet and deluxe, skylit bath; the efficient kitchen and charming breakfast nook; the sweeping outdoor deck.

First floor — 877 sq. ft.
Second floor — 910 sq. ft.
Basement — 877 sq. ft.
Garage — 458 sq. ft.

A Karl Kreeger Design

No. 20070

Screened Porch Offers Outdoor Living, Rain or Shine

No. 10672

This one-level Southwest-styled treasure would be at home in any neighborhood. A sheltered portico leads to the central foyer. To the left, the living and dining rooms run together into one spacious unit, brightened by the bow window at the front of the house, and sliders to the screened porch at the rear. The convenient kitchen serves the adjoining nook, dining room, and family room with ease. And, just off the family room, a hallway leads to the three rear bedrooms and full bath. The master suite, featuring a walk-in closet and full bath with an extra-large vanity, is just off the living room.

First floor — 1,912 sq. ft.
Porch — 255 sq. ft.
Garage — 435 sq. ft.

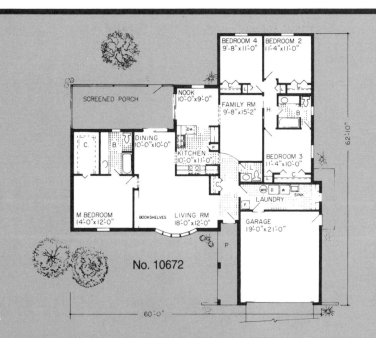

No. 10672

Facade Is Graced by Carriage Lights

No. 10650

From the curved banister to the bi-level study stairs, attention to detail characterizes the spacious interior rooms. Located off the twostory foyer, the high-ceilinged master suite features a luxurious whirlpool bath. Walk out to the redwood deck through atrium doors in the living room or breakfast nook. Formal dining and the powder room are just across the hall from the huge island kitchen. Bookcases line the balcony and study overlooking the beamed living room below. Three bedrooms and a bath share the second floor.

First floor — 2,049 sq. ft.
Second floor — 1,253 sq. ft.
Basement — 2,049 sq. ft.
Garage — 544 sq. ft.

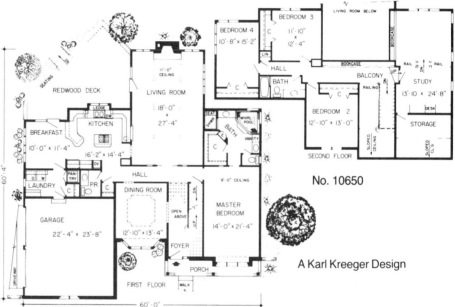

No. 10650

A Karl Kreeger Design

Simplicity in Design

No. 6687

Reminisent of past years of open porches and large rooms, this design appeals to the first time home owner. Simplicity can best describe this small ranch house with its kitchen and utility room appropriately positioned for economy of space. A formal dining area lists off from the kitchen, while an open living room with its wood-burning fireplace adds comfort and relaxation. A dressing table in the bath area is another added luxury in this design. The bedrooms are highlighted by four windows making the rooms brighter with natural lighting. Large closets are featured in the bedrooms.

Main floor — 1,380 sq. ft.
Porches — 240 sq. ft.

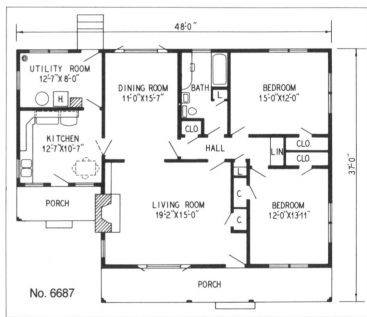

Relaxed and Economical Living

No. 21126

Well suited for the economy-minded small family or as a second home, this design is sure to please. To the left of a large front entry lies the living room, with deck access, a fireplace and a cathedral ceiling with exposed beams. The living room flows through an eating bar to the kitchen-dining area beyond. The dining room also adjoins the deck. To the right of the entry are two bedrooms and a full bath. Sliding glass doors and full length windows cloak the entire width of the rear of the house on this level. A touch of elegance is provided by a stairway spiraling to the second floor loft. Clerestory windows draw in the sun and illuminate this quiet, secluded room.

First floor — 1,082 sq. ft.
Loft — 262 sq. ft.

No materials list available

Recreation Room Welcomes You

No. 9964

This romantic chalet design would be equally appealing along an ocean beach or mountain stream. Restful log fires will add atmosphere in the sizable recreation room bordering the patio of this chalet. Upstairs, another fireplace warms the living and dining rooms which are accessible to the large wooden sun deck. Four bedrooms and two baths are outlined. The home is completely insulated for year round convenience and contains washer and dryer space.

First floor — 896 sq. ft.
Second floor — 457 sq. ft.
Basement — 864 sq. ft.

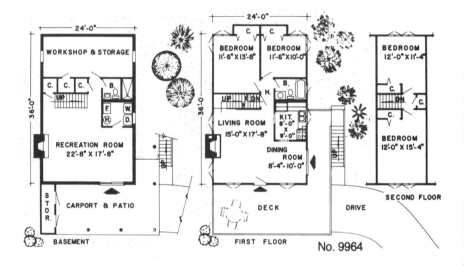

Tudor Grandeur for the Budget-Minded

No. 20354

Gracious living is within your reach if you choose this updated, three-bedroom Tudor. Distinguished by an elegant, centuries-old facade of stucco, brick, and multi-pane transom windows, and a plan that uses every inch of space, this home affords its owners all the amenities of a larger house. A two-story foyer divides the main floor into formal and family areas. Notice the built-ins throughout: window seats in the living and dining rooms, the convenient range-top island and planters that separate the expansive family areas, and the handy bar tucked into a corner of the sunroom off the breakfast nook. Your houseplant collection on the ledge above the stairwell will add a greenhouse feeling to the second floor hall that links the spacious bedrooms and two well-appointed baths.

First floor — 1,346 sq. ft.
Second floor — 1,196 sq. ft.
Basement — 1,346 sq. ft.
Garage — 840 sq. ft.

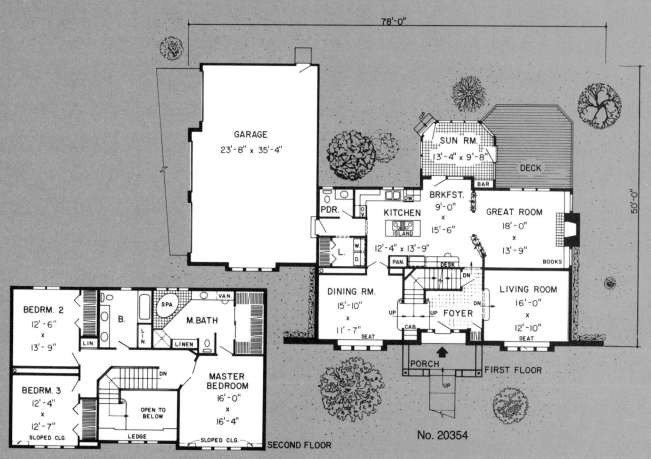

No. 20354

Tiled Halls and Entry Offer Charming Alternative

No. 10443

Large, elegant rooms within the core of this charming home are delineated by the unusual use of tile for the surrounding hall areas. Front placement of the garage muffles the street noise and provides privacy for the living and sleeping zones. The spacious kitchen has a pantry plus an angled peninsula which separates the room from the adjacent dining nook. Beamed ceilings accent the living room as do its fireplace, built-in bookcases and wet bar. The family room has easy access to the patio and the optional pool. Luxury is seen in the master suite with its double walk-in closet, private fireplace and elegantly appointed bath.

First floor-2,865 sq. ft.
Garage-501 sq. ft.

PLAN NO. 10443

A Karl Kreeger Design

A Home for Today and Tomorrow

No. 20109

This convenient, one-level plan is perfect for the modern family with a taste for classic design. Traditional Victorian touches in this three-bedroom beauty include a romantic, railed porch and the intriguing breakfast tower just off the kitchen. But, the step-saving arrangement of the kitchen between the breakfast and formal dining rooms, the wide-open living room with sliders to a rear deck, and the handsome master suite with its skylit, compartmentalized bath make this a home you'll love today and long into the future. Notice the convenient laundry location on the bedroom hall.

Main living area — 1,588 sq. ft.
Basement — 1,588 sq. ft.
Garage — 484 sq. ft.

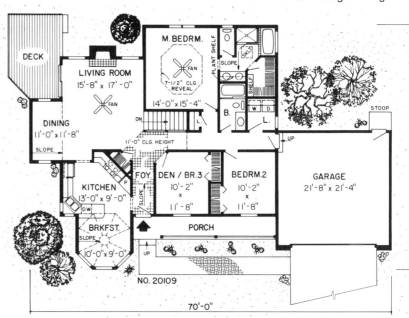

Central Patio Invites Outdoor Entertaining

No. 10446

Lattice accents greet guests in the tiled entry and separate it from the dining room. The large living room has a leaded-glass bay window, fireplace, built-in bookcases and wetbar. Double French doors lead to the patio from the family room which is also lighted by arched windows on its other walls. The kitchen, breakfast nook and utility area are adjacent to the dining room for easy serving, and just off the garage for fewer steps when unloading groceries. The bedrooms are grouped around one end of the patio so that the master suite has direct access to it.

First floor — 2,670 sq. ft.
Garage — 645 sq. ft.

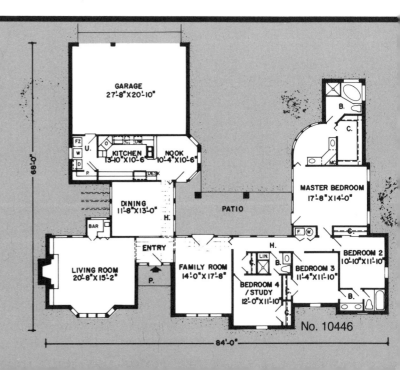

Enjoy the View

No. 20095

Step into the sunwashed foyer of this contemporary beauty, and you'll be faced with a choice. You can walk downstairs into a huge, fireplaced rec room with built-in bar and adjoining patio. Three bedrooms and a full bath complete the lower level. Or, you can ascend the stairs to a massive living room with sloping ceilings, a tiled fireplace, and a commanding view of the back yard. Sharing the view, a breakfast nook with sunny bay opens to an outdoor deck. The adjoining kitchen is just steps away from the formal dining room, which features recessed ceilings and overlooks the foyer. You'll also find the master suite on this level, just past the powder room off the living room.

Upper level — 1,448 sq. ft.
Lower level — 1,029 sq. ft.
Garage — 504 sq. ft.

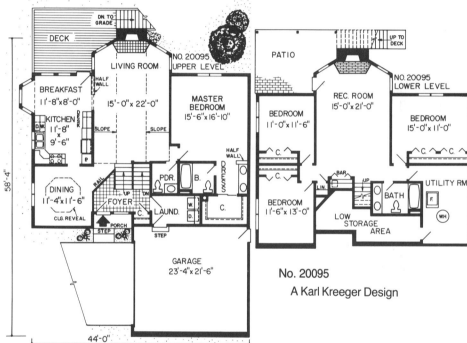

No. 20095

A Karl Kreeger Design

Plan Excellent Choice For Sloping Lot

No. 9714

Utilizing a sloping lot to create a striking design, this split foyer plan embodies outdoor living areas and highly livable lower level. Front-facing and opening to terrace, the family room dominates the lower level, which also includes bedroom, hobby room, and full bath with shower. Above a sun deck greets the living room and dining room, and a tiled country kitchen, complete with cooking island and built-in laundry, and three bedrooms and two full baths comprise the sleeping wing.

Main level – 1,748 sq. ft.
Lower level – 932 sq. ft.
Garage – 768 sq. ft.

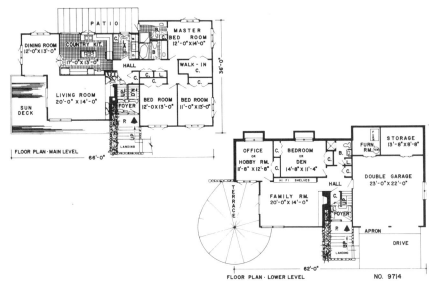

Simple, Easy To Build Passive Plan

No. 26950

The design of this plan allows for excellent air circulation between downstairs living areas and second level rooms. Ceilings rise two stories in the family, dining, and living areas and are open over balcony railings to upstairs bedrooms. The living room features deck access and wood burning fireplace. The conveniently arranged kitchen is highlighted by a generous pantry. A unique half round deck lies off the entry way and another roofed deck connects the garage and house. The shape of the double garage allows it to be entered from any of three directions that the home builder might choose.

First floor – 1,090 sq. ft.
Second floor – 580 sq. ft.
Garage – 484 sq. ft.

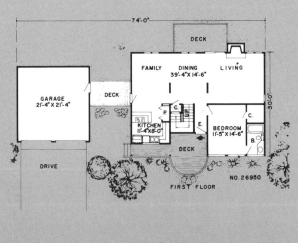

Glass Brings The Outdoors In

No. 9594

Adaptability is the outstanding characteristic of this modern two bedroom home, and the main evidence is a folding partition wall that can enclose part of the expansive dining room to form a guest room or den. When the partitions are not in use, the living room and dining room, separated from the terrace only by sliding glass doors, offer an immense area for entertaining or relaxing. The kitchen is distinguished by an exposed brick wall which encloses the built-in oven.

First floor-1,140 sq. ft.
Basement-1,140 sq. ft.
Garage-462 sq. ft.

TERRACE
20'-0" X 8'-0"

BEDROOM
11'-8" X 10'-8"

DEN or
GUEST RM.
9'-0" X 9'-0"

DINING ROOM
10'-0" X 12'-4"

KIT.
10'-0" X 9'-8"

DOUBLE GARAGE
22'-0" X 20'-0"

HALL

BEDROOM
14'-0" X 12'-0"

LIVING ROOM
20'-0" X 13'-0"

STORAGE

26'-0"

DRIVEWAY

WALK

NO. 9594

66'-4"

Superior Comfort and Privacy

No. 9828

Consider this refreshing design if you strive for the best. From the beautiful exterior of natural stone to the authentic slate floors in the foyer to the private patio off the master bedroom, this home demonstrates class. You'll appreciate fine touches like the two-way fireplace in between the living room and family room, the magnificent terrace, and the generous dimensions of the rooms. The breakfast nook enjoys a splendid view of the pool through a large bow window. Note the separate terrace entrances, including a mud room. Four bedrooms are grouped in a wing for privacy, while the maid's room is discretely placed. It can be built on a slab foundation.

First floor — 2,679 sq. ft.
Basement — 2,679 sq. ft.
Garage — 541 sq. ft.

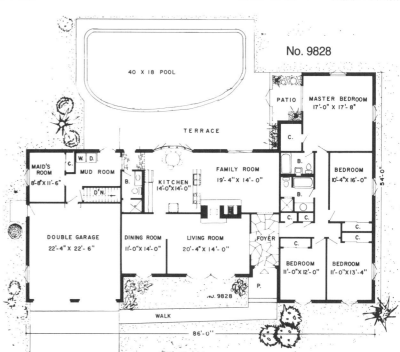

Compact Charmer Flooded with Sun

No. 20300

The clerestory window high over the covered porch of this inviting gem hints at the high excitement you'll find when you walk through the front door. From the soaring foyer to the sun room off the fireplaced living room and kitchen, this contemporary porch revival house is enveloped in warmth and sunlight. And, you'll find all the features you've been longing for: built-in media and china cabinets, an efficient U-shaped kitchen, a central yet concealed first-floor powder room, a skylit master bath with double vanities, and three spacious bedrooms with loads of closet space.

First floor — 909 sq. ft.
Second floor — 765 sq. ft.
Basement — 517 sq. ft.
Garage and stair — 479 sq. ft.

Classic and Convenient

No. 20110

Who said one-level homes had to be boring rectangles? Here's a clapboard and brick beauty with loads of curbside appeal. Step inside to a spacious living room dominated by a corner fireplace. A hallway off the foyer leads to two bedrooms, a full bath, and lots of closet space. At the rear of the house, you'll find a formal dining room and skylit breakfast nook adjoining the kitchen, a step-saving convenience for busy cooks. The rear deck is a nice spot for a barbecue, or just plain relaxing. And, when you really need an escape at the end of a hectic day, retire to your private master suite, complete with a double vanitied bath, a raised tub, and a walk-in shower.

First floor — 1,786 sq. ft.
Basement — 1,786 sq. ft.
Garage — 484 sq. ft.

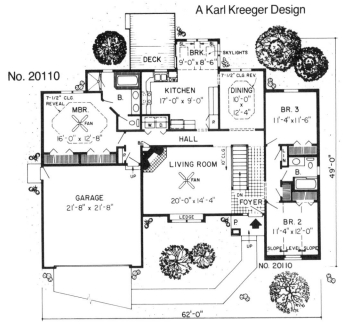

A Karl Kreeger Design

No. 20110

DECK
9'-0" x 8'-6"

BRK.

KITCHEN
17'-0" x 9'-0"

DINING
10'-0" x 12'-4"

BR. 3
11'-4" x 11'-6"

MBR.
16'-0" x 12'-8"

HALL

B.

GARAGE
21'-8" x 21'-8"

LIVING ROOM
20'-0" x 14'-4"

FOYER

BR. 2
11'-4" x 12'-0"

NO. 20110

62'-0"

49'-0"

Elegant Exterior Accents Spacious Design

No. 10459

Plenty of well organized storage makes this formal design as efficient as it is lovely. The luxurious master bedroom suite includes a five-piece bath plus individual walk-in closets. The two additional bedrooms share a walk-through five-piece bath. The rear patio can be entered from the master suite, the breakfast nook adjoining the kitchen, or from the living room. Bookshelves flank the living room fireplace. The kitchen is well located with access to both the dining room and family room for either formal or informal gatherings.

First floor — 2,520 sq. ft.
Garage — 614 sq. ft.

Updated Tudor

No. 20076

The traditional exterior of this four-bedroom classic only hints at the modern drama that unfolds inside. Flanked by formal dining and living rooms, the two-story foyer leads you directly into the expansive family room. There, the glass-walled view of the backyard is broken up only by a massive fireplace. Walk out to the deck from the family room or the huge island kitchen-breakfast room. The first-floor master suite is a convenience you're sure to appreciate. You won't have to travel very far to make coffee in the morning. The balcony overlooking the foyer links the upstairs bedrooms, each with a walk-in closet and nearby bath.

First floor — 2,030 sq. ft.
Second floor — 1,033 sq. ft.
Basement — 2,030 sq. ft.
Garage — 576 sq. ft.

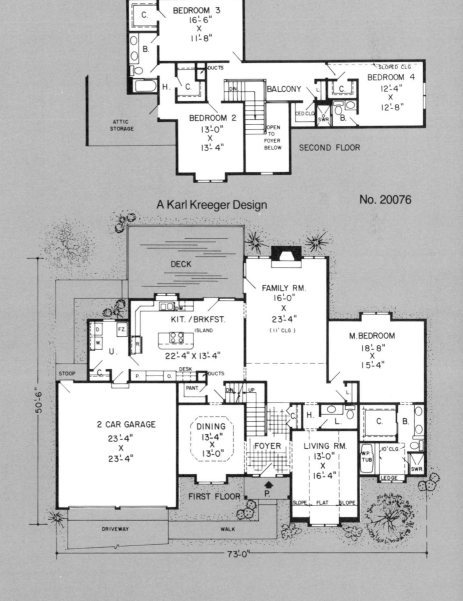

A Karl Kreeger Design   No. 20076

Fireplace A Feature

No. 9838

Family convenience is emphasized in this beautiful ranch style home. The owner's suite includes double closets and a private bath with a spacious built-in vanity. A two-way wood-burning fireplace between the living room and dining room permits the fire to be enjoyed from both rooms. An extra large garage possesses an abundance of extra storage space.

First floor-1,770 sq. ft.
Basement-1,770 sq. ft.
Garage-700 sq. ft.

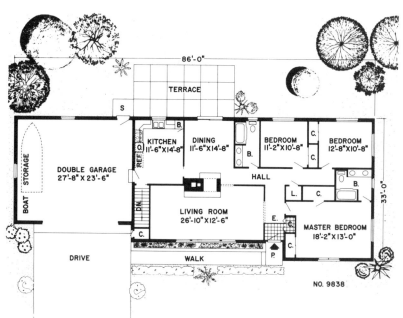

86'-0"

TERRACE

S

DOUBLE GARAGE
27'-8" X 23'-6"

BOAT STORAGE

REF.

KITCHEN
11'-6"X14'-8"

DINING
11'-6"X14'-8"

B.

BEDROOM
11'-2"X10'-8"

BEDROOM
12'-8"X10'-8"

B.

C.

HALL

33'-0"

DN.

LIVING ROOM
26'-10"X12'-6"

L. C.

C.

B.

MASTER BEDROOM
18'-2"X13'-0"

E.

C.

DRIVE

WALK

P.

NO. 9838

Family Room Forms Core

No. 1064

The family room forms the core of this plan. Creating the focal point in this room is a heat circulating fireplace, encased in masonry and faced with cut stone. Bookshelves, a T.V. shelf and wood storage area fit into the stone flanking the fireplace. The family room flows through an eating bar to the kitchen. A utility room is handily tucked around the corner behind the kitchen. Secluded on the other side of the family room are three bedrooms, a bath and master bedroom suite.

First floor-1,954 sq. ft.
Garage-431 sq. ft.

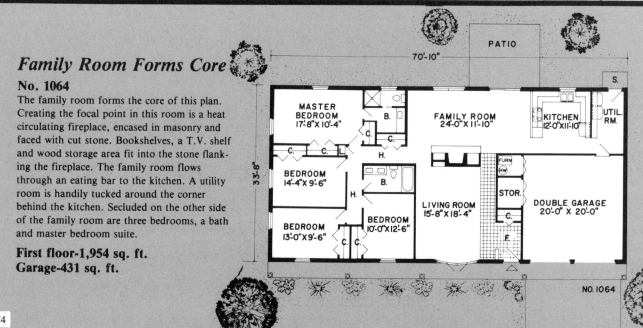

PATIO

70'-10"

S.

MASTER BEDROOM
17'-8"X 10'-4"

B.

FAMILY ROOM
24'-0"X 11'-10"

KITCHEN
12'-0"X11'-10"

UTIL. RM.

C. C.

C. C. L.

H.

33'-8"

BEDROOM
14'-4"X 9'-6"

B.

FURN.
HW

H.

LIVING ROOM
15'-8"X18'-4"

STOR.

DOUBLE GARAGE
20'-0" X 20'-0"

BEDROOM
13'-0"X 9'-6"

C. C.

BEDROOM
10'-0"X12'-6"

C.

F.

NO. 1064

Colonial Detailing Enlivens Exterior

No. 10020

Impressive Colonial columns punctuate the semi-circular porch and fuse with the bow windows and brick to create an exceptional facade. Inside, the floor plan is a study in modern living. Fireplaces grace both living room and family room, which opens to an expansive terrace. A formal dining room adjoins the highly functional kitchen, and the 21-foot master bedroom boasts a lavish full bath and double closets. Two front bedrooms are accented with lovely bow windows.

First floor-2,512 sq. ft.
Basement-2,512 sq. ft.
Garage-648 sq. ft.

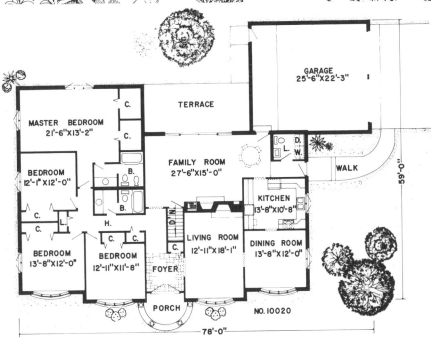

GARAGE 25'-6"X22'-3"

MASTER BEDROOM 21'-6"X13'-2"

TERRACE

BEDROOM 12'-1" X12'-0"

FAMILY ROOM 27'-6"X15'-0"

KITCHEN 13'-8"X10'-8"

WALK

BEDROOM 13'-8"X12'-0"

BEDROOM 12'-11"X11'-8"

LIVING ROOM 12'-11"X18'-1"

DINING ROOM 13'-8"X12'-0"

FOYER

PORCH

NO. 10020

78'-0"

59'-0"

Sun Deck, Covered Patio Invite Outdoor Living

No. 9840

Encircling part of three sides of this home, an expansive sun deck spills off the living and dining room and allows an unparalleled view of lake or mountain surroundings. Beneath the sun deck, a stone patio balances the stone siding of the family room and is reached via sliding glass doors. The first level also includes a large hobby room, utility and storage room and half bath. Two bedrooms, a full bath, and kitchen with breakfast bar complete the upstairs plan, and a substantial sleeping loft with closet comprises the third level.

First floor-1,120 sq. ft.
Lower level-1,120 sq. ft.
Upper level-340 sq. ft.

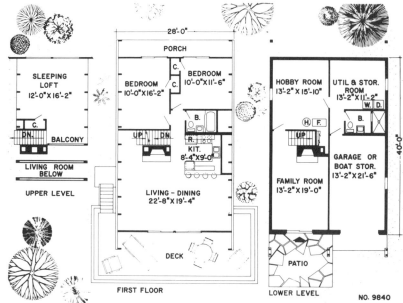

Building A-frame Can Be Weekend Project

No. 7664

Easy to apply red cedar shake shingles are specified for the roof of this A-frame cabin and help make building it yourself a feasible and rewarding weekend project. Constructed on a concrete slab, the cabin exudes relaxed informality through the warm natural tones of exposed beams and unfinished wood interior.

Main floor-560 sq. ft.
Upper level-240 sq. ft.

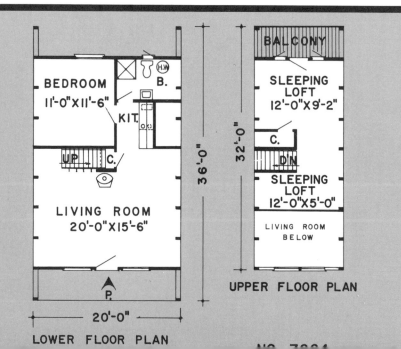

Chalet Can Be Finished As Needed

No. 10026

Swiss Chalet inspired, this home allows the possibility of using it while completing the attic bedroom or lower bedroom and family room at some later date. The first floor, housing living room, kitchen, full size bedroom and bath and even a laundry would make a more than comfortable retreat until the home could be finished.

First floor-1,052 sq. ft.
Second floor-628 sq. ft.
Lower level-1,052 sq. ft.

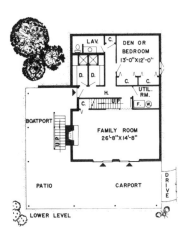

LOWER LEVEL

FIRST FLOOR
NO. 10026

Home Recalls Southern Plantation

No. 9850

Magnificent white columns, shutters, and small paned windows combine to create images of the pre-Civil War South in this generously-proportioned design. Inside, the opulent master bedroom suite, with plentiful closet space, a full bath and study, suggests modern luxury. Fireplaces enhance the formal living room and sizable family room, which skirts the lovely screened porch. The formal dining room boasts build-in china closets.

First floor-2,466 sq. ft.
Basement-1,447 sq. ft.
Garage-664 sq. ft.

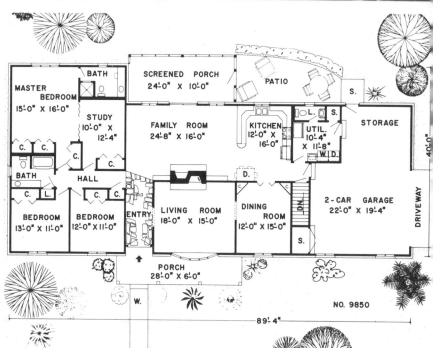

Semicircular Terrace Offers Access

No. 9882

Spanning four rooms to the rear of the home, the semi-circular terrace in this plan is accessible through sliding glass doors from the living room, dining room and family room. The sunken living room with fireplace borders the formal dining room, and a kitchen with laundry space is situated to serve both dining room and family room. Three of the bedrooms, including the master bedroom which merits a bath and large closet, face front and enjoy lovely bay windows.

First floor-2,212 sq. ft.
Basement-2,212 sq. ft.
Garage-491 sq. ft.

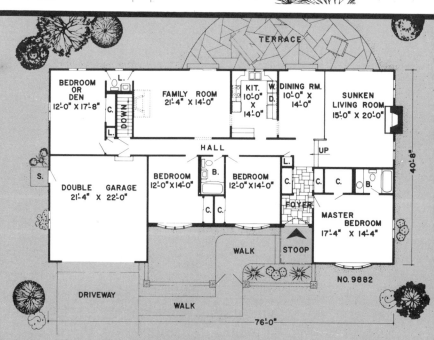

The Home Of A Lifetime

No. 9950

Distinctive as this home may appear, with its deck-encircled hexagonal living room, its construction will actually prove practical. Besides the living room, which exhibits exposed beams and a cathedral ceiling, the main level emcompasses four bedrooms, two baths, dining room and kitchen. On the lower level, an enormous family room opens to a patio, with built-in barbecue. Another bedroom, den and bath with shower are detailed. Boat storage is also provided on this level.

First floor-1,672 sq. ft.
Lower level-1,672 sq. ft.
Garage-484 sq. ft.

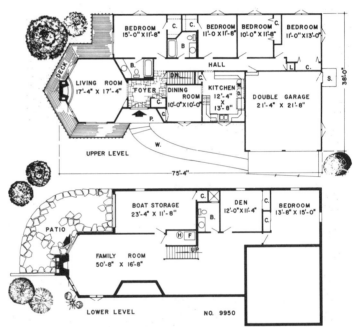

UPPER LEVEL

BEDROOM 15'-0" X 11'-8"
BEDROOM 11'-0 X 11'-8"
BEDROOM 10'-0" X 11'-8"
BEDROOM 11'-0"X13'-0"
HALL
LIVING ROOM 17'-4" X 17'-4"
FOYER
DINING ROOM 10'-0"X10'-0"
KITCHEN 12'-4" X 13'-8"
DOUBLE GARAGE 21'-4" X 21'-8"
DECK
38'-0"
75'-4"

LOWER LEVEL

BOAT STORAGE 23'-4" X 11'-8"
DEN 12'-0"X11'-4"
BEDROOM 13'-8" X 15'-0"
PATIO
FAMILY ROOM 50'-8" X 16'-8"
NO. 9950

Convenience and Beauty Built into Every Room

No. 20358

To enjoy the ingenious plan of this gracious brick beauty, stand in the second-floor loft and look down on the two-story foyer, the open staircase, and towering great room with built-in bar and rear patio access. You won't see the private study tucked away from the action at the front of the house, but you'll enjoy its quiet atmosphere. Directly overhead, the guest room enjoys its own private bath. Step down the hall past two book-lined bedrooms, linked by an adjoining full bath, to the master suite, an elegant retreat you'll relish at the end of the day. Downstairs, a well-appointed island kitchen shares the backyard view with the breakfast room just across the counter. And, it's just steps away from the formal dining room and the glass-walled sun porch.

First floor — 2,104 sq. ft.
Second floor — 1,603 sq. ft.
Basement — 2,238 sq. ft.
Garage — 840 sq. ft.

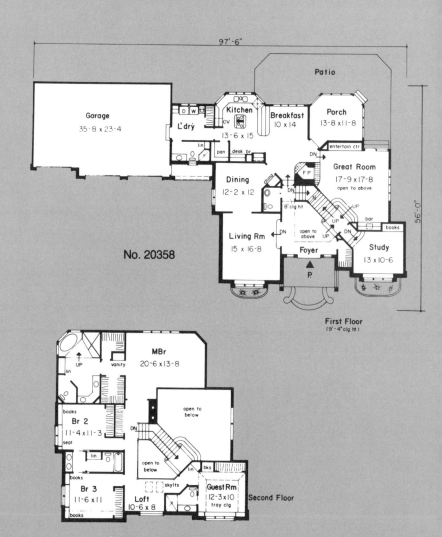

No. 20358

Central Courtyard Features Pool

No. 10507

Created for gracious living, this design is organized around a central courtyard complete with pool. Secluded near one corner of the courtyard is the master bedroom suite which is accented with a skylight, spacious walk-in closet and a bath which also accommodates swimming enthusiasts. The living room, dining room and kitchen occupy another corner. The well located kitchen easily serves the patio for comfortable outdoor entertaining. The family room plus two more bedrooms complete the design.

First floor — 2,194 sq. ft.
Garage — 576 sq. ft.

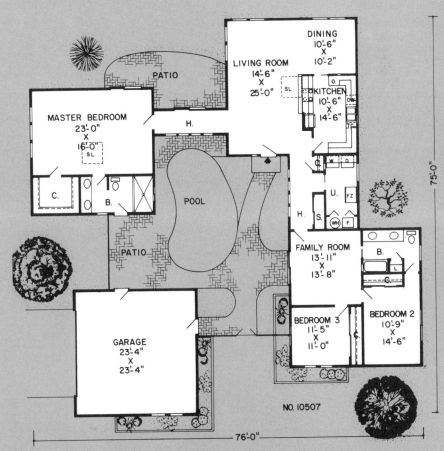

DINING
10'-6"
X
10'-2"

LIVING ROOM
14'-6"
X
25'-0"

KITCHEN
10'-6"
X
14'-6"

PATIO

H.

MASTER BEDROOM
23'-0"
X
16'-0"
SL.

C.

B.

POOL

PATIO

U.

FZ.

H.

S.

WH.

F.

FAMILY ROOM
13'-11"
X
13'-8"

B.

L.

C.

GARAGE
23'-4"
X
23'-4"

BEDROOM 3
11'-5"
X
11'-0"

BEDROOM 2
10'-9"
X
14'-6"

C.

NO. 10507

75'-0"

76'-0"

Master Bedroom Suite Accentuates Luxury

No. 9870

Adorned with pillars and a bow window, this French Provincial design becomes an exercise in elegance, crowned by the master bedroom suite. Placed to allow full privacy, the master bedroom incorporates a segmented bath, large walk-in closet, and sitting room with its own closet. A firelit living room and dining room augment an appealing family room, which opens to the terrace. Beyond the kitchen, a laundry room, half bath, and closet space add to the charm.

First floor — 2,015 sq. ft.
Basement — 2,015 sq. ft.
Garage — 545 sq. ft.

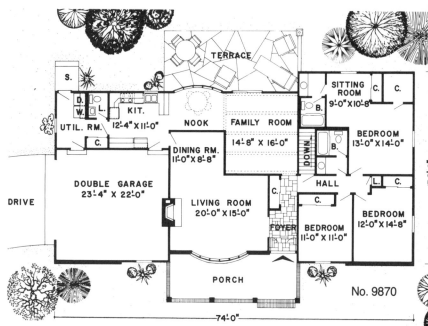

Master Suite Features Cozy Hearth

No. 10635

Columns adorn the classic entry of this traditional colonial dwelling. A hallway, flanked by the living room and beamed family room with fireplace, leads directly into the convenient island kitchen. Eat in the formal dining room or sunny dinette. Sliding glass doors lead to the patio for outside entertaining. Four bedrooms and two baths lie at the top of the central staircase.

First floor — 1,280 sq. ft.
Second floor — 1,224 sq. ft.
Basement — 1,283 sq. ft.
Garage — 576 sq. ft.

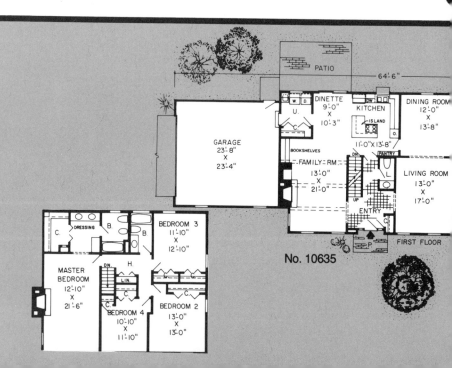

Exterior Promise Of Luxury Fulfilled

No. 9998

Graceful Spanish arches and stately brick suggests the right attention to detail that is found inside this expansive three bedroom home. The plush master bedroom suite, a prime example, luxuriates in a lounge, a walk-in closet and a private bath. Exposed rustic beams and a cathedral ceiling heightens the formal living room, and an unusually large family room savors a wood-burning fireplace. In addition to the formal dining room, a kitchen with dinette and access to the terrace is planned.

First floor — 2,333 sq. ft.
Basement — 2,333 sq. ft.
Garage — 559 sq. ft.

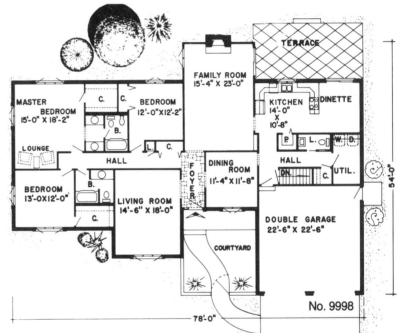

TERRACE

FAMILY ROOM
15'-4" X 23'-0"

KITCHEN
14'-0"
X
10'-8"

DINETTE

MASTER
BEDROOM
15'-0" X 18'-2"

C. C.

BEDROOM
12'-0"X12'-2"

B.

L. C.

P. L. W.D.

LOUNGE

HALL

FOYER

DINING
ROOM
11'-4" X 11'-8"

HALL

DN.

UTIL.

C.

BEDROOM
13'-0X12'-0"

B.

LIVING ROOM
14'-6" X 18'-0"

DOUBLE GARAGE
22'-6" X 22'-6"

C.

COURTYARD

No. 9998

78'-0"

54'-0"

Mudroom Separates Garage and Kitchen

No. 9812

Gardening and woodworking tools will find a home in the storage closet of the useful mudroom in this rustic detailed ranch. Besides incorporating a laundry area, the mudroom will prove invaluable as a place for removing snowy boots and draining wet umbrellas. The family room appendages the open kitchen and flows outward to the stone terrace. The master bedroom is furnished with a private bath and protruding closet space, and the living room retains a formality by being situated to the left of the entryway.

First floor — 1,396 sq. ft.
Basement — 1,396 sq. ft.
Garage — 484 sq. ft.

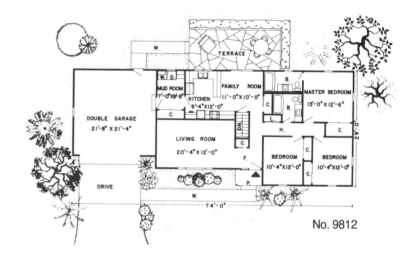

No. 9812

Wooden Decks are Nice for Summer Dining

No. 9308

Variegated brick, rich wood siding, and diamond light windows layer the exterior of this split foyer plan. Inside, four bedrooms and a den, plus a large recreation room provide space for privacy and relaxation. Besides the recreation room, a den, bedroom, utility and bath are found on the lower level. Upstairs, the comfortable living room enjoys a fireplace, and the dining room includes sliding glass doors to the elevated wooden deck.

Upper level — 1,440 sq. ft.
Lower level — 1,344 sq. ft.
Garage — 497 sq. ft.

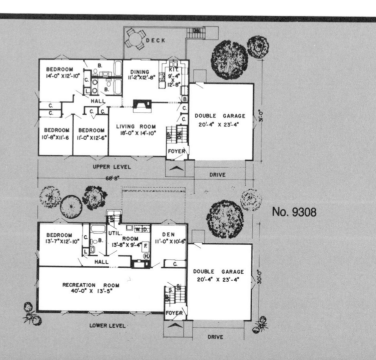

No. 9308

Double Doors Give Spanish Welcome

No. 10108

Massive double doors open to the foyer of this multi-arched Spanish design and balance three sets of double doors opening to a second floor balcony. Spanning over 27 feet, the living room occupies the entire area to the right of the foyer, while the kitchen and family room edge the left side. Hallway, bath, and laundry niche separate the areas and buffer noises. Three large bedrooms boast two baths.

First floor — 1,176 sq. ft.
Second floor — 1,176 sq. ft.
Basement — 1,176 sq. ft.
Garage — 576 sq. ft.

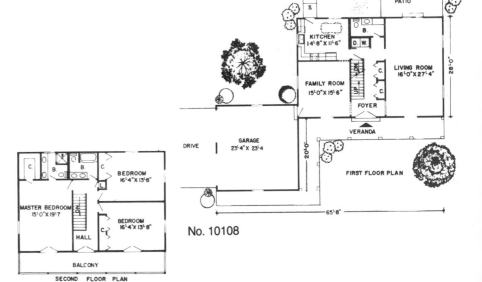

No. 10108

SECOND FLOOR PLAN

FIRST FLOOR PLAN

Gingerbread Charm

No. 10690

Victorian elegance combines with a modern floor plan to make this a dream house without equal. A wrap-around porch and rear deck add lots of extra living space to the roomy first floor, which features a formal parlor and dining room just off the central entry. Informal areas at the rear of the house are wide-open for family interaction. Gather the crew around the fireplace in the family room, or make supper in the kitchen while you supervise the kids' homework in the sunwashed breakfast room. Three bedrooms, tucked upstairs for a quiet atmosphere, feature skylit baths. And, you'll love the five-sided sitting nook in your master suite, a perfect spot to relax after a luxurious bath in the sunken tub.

First floor — 1,260 sq. ft.
Second floor — 1,021 sq. ft.
Basement — 1,186 sq. ft.
Garage — 840 sq. ft.

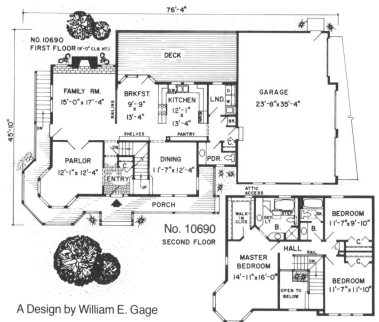

A Design by William E. Gage

Open-Beamed Ceilings Offered in Plan

No. 10573

Expansive beautiful ceilings are offered in this spacious design. The exterior is built with a brick and stucco frontage and wood veneer siding on the side and rear elevations. It also has a shake shingle roof. On the first floor, a large foyer is available with closet space. From the foyer and to the left lie the living and dining rooms. The living room has a large bay window. The dining room is more formal and has a decorative raised ceiling. From the dining room lies the kitchen with its own pantry, a beautiful, open-beamed ceiling, and a bay-windowed breakfast nook. Another feature of the first floor is the sunken family room that has a large wood-burning fireplace and massive open beams hanging from its ceiling.

First floor — 1,306 sq. ft.
Second floor — 1,248 sq. ft.
Basement — 1,338 sq. ft.
Garage — 540 sq. ft.

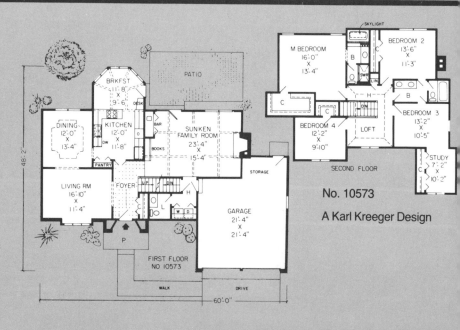

No. 10573

A Karl Kreeger Design

You'll Enjoy Peace and Quiet

No. 25002

The excellent design of the floor plan buffers living and sleeping areas with stairway, master bath, closets, and a hall. The bedrooms are clustered together, yet none shares a wall with another or with the living room. The family playroom is downstairs along with a bedroom, bath, laundry, and storage. A large fireplace wall in the living room and dining room create a feeling of warmth, while the cathedral ceiling with dark contrasting beams gives a sense of spaciousness.

Main level — 2,263 sq. ft.
Lower level — 1,290 sq. ft.
Garage — 528 sq. ft.

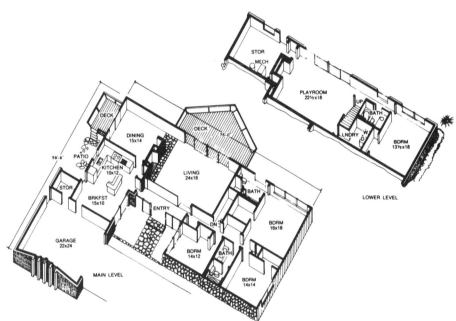

Central Atrium Highlights Well-organized Plan

No. 10464

Bring the outdoors in no matter what the season with glass-walled atrium incorporated into this elegant plan. The tiled family room carries out the indoor-outdoor living scheme and open room arrangement. The front living room has a large fireplace flanked with bookcases plus access to the dining room which is easily entered from the kitchen. A breakfast nook and convenient laundry area complete the functional areas of this home. Each of the spacious bedrooms has it own walk-in closet and bath. The master suite has a separate dressing room with five-piece bath.

First floor — 2,222 sq. ft.
Garage — 468 sq. ft.

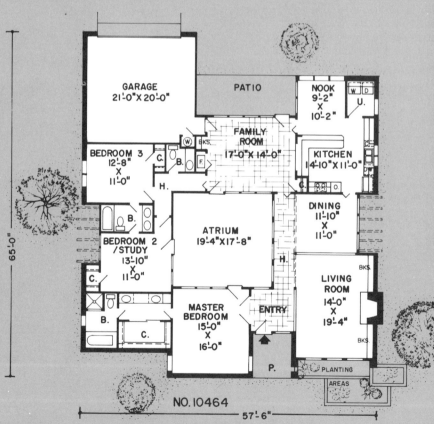

A *View from Every Room*

No. 20361

The impressive facade of this beautiful home hints at the sunny, open atmosphere inside. The two story foyer, flanked by a private study and formal living room, is dominated by an angular staircase to the bedroom floor. Step past the powder room to the rear of the house, and discover the kitchen of your dreams. Notice the cooktop island, built-ins throughout, and sink overlooking the rear patio. The glass-walled breakfast room, three season porch, and towering, fireplaced family room share a backyard view. Upstairs, the balcony overlooking the family room links three spacious bedrooms and two full baths, including the master suite with its private garden tub, double vanities, and room-size closet.

First floor — 1,465 sq. ft.
Second floor — 1,031 sq. ft.
Basement — 1,465 sq. ft.
Garage — 746 sq. ft.

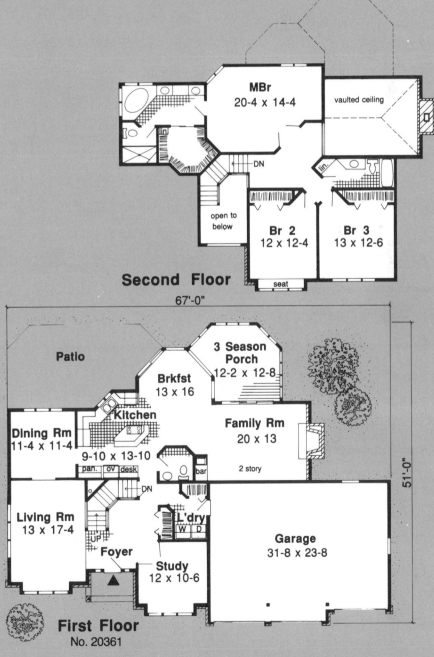

Second Floor

- MBr 20-4 x 14-4
- vaulted ceiling
- DN
- open to below
- lin.
- Br 2 12 x 12-4
- Br 3 13 x 12-6
- seat

67'-0"

First Floor
No. 20361

51'-0"

- Patio
- Brkfst 13 x 16
- 3 Season Porch 12-2 x 12-8
- Kitchen 9-10 x 13-10
- Dining Rm 11-4 x 11-4
- Family Rm 20 x 13
- 2 story
- pan. ov desk
- DN
- bar
- Living Rm 13 x 17-4
- L'dry W D
- Garage 31-8 x 23-8
- UP
- Foyer
- Study 12 x 10-6

Angular Fireplace Adds Interest

No. 20125

With its spacious, garage-level shop area, this attractive brick and wood-sided classic is the perfect abode for the home hobbyist. The main floor active space surrounds a central staircase. Formal areas off the foyer at the front of the house are ideal for entertaining. Your guests will enjoy the cozy atmosphere of the fireplaced living room, and the quiet elegance of the formal dining room. The kitchen, breakfast bay and utility room share a backyard view, and access to the rear deck. With its raised tub, double vanities, and step-in shower, the first-floor master suite is a private, yet convenient retreat you're sure to appreciate. Two bedrooms upstairs share another full bath.

First floor — 1,340 sq. ft.
Second floor — 455 sq. ft.
Basement — 347 sq. ft.
Garage — 979 sq. ft.

No. 20125
First Floor

A Karl Kreeger Design

Modified Cape for Family Living

No. 10634

With a graceful porch sheltering three sides of this inviting home and a patio off the back, you can enjoy all your summer evenings outside. Walk out for a breath of fresh air after enjoying the formal dining room or the sunny breakfast nook. Then enjoy the walk across the central foyer from the spacious living room. Sharing the second floor with three bedrooms and two baths, the master suite features a hexagonal sitting room.

First floor — 1,182 sq. ft.
Second floor — 1,164 sq. ft.

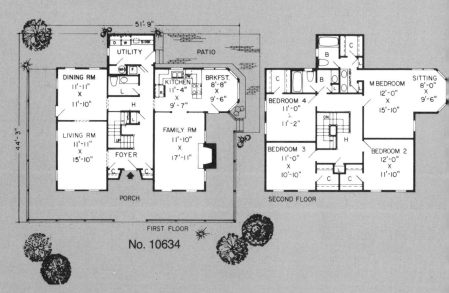

No. 10634

Timeless Elegance

No. 20105

The handsome Tudor exterior of this four-bedroom classic is mirrored by an exciting interior plan of extraordinary beauty. Step through the foyer, flanked by a formal dining room and library, and past the stairway to a massive living room characterized by high ceilings, abundant windows, and access to a private rear deck. With two-way access to the bar and fireplace, both living and hearth rooms share easy entertaining and a cozy atmosphere. The adjoining kitchen, with its handy breakfast bar and nearby pantry, is a marvel of convenience. Look at the recessed ceilings, twin walk-in closets, and luxurious bath in the first-floor master suite. Upstairs, three ample bedrooms enjoy walk-in closets and adjoining baths.

First floor — 2,080 sq. ft.
Second floor — 1,051 sq. ft.
Basement — 2,080 sq. ft.
Garage — 666 sq. ft.

A Karl Kreeger Design

No. 20105

Rustic Design Blends with Hillside

No. 10012

Naturally perfect for a woodland setting, this redwood decked home will adapt equally well to a lake or ocean setting. A car or boat garage is furnished on the lower level. Fireplaces equip both the living room and the 36-foot long family room which opens onto a shaded patio. A laundry room adjoins the open kitchen which shares the large redwood deck encircling the living and dining area. Two bedrooms and two full baths on the first floor supplement another bedroom and half bath on the lower level.

First floor — 1,198 sq. ft.
Basement — 1,198 sq. ft.

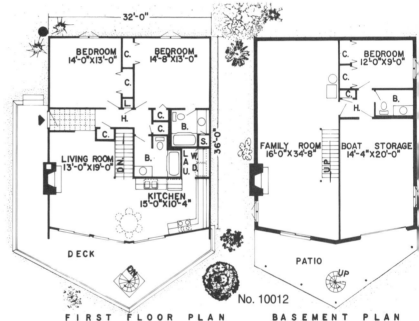

FIRST FLOOR PLAN   BASEMENT PLAN

Energy-Saving Sunroom Warms Classic Tudor

No. 10735

Here's a gracious family castle in a traditional style. From the dual-access curving stairway to the fireplaced living and family rooms with exposed beams, you'll find elegant touches everywhere. Look at the upstairs bedrooms with conveniently adjoining baths, the built-in bookshelves in the loft and study, and the angular bay windows and recessed ceilings in the dining room and master suite. But, this house isn't just beautiful. The island kitchen is designed for convenience. The sun room saves your energy dollars by capturing heat in its tile floor. With a private hot tub and study, the first-floor master suite is a luxurious retreat for its lucky occupant.

First floor — 3,332 sq. ft.
Sun room — 340 sq. ft.
Second floor — 1,218 sq. ft.
Basement — 3,672 sq. ft.
Garage — 1,137 sq. ft.

A Karl Kreeger Design

Home Exterior Blends with Vacation Sites

No. 10150

This two story rough-frame home blends in with its surroundings near any beach area or mountain resort. Ground level entry is provided to the family room. The kitchen opens onto a living-dining room combination, lighted by large windows and doors opening onto a three sided deck.

Upper level — 1,008 sq. ft.
Lower level — 652 sq. ft.
Garage — 356 sq. ft.

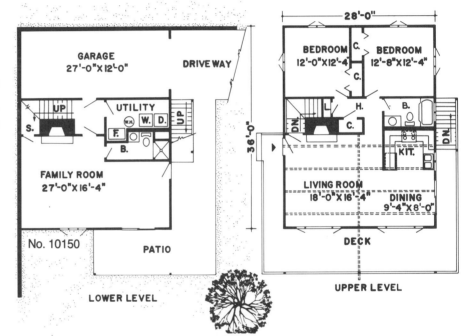

GARAGE 27'-0"X12'-0"

DRIVE WAY

UTILITY

UP

S.

UP

W.H. W. D.

F.

B.

FAMILY ROOM 27'-0"X16'-4"

No. 10150

PATIO

LOWER LEVEL

36'-0"

28'-0"

BEDROOM 12'-0"X12'-4"

C.

BEDROOM 12'-8"X12'-4"

C.

DN

L

H.

C.

B.

KIT.

LIVING ROOM 18'-0"X16'-4"

DINING 9'-4"X8'-0"

DN

DECK

UPPER LEVEL

Rustic Exterior; Complete Home

No. 10140

Rustic though it is in appearance, the interior of this cabin is quiet, modern and comfortable. Small in overall size, it still contains three bedrooms and two baths in addition to a large, two story living room with exposed beams. As a hunting or fishing lodge or a mountain retreat, this compares well.

First floor-1,008 sq. ft.
Second floor-281 sq. ft.
Basement-1,008 sq. ft.

Rustic Ranch Features Fireplace

No. 9076

Natural wood siding and stone chimney transport this three bedroom home deep into the wilderness, where its fireplace warms the living and dining rooms. A front porch translates a certain old-fashioned, homey comfort, but the interior claims certain modern touches, such as the master bedroom's private bath. A full bath off the hall serves the other bedrooms. Closets are plentiful, included even in the living room, and additional storage can be found in the full basement.

First floor-1,140 sq. ft.
Basement-1,140 sq. ft.

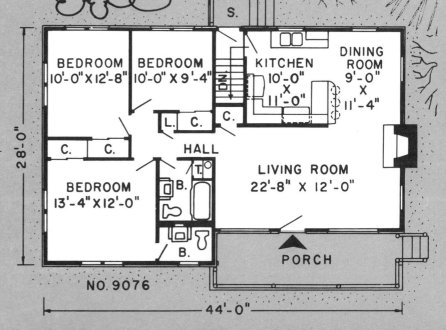

Rustic Ranch Integrates Outdoors

No. 10142

Appendaging a 31-foot redwood deck at rear and a long front porch, this ranch plan offers a woodsy appeal and plenty of involvement with the outdoors. Inside, the floor plan caters to the relaxed lifestyle of the seventies. Flanking the large foyer is the spacious sunken living room, warmed by a wood-burning fireplace.

First floor-1,705 sq. ft.
Basement-1,705 sq. ft.
Garage-576 sq. ft.

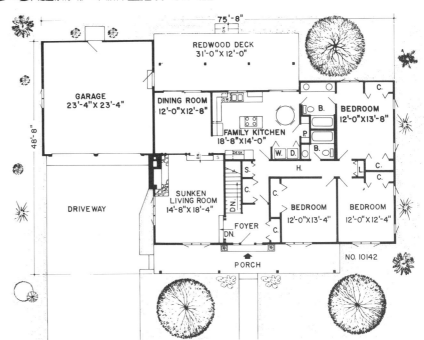

GARAGE
23'-4" X 23'-4"

DRIVEWAY

REDWOOD DECK
31'-0" X 12'-0"

DINING ROOM
12'-0" X 12'-8"

FAMILY KITCHEN
18'-8" X 14'-0"

BEDROOM
12'-0" X 13'-8"

SUNKEN
LIVING ROOM
14'-8" X 18'-4"

FOYER

BEDROOM
12'-0" X 13'-4"

BEDROOM
12'-0" X 12'-4"

PORCH

NO. 10142

75'-8"

48'-8"

Angular Design Is Strikingly Contemporary

No. 10469

The living room is the focal point of this contemporary design and incorporates several innovative features. Its vaulted ceiling is highlighted with exposed beams, and the angled front has up to four levels of windows which are operated by remote control. A wood-burning fireplace and built-in bookshelves enhance the rear wall of the room. The kitchen, informal serving area and dining room occupy the remainder of the first floor. The second floor is reserved for the three spacious bedrooms. The master bedroom also has a beamed ceiling plus its own fireplace.

First floor-989 sq. ft.
Second floor-810 sq. ft.
Garage-538 sq. ft.

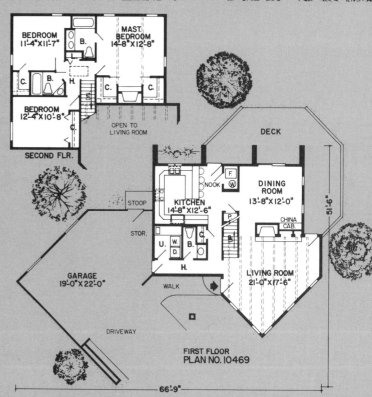

Balcony Overlooks Dining Room And Foyer

No. 10531

Extending between the two second floor bedrooms is a bridge-like balcony which accents this home's stately appearance. Each of these two large bedrooms has its own walk-in closet and private bath. The first floor master suite features two huge walk-in closets, an L-shaped five-piece bath, and a sitting room with a bay window. The sunken great room features a bar, fireplace, built-ins for stereo and television all crowned by a sloping, beamed ceiling. Both the dining room and the foyer have cathedral ceilings and are overlooked by the second floor bridge. The fully equipped kitchen opens onto an octagonal breakfast nook.

First floor—2,579 sq. ft.
Second floor—997 sq. ft.
Basement—2,579 sq. ft.
Garage & storage—1,001 sq. ft.

Redwood Bridge Fronts Contemporary

No. 10148

Leading to double entrance doors and a lavish foyer, a redwood bridge expresses the unique, natural flavor of this three bedroom contemporary. Immediately visible from the foyer is the fireplace lighting the expansive sunken living room. Redwood deck beyond is accessible through two pairs of sliding glass doors.

First floor-2,050 sq. ft.
Basement-2,050 sq. ft.
Garage-440 sq. ft.

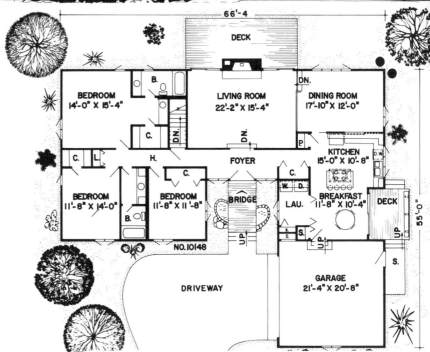

Passive Contemporary Design Features Sunken Living Room

No. 26112

Wood adds its warmth to the contemporary features of this passive design. Generous use of southern glass doors and windows, an air lock entry, skylights and a living room fireplace reduce energy needs. R-26 insulation is shown for floors and sloping ceilings. Decking rims the front of the home and gives access through sliding glass doors to a bedroom/den area and living room. The dining room lies up several steps from the living room and is separated from it by a half wall. The dining room flows into the kitchen through an eating bar. A second floor landing balcony overlooks the living room.

First floor-911 sq. ft.
Second floor-560 sq. ft.

Balcony Enriches
Facade, Bedrooms

No. 10128

Two bedrooms enjoy a bonus in the 23-foot balcony that fronts this split-level plan. Stone veneer, ornamental iron railings, and French doors create an eye-catching exterior, while effective zoning distinguishes the interior. Living areas are cozy and include firelit living room, well-proportioned dining room open to the terrace.

Living levels–1,344 sq. ft.
Garage levels–720 sq. ft.

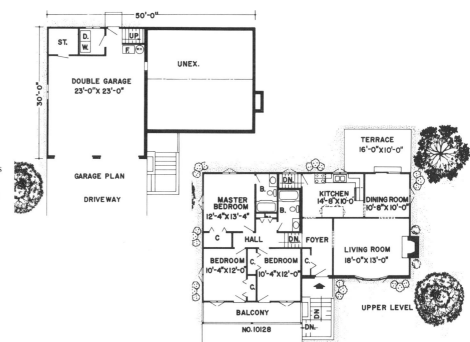

50'-0"

ST. D. W. UP. F.

DOUBLE GARAGE
23'-0"X 23'-0"

UNEX.

30'-0"

GARAGE PLAN

DRIVEWAY

TERRACE
16'-0"X10'-0"

MASTER BEDROOM
12'-4"X13'-4"

KITCHEN
14'-8"X10'-0"

DINING ROOM
10'-8"X10'-0"

C

HALL DN. FOYER

B. B. DN.

LIVING ROOM
18'-0"X13'-0"

BEDROOM
10'-4"X12'-0"

BEDROOM
10'-4"X12'-0"

C. C. C.

UPPER LEVEL

BALCONY

NO. 10128 DN.

SOLAR HOME

Contemporary Convenience Fills Colonial

No. 9762

Handsome white columns mark the entrance to this delightful colonial, which harmonizes a traditonal facade with an up-to-date interior. The split foyer arrangement is a practical choice that permits easy access to the sprawling family room and hobby shop below. Upstairs, the master bedroom profits by the extensive bath and dressing area. The carefully calculated kitchen chooses a breakfast bar, desk, and copious cabinet space. The separate dining room spills out to a raised terrace via sliding glass doors.

First floor — 1,920 sq. ft.
Basement — 1,426 sq. ft.
Garage — 494 sq. ft.

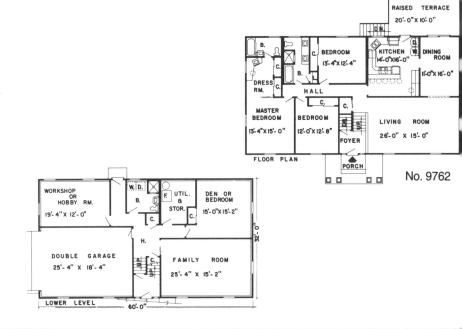

No. 9762

Living Room Encourages Entertaining

No. 9846

Radiating all the charm and welcome of a French country home, this four bedroom design is highlighted by a generously proportioned living room with fireplace. Its sliding glass doors connect to the terrace and permit open, enjoyable entertaining. A formal dining room and kitchen with laundry space border the living room and the set-off family room. The master bedroom enjoys a bath and huge closet, while three more bedrooms and another bath are included.

First floor — 2,022 sq. ft.
Basement — 2,022 sq. ft.
Garage — 576 sq. ft.

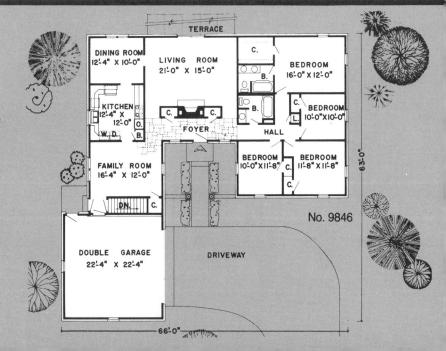

No. 9846

Colonial Ranch Style, Enriched Interior

No. 9864

Endowed with the trimmings of a traditional Colonial, this three-bedroom ranch style becomes doubly attractive with the addition of modern features. For example, the sizable master bedroom annexes a full bath with shower, walk-in closet and spacious dressing area. Warmed by a wood-burning fireplace, the living room spills onto a large redwood deck via sliding glass door. A functional kitchen is separated from the family room by a cooking peninsula, and a utility room and hobby shop edge the double garage.

First floor-1,612 sq. ft.
Basement-1,612 sq. ft.
Garage, utility and storage-660 sq. ft.

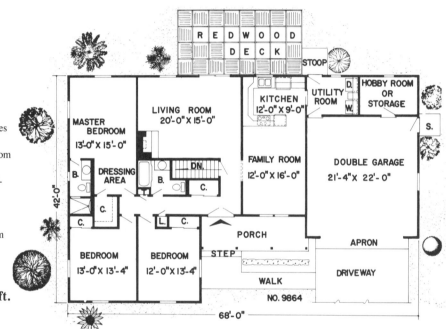

REDWOOD DECK

STOOP

MASTER BEDROOM 13'-0" X 15'-0"

LIVING ROOM 20'-0" X 15'-0"

KITCHEN 12'-0" X 9'-0"

UTILITY ROOM

D. W.

HOBBY ROOM OR STORAGE

S.

B.

DRESSING AREA

DN.

FAMILY ROOM 12'-0" X 16'-0"

DOUBLE GARAGE 21'-4" X 22'-0"

C.

B.

C.

C.

42'-0"

C.

L. C.

BEDROOM 13'-0" X 13'-4"

BEDROOM 12'-0" X 13'-4"

STEP

PORCH

APRON

WALK

DRIVEWAY

NO. 9864

68'-0"

Master Bedroom Merits Deck

No. 10270

Consider this home for the family with hobbies. With plenty of living space in an easy-to-clean single level design and accommodations for a workshop and outdoor activities, this design is perfectly practical. Admire the elegant touches too, like the huge bow windows, the deluxe master bath with corner tub, and two appealing decks. The family kitchen boasts an efficient layout that simplifies daily meals. First floor laundry facilities save time and steps. This home can be built on a slab foundation.

First floor — 2,202 sq. ft.
Basement — 2,016 sq. ft.
Garage & workshop — 677 sq. ft.

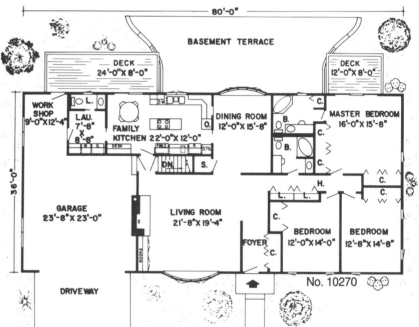

Underground Delight

No. 10376

This three bedroom, underground masterpiece is designed to fight the high cost of living through its many energy-saving features, including the use of passive solar energy. The large master bedroom on one end shows an abundance of closets. Each of the three bedrooms has sliding glass doors to the front lawn. Also featured in this area is a multi-purpose room, easily converted to individual use, graciously separated from the entry way by ornately carved wood room dividers. The plan calls for 2 baths, one delightfully designed with a whirlpool. The family room opens to a greenhouse via sliding glass doors. A two car garage completes this home.

Living area — 2,086 sq. ft.

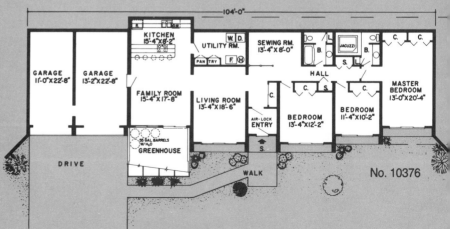

Double-closeted Bedrooms Highlight Plan

No. 10234

Generously proportioned bedrooms, with double closets and bordering laundry and full bath, promise livability in this trim leisure plan. For entertaining, the 22-ft living room expands via two sets of sliding glass doors to the large balcony. A spacious kitchen offers dining space and pantry and opens to the wooden deck for easily-prepared outdoor meals. Lower level shows garage, workbench, and storage for camper or trailer.

**Upper level-1,254 sq. ft.
Lower level-1,064 sq. ft.**

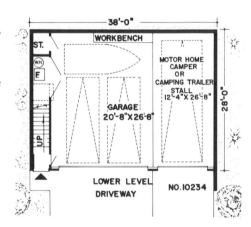

LOWER LEVEL
DRIVEWAY   NO. 10234

UPPER LEVEL

SOLAR HOME

Contemporary Tudor Castle

No. 10620

Touches of old England abound in this elegant 4 bedroom, 3 1/2 bath home. Find wonderful angles, a large fireplace and rough-hewn beams in the two-story great room. Octagonal recessed ceilings in the master bedroom and formal dining room, and a library with built-in bookcase are traditional features borrowed from long ago. But, the luxury of a sunken skylit tub in the master suite and soaring views of the great room and foyer from the balcony are strictly contemporary. The kitchen features a convenient island design and a walk-in pantry for extra storage, with easy access to the laundry room and garage.

First floor — 2,268 sq. ft.
Second floor — 994 sq. ft.
Basement — 2,268 sq. ft.
Garage — 603 sq. ft.

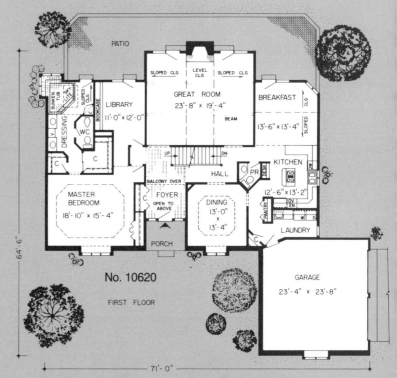

No. 10620

FIRST FLOOR

A Karl Kreeger Design

SECOND FLOOR

Private Court With Hot Tub Outside Master Bedroom

No. 10534

Adjoining the luxurious master suite of this stately home is a private court complete with hot tub. Secluded from the rest of the first floor this suite is comprised of a spacious bedroom, oversized walk-in closet and five-piece bath. Just down the hall is the cozy library which opens onto the two-story foyer through French doors. Other elegant touches on the first floor include a morning room with built-ins, a bar with wine storage, and a sun porch with French doors into the dining room. The living room and foyer rise to the second floor which encompasses three large bedrooms and two full baths.

First floor—2,486 sq. ft.
Second floor—892 sq. ft.
Basement—2,486 sq. ft.
Garage—576 sq. ft.

SECOND FLOOR PLAN

FIRST FLOOR PLAN

Dramatic Shape and Features

No. 10274

If your lot is the right shape, build this magnificent plan. A dramatically positioned fireplace forms the focus of a contemporary living area. Kitchen, dining, and living spaces are fashioned into a huge central room that flows from the heart of the home through sliding doors to the dramatic deck. The many flexible decorating options, such as screens and room dividers or conversational groupings, are impressive. A huge master bedroom and two roomy bedrooms are tucked in a wing away from the main area for privacy.

First floor — 1,783 sq. ft.
Garage — 576 sq. ft.

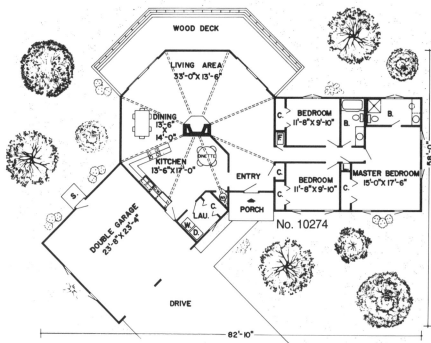

One-floor Living, Tudor Style

No. 20099

You'll find an appealing quality of open space in every room of this unique one-level home. Angular windows and recessed ceilings separate the two dining rooms from the adjoining island kitchen without compromising the airy feeling. A window-wall that flanks the fireplace in the soaring, skylit living room unites interior spaces with the outdoor deck. The sunny atmosphere continues in the master suite, with its bump-out window and double-vanitied bath, and in the two bedrooms off the foyer.

First floor — 2,020 sq. ft.
Basement — 2,020 sq. ft.
Garage — 534 sq. ft.

A Karl Kreeger Design

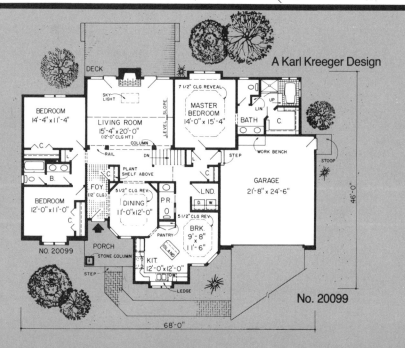

Ranch Style Favors Living Room

No. 6360

Stretching over 22 feet to span the width of this ranch design, the living room enjoys expanses of windows, a wood-burning fireplace, and access to the terrace. A separate dining room with plenty of windows and an efficient kitchen with abundant counter space border the living room.

House — 1,293 sq. ft.
Basement — 767 sq. ft.
Garage — 466 sq. ft.
Terrace — 92 sq. ft.

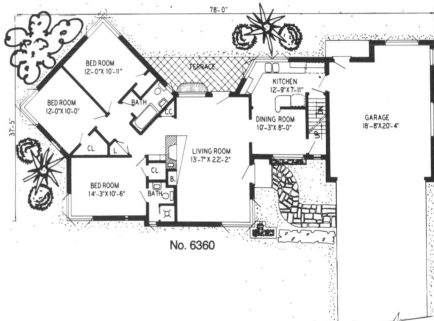

No. 6360

Wonderful Views Everywhere

No. 20068

Consider this home if your backyard is something special in each season. Both living and dining areas offer broad views across the deck to the beautiful scene beyond. Even the balcony on the second floor captures it all. The open floor plan in the interior of the home brings the view to the kitchen and front hall as well. The master bedroom, with a fabulous walk-in closet and lavish bath, maintains its privacy to the side while indulging in the view of the backyard. The second floor bedrooms are notable for the huge closets.

First floor — 1,266 sq. ft.
Second floor — 489 sq. ft.
Basement — 1,266 sq. ft.
Garage — 484 sq. ft.

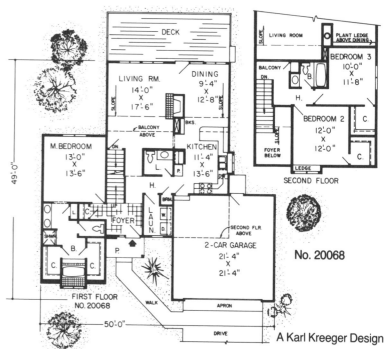

A Karl Kreeger Design

Eye-catching Angle Marks Vacation Plan

No. 10224

Fronted by a redwood deck, an exceptional exterior blends with a practical floor plan in this refreshing leisure home plan. The entry and lounge is equipped with closets and bordered by a bedroom on one side and the living room on the other. A corridor kitchen and dining area open to a handy porch. Upstairs, the bunk room offers ample sleeping space for guests and, with the hobby room, boasts an enjoyable second story deck.

First floor — 1,012 sq. ft.
Second floor — 406 sq. ft.

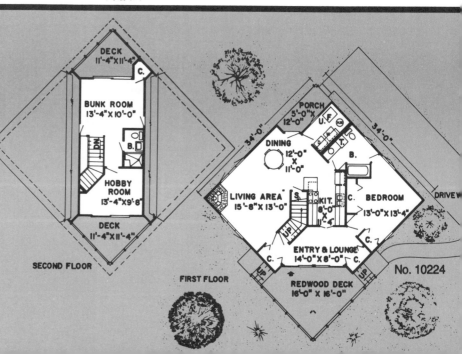

Elegant Master Suite
Crowns Victorian

No. 20351

Gingerbread trim, round-top windows, and a two-story bay window bring a Victorian flavor to this modern plan. A fireplace adds a cozy charm to the angular living room just off the foyer. Walk past the stairs and the handy powder room to the rear of the house. Flanked by the formal dining and family rooms, the convenient kitchen lets the cook enjoy family activities and prepare dinner, too! You'll appreciate the outdoor living space the rear deck adds. But, when there's a chill in the air, you can light a fire and enjoy the view from the window seat in the family room. Three upstairs bedrooms include the bayed master suite, which features loads of closet space, a raised whirlpool tub, and a step-in shower for busy mornings.

First floor — 1,304 sq. ft.
Second floor — 1,009 sq. ft.
Basement — 1,304 sq. ft.
Garage — 688 sq. ft.

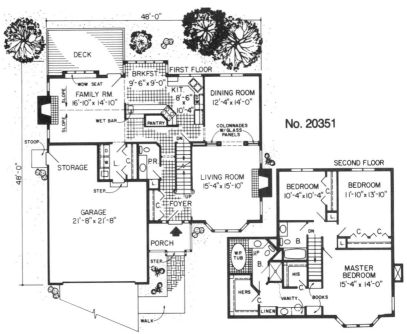

No. 20351

Colonial Charmer Fit for a Crowd

No. 20101

Imagine entertaining in this spacious masterpiece! Throw open the double doors between the front parlor and fireplaced family room and you've got an expansive room that can handle any crowd. There's room for an army of cooks in the bayed kitchen-breakfast room combination. And, when the oven overheats the room, head out to the adjoining deck for a breath of fresh air. Store extra supplies in the room-sized pantry on the way to the elegant, formal dining room. The adjacent breezeway contains a handy powder room and laundry facilities. Four bedrooms are tucked upstairs, away from the action. Look at the magnificent master suite. Recessed ceilings, a skylit shower, and double vanities make this room both luxurious and convenient.

First floor — 1,109 sq. ft.
Second floor — 932 sq. ft.
Basement — 1,109 sq. ft.
Garage — 552 sq. ft.

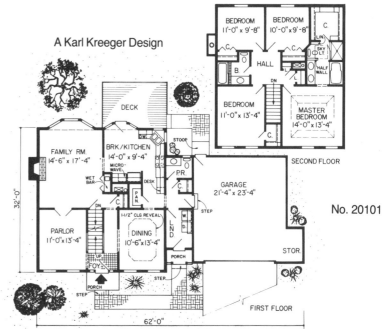

A Karl Kreeger Design

No. 20101

Bay Windows and Skylights Brighten this Tudor Home

No. 10673

Step from the arched fieldstone porch into the two-story foyer, and you can see that this traditional four bedroom home possesses a wealth of modern elements. Behind double doors lie the library and fireplaced living room, bathed in sunlight from two skylights in the sloping roof. Step out to the brick patio from the laundry room or bay-windowed breakfast room. For ultimate relaxation, the master bedroom suite contains a whirlpool tub. One bedroom boasts bay windows; another features a huge walk-in closet over the two car garage.

First floor — 1,265 sq. ft.
Second floor — 1,210 sq. ft.
Basement — 1,247 sq. ft.
Garage — 506 sq. ft.

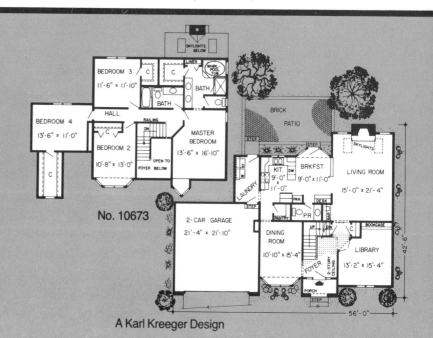

No. 10673

A Karl Kreeger Design

110

SOLAR HOME

Master Suite Crowns Plan

No. 10394

The master bedroom suite occupies the entire second level of this passive solar design. The living room rises two stories in the front, as does the foyer, and can be opened to the master suite to aid in air circulation. Skylights in the sloping ceilings of the kitchen and master bath give abundant light to these areas. Angled walls, both inside and out, lend a unique appeal. An air lock entry, 2x6 exterior studs, 6-inch concrete floor, and generous use of insulation help make this an energy efficient design.

First floor — 1,306 sq. ft.
Second floor — 472 sq. ft.
Garage — 576 sq. ft.

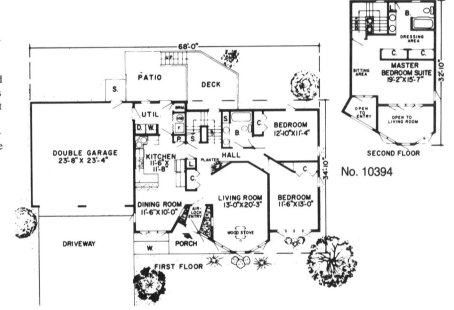

No. 10394

Open Living Area Highlights Well-zoned Plan

No. 10523

A feeling of spaciousness is created by the centrally located living and dining areas which both have a view of the hearthed fireplace. The galley-style kitchen features a pantry, a bump-out window over the sink, and easy access to the combined laundry/utility room. The breakfast nook, which overlooks the deck, is flooded with light from the uniquely arranged windows. The three bedrooms and two baths are on the other side of the core of activity rooms. The master bedroom has a private bath plus a double vanity, walk-in and a walk-in closet in the dressing area.

First floor — 1737 sq. ft.
Basement — 1737 sq. ft.
Garage — 584 sq. ft.

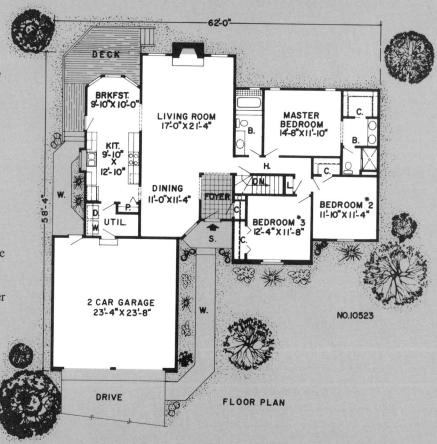

FLOOR PLAN

Hearth Room Highlights Four-bedroom Plan

No. 10527

Expanding the dream kitchen of this lovely home is the cozy hearth room. Its fireplace is flanked by windows, and its unusual ceiling adds to its unique setting. In addition to the formal living and dining rooms on the first floor, there is the large, sunken family room. Highlighting this welcoming room are a built-in bar and a fireplace flanked by bookcases. Upstairs are four large bedrooms. The master bedroom features two walk-in closets and a five-piece bath. Bedrooms two and three share a bath but have individual basins, and bedroom four has its own private bath.

First floor — 1,697 sq. ft.
Second floor — 1,624 sq. ft.
Basement K— 1,697 sq. ft.
Garage — 586 sq. ft.

SECOND FLOOR

FIRST FLOOR
NO. 10527

Outdoor-Lovers' Delight

No. 10748

This one-level charmer packs a lot of convenience into a compact space. From the shelter of the front porch, the foyer leads three ways: right to the bedroom wing, left to the roomy kitchen and dining room, or straight ahead to the massive living room. You'll appreciate the quiet atmosphere in the sleeping wing, the elegant recessed ceilings and private bath in the master suite, and the laundry facilities that adjoin the bedrooms. You'll enjoy the convenience of a kitchen with a built-in pantry and adjacent dining room. And, you'll love the airy atmosphere in the sunny, fireplaced living room, which features a cooling fan, high ceilings, and double French doors to the huge, wrap-around porch.

Living area — 1,540 sq. ft.
Porches — 530 sq. ft.

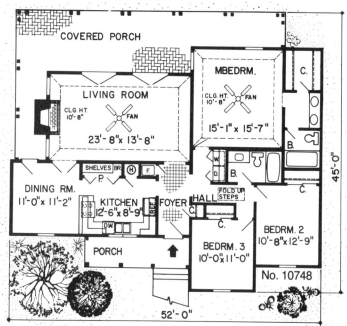

Passive Solar with Unique Great Room

No. 10380

Expanses of glass and rugged exposed beams dominate the front of this design's six-sided living center, creating a contemporary look that would be outstanding in any setting. Angled service and sleeping wings flow to the right and left, creating unusual shaped rooms and leaving nooks and crannies for storage. Spiral stairs just inside the tiled entry rise to a loft overlooking the great room. All rooms have sloped ceilings with R-38 insulation while sidewalls call for R-24. Living and dining possibilities are expanded by use of the rear patio and deck. A full basement lies under the house.

First floor — 2,199 sq. ft.
Loft — 336 sq. ft.
Garage — 611 sq. ft.
Basement — 2,199 sq. ft.

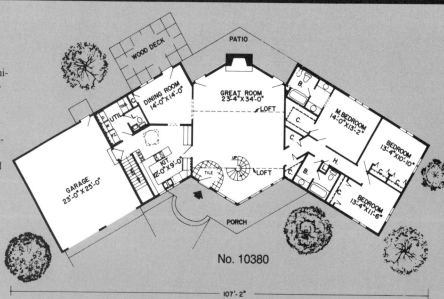

Railing Divides Living Spaces

No. 10596

This one-level design is a celebration of light and open space. From the foyer, view the dining room, island kitchen, breakfast room, living room, and outdoor deck in one sweeping glance. Bay windows add pleasing angles and lots of sunshine to eating areas and the master suite. And, a wall of windows brings the outdoors into the two back bedrooms.

Upper floor — 1,740 sq. ft.
Basement — 1,377 sq. ft.
Garage — 480 sq. ft.

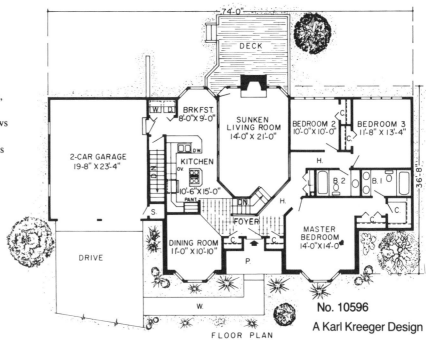

74'-0"

DECK

BRKFST.
8'-0" X 9'-0"

SUNKEN LIVING ROOM
14'-0" X 21'-0"

BEDROOM 2
10'-0" X 10'-0"

BEDROOM 3
11'-8" X 13'-4"

2-CAR GARAGE
19'-8" X 23'-4"

KITCHEN
10'-6" X 15'-0"

36'-8"

B.2

B.1

DRIVE

FOYER

MASTER BEDROOM
14'-0" X 14'-0"

DINING ROOM
11'-0" X 10'-10"

P.

W.

No. 10596

FLOOR PLAN

A Karl Kreeger Design

SOLAR HOME

Cathedral Window Graced by Massive Arch

No. 20066

A tiled threshold provides a distinctive entrance into this spacious home. There's room for gracious living everywhere, from the comfortable living room with a wood-burning fireplace and tiled hearth, to the elegant dining room with a vaulted ceiling, to the outside deck. Plan your meals in a kitchen that has all the right ingredients: a central work island, pantry, planning desk, and breakfast area. A decorative ceiling will delight your eye in the master suite, which includes a full bath and bow window.

First floor — 1,850 sq. ft.
Basement — 1,850 sq. ft.
Garage — 503 sq. ft.

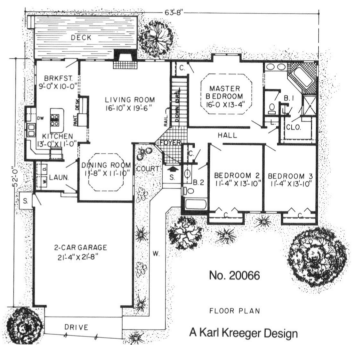

Contemporary Castle

No. 10697

With glass walls in every room, this gracious home deserves a beautiful setting. Whether you're swimming, entertaining, or just want to relax, you'll find a perfect spot — patios and a deck surround living spaces upstairs and down. And, this house isn't just beautiful. Convenient features abound throughout. Notice how eating areas flank the roomy island kitchen and utility areas, and how the family and living rooms share a wetbar and back-to-back fireplaces. Every bedroom adjoins a bath, but the master suite, with its recessed ceilings, private sitting room with a walled patio, and double walk-in closets is a luxurious retreat that's hard to resist.

First floor — 2,740 sq. ft.
Second floor — 948 sq. ft.
Garage — 522 sq. ft.

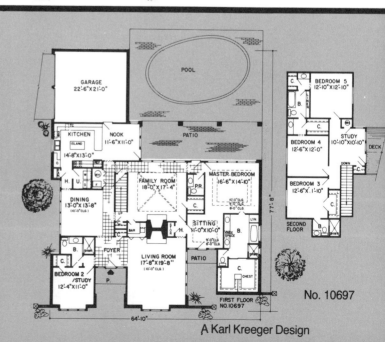

Three Levels of Spacious Living

No. 10396

This passive solar design is suitable for vacation or year round living. The rear or southern elevation of the home is highlighted by an abundance of decks and glass. A minimum of windows are found on the north, east and west sides. The basement level has a large shop, storage and recreation areas, plus a bedroom. The first level living room is two steps up from the rest of the first floor, with two stories of glass on its southern wall. An angled wall lends character to the kitchen-dining area. The master suite occupies the entire second level with its own bath, dressing area, walk-in closet, storage nook and private deck.

First floor — 886 sq. ft.
Second floor — 456 sq. ft.
Basement — 886 sq. ft.

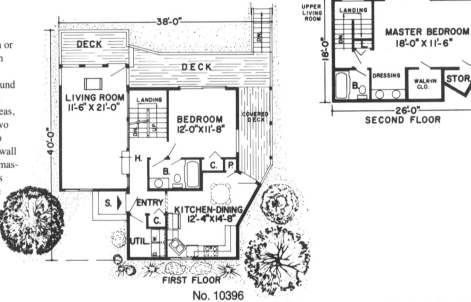

SOLAR HOME

No. 10396

A Stylish and Clever Exterior

No. 10611

A stylish and clever exterior make this mid-size home seem even larger and more expensive than it is. And inside, an ingenious use of compartmentalized design contributes to that feeling. An oversize foyer with double coat closets is the starting point. From there, each secluded, separate room stretches the dimensions of the house. The elongated living room with double windows, the large, offset family room with screened porch, and the secluded den are good examples. Upstairs are 4 spacious bedrooms and additional attic storage. Popular features like 1st floor laundry facilities and brick patio complete an outstanding plan.

First floor — 1,755 sq. ft.
Second floor — 1,334 sq. ft.
Basement — 1,755 sq. ft.
Garage — 692 sq. ft.

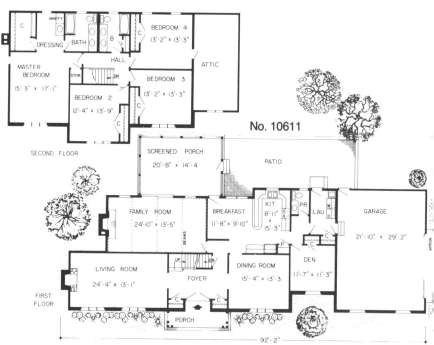

No. 10611

Feature-packed Living Space

No. 10509

This well-zoned plan incorporates features usually found in much larger houses and does it with style. The living areas extend from the extremely efficient kitchen into the living room and around the corner into the dining area. The living room is accented by sliding doors to the patio and a fireplace with an extended hearth. Separating the living areas from the three bedrooms is the placement of the entry, the laundry and the master bath. The large and inviting master suite has a dressing area, walk-in closet and private patio. The third bedroom features a built-in dressing table. You'll find that this home receives you well.

First floor — 1,464 sq. ft.
Garage — 528 sq. ft.

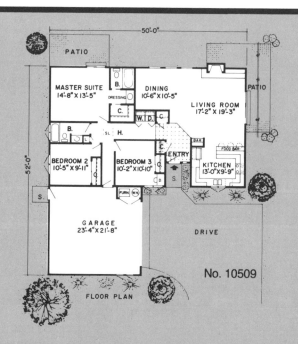

No. 10509

FLOOR PLAN

Perfect For Entertaining

No. 20050

As guests enter the two-story, tiled foyer, they are immediately welcomed by the expansive living room with its sloped ceiling and cheery fireplace. Lead them into the dining room and serve them from the adjacent kitchen. There's even room for more than one cook in this roomy kitchen which opens onto a covered deck for outdoor meals. The first floor master bedroom features a large, five-piece bath and double closets. Upstairs are two more bedrooms with roomy closets, an additional bath and room for storage in the attic.

First floor — 1,303 sq. ft.
Second floor — 596 sq. ft.
Basement — 1,303 sq. ft.
Garage — 460 sq. ft.

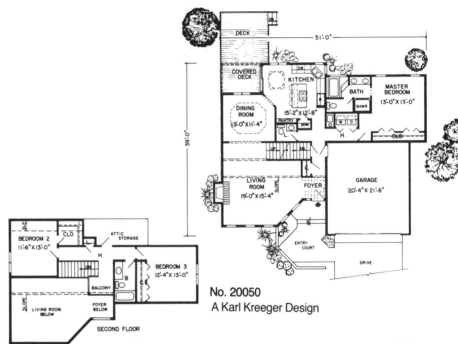

No. 20050
A Karl Kreeger Design

Formal Entry, Luxury Master Suite, Plus Room to Expand

No. 10525

In addition to the three, well-designed bedrooms, the second floor of this traditional design features a large unfinished area which could be a study, hobby center or even a fully equipped exercise room. The luxury master suite has two walk-in closets in the dressing area plus a conveniently arranged five-piece bath which features a circular window above the tiled tub enclosure. The first floor is composed of formal dining and living rooms on either side of the tiled foyer with the family areas organized along the back overlooking the patio. The cozy family room has a fireplace, built-in bookcase and opens onto the patio. The kitchen features a bump-out window over sink and shares a snack bar with the bright and cherry breakfast nook.

First floor — 1219 sq. ft.
Second floor — 1010 sq. ft.
Basement — 1219 sq. ft.
Garage — 514 sq. ft.

BEDROOM #2
10'-0" X 11'-10"

MASTER BEDROOM
15'-4" X 15'-4"

UNFINISHED AREA

BEDROOM #3
11'-8" X 11'-8"

MAST. BATH

DRESSING

30'-0"

SECOND FLOOR PLAN

55'-0"

PATIO

KIT.
10'-0" X 11'-0"

BRKFST.
10'-2" X 10'-6"

LAUN.

FAMILY ROOM
20'-10" X 15'-4"

LAV.

GARAGE
22'-8" X 21'-8"

DINING ROOM
11'-8" X 11'-8"

FOYER

LIVING ROOM
11'-4" X 17'-4"

PORCH

DRIVE

FIRST FLOOR PLAN

NO. 10525

Natural Lighting Built In Design

No. 10547

Clever use of skylights in the foyer and master bedroom's bath area add creative natural lighting to this home. The sun room is a passive solar feature which if turned to the south will help heat the house. Unique in design, this ranch incorporates many options. Its' large kitchen and breakfast area with an adjoining laundry offers convenience as a priority. The open dining and living area's display a profound sense of expansiveness, while a more formal dining area may be added by partioning off the area. The master bedroom with its adjoining bath offers both a tub and a shower plus a walk-in closet.

First floor—1,607 sq. ft.
Second floor—623 sq. ft.
Basement—1,542 sq. ft.
Garage—484 sq. ft.

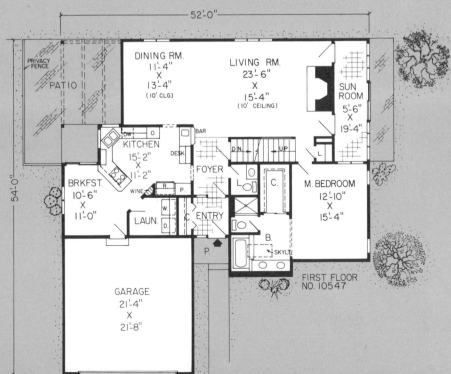

SECOND FLOOR

FIRST FLOOR
NO. 10547

Accent on Luxury

No. 10655

Your houseguests may never want to leave this updated 5 bedroom manor home. Sturdy brick construction and elegant detailing — such as recessed octagonal ceilings, built in cabinets, shelves, and pantry — make this a special place. Extra amenities include the hexagonal sunny breakfast room with access to the deck, two powder rooms, guest bedroom, and full bath all on the first floor. The soaring two story foyer, flanked by the library and dining room, offers a view of the curved staircase and a glimpse of the wood-beamed great room beyond. Walk up the stairs and find a huge master bedroom suite with skylit bath, along with three more bedrooms and two full baths.

First floor — 2,526 sq. ft.
Second floor — 2,062 sq. ft.
Basement — 2,493 sq. ft.
Garage — 976 sq. ft.

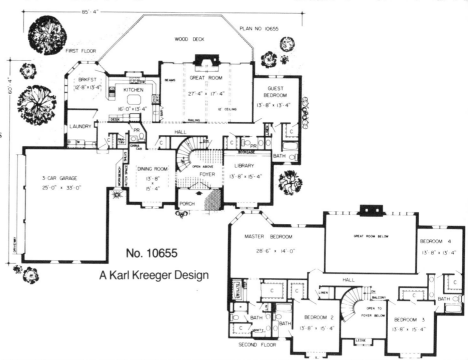

No. 10655
A Karl Kreeger Design

Living Areas Warmed by Massive Fireplace

No. 10752

Here's a handsome home for the family that enjoys one-level living. Skylights, sloping ceilings, and an absence of walls give active areas an irresistable, spacious atmosphere. And, with a floor-to-ceiling window wall in the living room and French doors in the dining room, interior spaces enjoy a pleasing unity with the great outdoors. Whether you're in the mood for formal or informal dining, the centrally located kitchen will make mealtime a breeze. Three bedrooms, each featuring a walk-in closet, occupy their own quiet wing off the foyer. The front bedrooms share a full bath with double vanities. The master suite at the rear of the house enjoys a private bath.

First floor — 1,705 sq. ft.
Garage — 488 sq. ft.

No. 10752

Garden Room Brings the Outdoors In

No. 10423

This floor plan flows with unmatched character throughout its entirety. Spiral stairs, leading to a bay-windowed second floor loft, catch your eye as you enter. Highlighting the quieter living areas is the master bedroom suite. A fireplace and split his and her closet and bath area with sunken tub are found here. Sharing two of its inside walls of windows with the eight-sided eating nook and fire-placed living room, the garden room can become your haven for plants as well as a focus of interest of the home.

First floor — 2,506 sq. ft.
Loft — 267 sq. ft.
Garage — 521 sq. ft.
Patio & porch — 155 sq. ft.

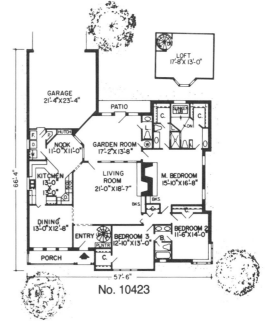

No. 10423

Good Things Come in Small Packages

No. 20303

Do you have a small lot, or a limited budget? Here's a compact gem that won't break the bank, and provides plenty of room for the whole family. And, this distinctive plan is an energy saver, too. Look at the air-lock vestibule entry that keeps the chill outside, and the skylights in both baths that let the sun help with the heating bills. There's a cozy sitting nook in the living room. A matching nook off the kitchen is a perfect spot for family meals. To insure quiet bedtimes, the central staircase separates the downstairs bedrooms from active areas. But for maximum privacy, escape upstairs to the master suite, which features double vanities, as well as a walk-in shower and tub.

First floor — 861 sq. ft.
Second floor — 333 sq. ft.
Basement — 715 sq. ft.

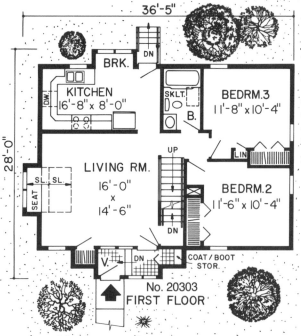

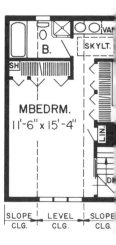

Three Bedroom Design Features Sloped Ceilings

No. 10505

The luxurious master suite of this uniquely designed, three bedroom home is secluded on an upper floor. It is linked to the stairway by a balcony which overlooks the first floor family room and central hall. Additionally it features a full wall of double closets, a sloped ceiling and a private fireplace. The octagonal, five-piece bath also features a sloped ceiling. The octagonal treatment is carried out in the first floor nook which adjoins the kitchen and in the arrangement of the casement windows in the living room. The family room boasts a corner fireplace and has its own sloped ceiling. Two additional bedrooms, each with a large closet, a four-piece bath, and a conveniently located laundry room complete this unusual and inviting home.

First floor — 1,704 sq. ft.
Second floor — 561 sq. ft.
Garage — 439 sq. ft.

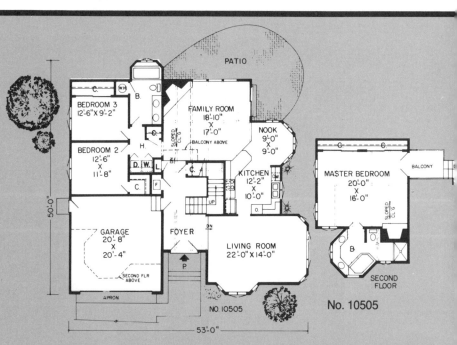

Enjoy a Crackling Fire on a Chilly Day

No. 10683

From the dramatic, two-story entry to the full-length deck off the massive great room, this is a modern plan in a classic package. Cathedral ceilings soar over the formal dining and sunken living rooms, separated by an open railing. The corner kitchen efficiently serves formal and family eating areas. Can't you imagine a table overlooking the deck in the sunken great room's sunny bay? Up the angular staircase, two bedrooms, each with a huge closet, share a full bath. You'll have your own, private bath, including double vanities and a sun-splashed raised tub, in the master suite at the rear of the house.

First floor — 990 sq. ft.
Second floor — 721 sq. ft.
Basement — 934 sq. ft.
Garage — 429 sq. ft.

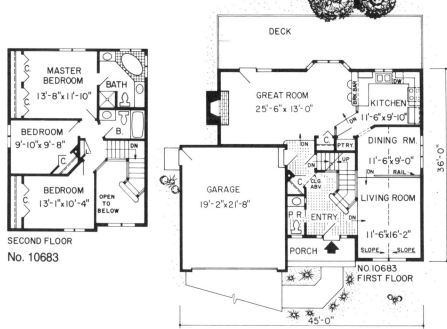

SECOND FLOOR

No. 10683

MASTER BEDROOM 13'-8"x11'-10"
BATH
BEDROOM 9'-10"x 9'-8"
BEDROOM 13'-1"x10'-4"
OPEN TO BELOW

DECK
GREAT ROOM 25'-6" x 13'-0"
KITCHEN 11'-6"x9'-10"
BRK. BAR
DW
DINING RM. 11'-6"x9'-0"
GARAGE 19'-2"x21'-8"
PT RY.
UP
C.
CLG. ABV.
LIVING ROOM 11'-6"x16'-2"
P.R.
ENTRY
RAIL
SLOPE SLOPE
PORCH
NO. 10683 FIRST FLOOR
36'-0"
45'-0"

Kitchen Is Homemaker's Haven

No. 10417

Inside and out, this design speaks of space and luxury. Outside, cedar shake roofing contrasts nicely with brick veneer to compliment arched and leaded windows and false dormers. Double entry doors usher you into a two-story entrance with staircase curving gently to second level rooms. Ten ft. ceilings throughout the lower level and nine ft. ceilings upstairs add to the spaciousness already created by large sized rooms. What homemaker wouldn't be excited about the kitchen features — 60 sq. ft. of counter space, 5 × 6 step-saving island cooking range, desk area, windowed eating nook and nearby patio access? A combination full bath and utility room, which can be entered from the house, garage or yard.

First floor – 3,307 sq. ft.
Second Floor – 837 sq. ft.
Garage – 646 sq. ft.
Porch & Patios – 382 sq. ft.

Large Covered Patio For Outdoor Enjoyment

No. 10436

Beauty and character flow from every area of this design. The double entry, set off by brickwork arches, ushers you into a large foyer with curving staircase. The family room and fireplaced living room share a bar and with the patio, are sunken 12 inches lower than the adjoining rooms. On yet a third level are the utility room and garage which lie up 12 inches. In addition to the lower level master suite, three additional bedrooms are located upstairs and complete the sleeping accommodations. Each bedroom has direct access to a bath, and the largest of the three boasts a bay window and adjoining library.

First floor-2,277 sq. ft.
Second floor-851 sq. ft.
Garage-493 sq. ft.

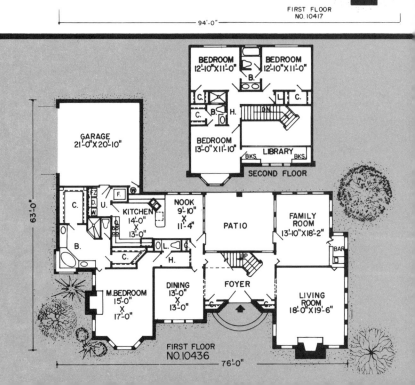

126

Two Fireplaces Featured

No. 10431

It's the little details that can add interest and character to a design and set it apart from others. Master bedroom suite on the right balances the living room on the left (both with bay windows), giving the front elevation a feeling of symmetry. The front entry between them features double entry doors flanked by side lights. The living room, decorated by a raised hearth fireplace, flows through a graceful arch doorway to formal dining room beyond. The family woodchopper will be kept busy supplying this fireplace and an additional one in the family room, with wood. Every nook and cranny in the floor plan seems to boast of storage and closet space or an added extra such as a bar in the family room or pantry right outside the kitchen. Dormers dress up the exterior and shed light onto the staircase inside. Additional natural light is given to the home by skylights in two of the three bathrooms.

First floor – 2,108 sq. ft.
Second Floor – 509 sq. ft.
Garage – 532 sq. ft.

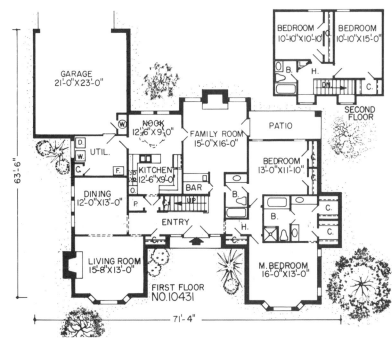

FIRST FLOOR NO.10431

GARAGE 21'-0"X23'-0"

NOOK 12'-6"X9'-0"

FAMILY ROOM 15'-0"X16'-0"

PATIO

UTIL.

KITCHEN 12'-6"X9'-0"

BAR

DINING 12'-0"X13'-0"

ENTRY

LIVING ROOM 15'-8"X13'-0"

M. BEDROOM 16'-0"X13'-0"

BEDROOM 13'-0"X11'-10"

63'-6"

71'-4"

SECOND FLOOR

BEDROOM 10'-10"X10'-10"

BEDROOM 10'-10"X15'-0"

Comfort and Convenience in an Elegant Setting

No. 20363

Transom windows, skylights, and an open plan combine to make this sturdy brick classic a sun-filled retreat you'll love coming home to. The soaring ceilings of the foyer are mirrored in the fireplaced family room, a perfect place for informal gatherings. Its proximity to the island kitchen with built-in bar and adjoining breakfast room makes your mealtime efforts easier. When you want to entertain in style, choose the formal living and dining rooms just inside the front door. Down a short hall off the foyer, you'll find a luxurious master suite featuring a vaulted bath with garden spa. Enjoy the family room view from the upstairs balcony that leads to two more bedrooms and a full bath with double vanities.

First floor — 1,859 sq. ft.
Second floor — 579 sq. ft.
Basement — 1,859 sq. ft.
Garage — 622 sq. ft.

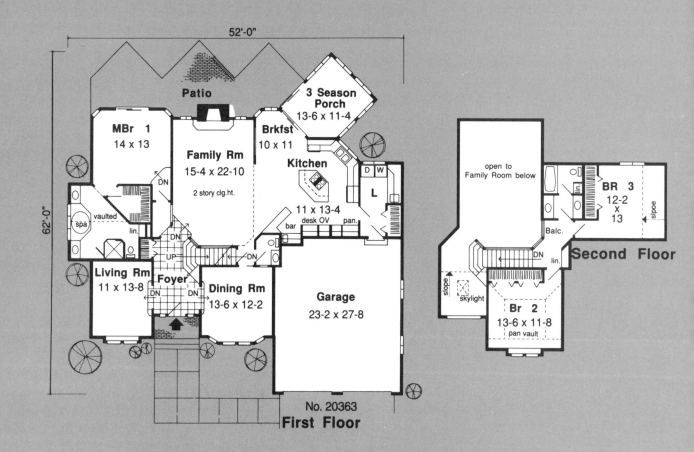

No. 20363
First Floor

Second Floor

Sunny and Spacious

No. 20302

The wood detailing that radiates from the half round window of this inviting family home hints at the sunny atmosphere you'll find inside. Walking through the vestibule past the formal and family dining rooms, you'll encounter a two-way fireplace that warms the living and family rooms at the rear of the house. Notice the double sliders that link both rooms to a massive rear deck, and the pass-through convenience afforded by the U-shaped kitchen. Tucked behind the garage for privacy, the first-floor master suite features a skylit bath with double vanities and a luxurious spa tub. And, upstairs, three bedrooms open to a skylit lounge with a bird's-eye view of the family room.

First floor — 1,510 sq. ft.
Second floor — 820 sq. ft.
Basement — 1,284 sq. ft.
Garage — 430 sq. ft.

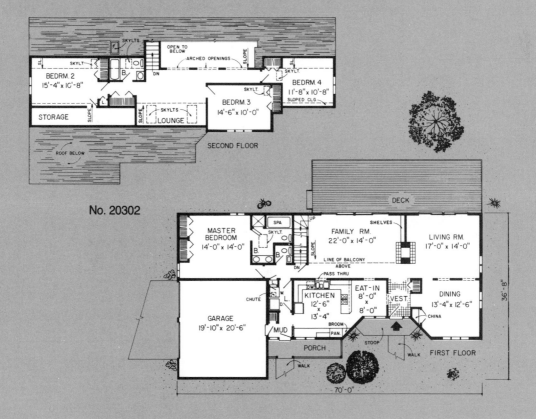

Traditional Energy-Saver

No. 20071

Take advantage of a southern exposure and save on energy costs in this beautiful family Tudor. Heat is stored in the floor of the sun room, adjoining the living and breakfast rooms. When the sun goes down, close the French doors and light a fire in the massive fireplace. State-of-the-art energy saving is not the only modern convenience in this house. You'll love the balcony overlooking the soaring two-story foyer and living room. In addition to providing great views, the balcony links the upstairs bedrooms. You're sure to enjoy the island kitchen, centrally located between formal and informal dining rooms. And, you'll never want to leave the luxurious master suite, with its double vanities and step-up whirlpool.

First floor — 2,186 sq. ft.
Second floor — 983 sq. ft.
Basement — 2,186 sq. ft.
Garage — 704 sq. ft.

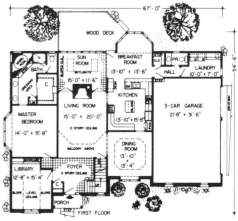

No. 20071

A Karl Kreeger Design

Glass-walled Family Room Invites Entertaining

No. 10466

With convenient access through the breakfast nook, a well-stocked wetbar opens into both the living room and the family room. The beamed ceiling of the living room plus its hearth-rimmed fireplace will appeal to family and guests alike. The kitchen sink is bathed in light from the corner greenhouse windows and flanked by plenty of cabinet and counter space. The four bedrooms of this well-organized plan are located along one wall of the home. The master suite features a corner window-seat and a dressing room with its own skylight.

First floor — 2,285 sq. ft.
Garage — 483 sq. ft.

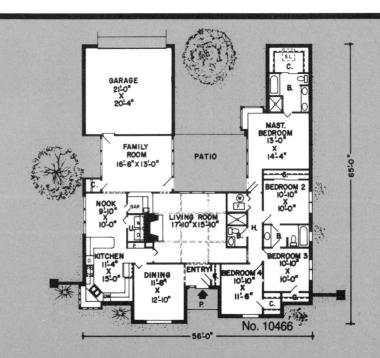

No. 10466

Morning Room Adds
Gracious Accent

No. 10445

Tiled floors unify the dining and food preparation areas of this masterful design. Located off the well organized kitchen is a morning room that's perfect for an elegant brunch or some private time before the day begins. Highlighted by a solarium, this octagonal room opens onto the centrally located living room that features built-in bookcases, a fireplace and a wetbar. The family room design employs more tile accents and opens onto the patio. The secluded master bedroom suite features a sunken tub, a small greenhouse for the plant enthusiast and roomy closets.

First floor-2,466 sq. ft.
Garage-482 sq. ft.

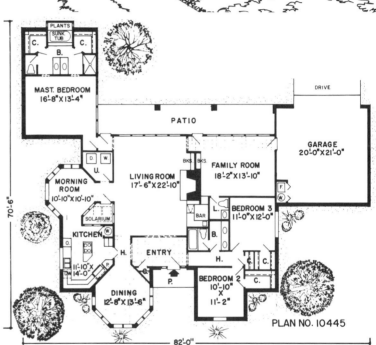

Traditional Sun Catcher

No. 20096

Windows and skylights in all shapes and sizes lend this home an airy, cozy feeling. From the two-story foyer to the skylit breakfast nook off the island kitchen, active areas are arranged in an open plan just perfect for entertaining. In warm weather, you'll enjoy the huge rear deck, accessible from both the living and breakfast rooms. Overnight guests will appreciate the full bath adjoining the downstairs den. Upstairs, three bedrooms open to a balcony overlooking the floor below. Look at the master suite. A walk-in closet and shower, double vanities, and a raised, skylit tub make this spacious area a luxurious retreat.

First floor — 1,286 sq. ft.
Second floor — 957 sq. ft.
Basement — 1,286 sq. ft.
Garage — 491 sq. ft.

A Karl Kreeger Design

No. 20096

Extraordinary Exterior Draws Attention

No. 10442

Reminiscent of lordly manor houses, this home also features many more contemporary pleasures such as a sunken master bedroom with dressing areas; the outdoor enjoyment provided by decks, porches and patios; and a second-story bridge overlooking the cathedral-ceilinged living room. Featuring 2,069 sq. ft. of well-organized living space on the first floor and 860 sq. ft. in the upper story, this splendid residence is designed with two bedrooms and a game room on the second story. The game room is accented by a wetbar and its own fireplace.

First floor — 2,069 sq. ft.
Second floor — 860 sq. ft.
Garage — 600 sq. ft.

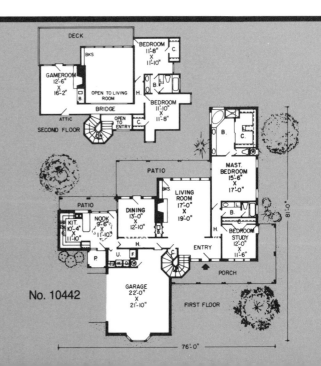

No. 10442

Light and Airy

No. 10745

Diagonal siding accentuates the multiple roof lines in this airy, three-bedroom beauty. Standing in the foyer, you can glance down the stairs that lead to a full basement, or let your eye follow the soaring ceiling to its peak over the kitchen, great room and dining room. The open plan and cathedral ceilings give living areas a spacious feeling. And, with the added outdoor living space the rear deck provides, you'll have plenty of room for entertaining. When your arms are full of groceries, you'll appreciate the convenience of the pantry located just off the garage entry. And, you'll also enjoy the quiet atmosphere in the bedrooms, tucked away in their own wing for maximum privacy.

Main living area — 1,643 sq. ft.

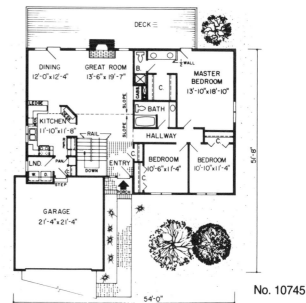

No. 10745

Surround Yourself with Luxury

No. 10615

A magnificent home in every detail, this stately 5 bedroom residence surrounds you with thoughtful luxury. Enter the oversized, tiled foyer and view the grand staircase whose landing splits the ascent into separate wings and creates an aura of privacy for a guest or live-in relative in bedroom 4. Serenity reigns throughout the home thanks to the courtyard plan that insulates the master bedroom complex and bedroom 2 from the main living areas. The kitchen is designed to serve the eating areas and family room and reserve the vast living room for more formal entertaining. Most of the home shares access to, and wonderful views of, the patio, covered by the 2nd floor deck, and pool area.

First floor — 4,075 sq. ft.
Second floor — 1,179 sq. ft.
Garage — 633 sq. ft.

No. 10615

Bridge Forms Focal Point

No. 10419

Wrap around stairs and a bridge hold the central position for both location and interest in the floor plan. The bridge functions to connect the stairway with second floor bedrooms, crossing the open space created by the two-story ceilings of the family room and entryway. Double hung windows cover both stories of the rear wall of the family room, looking out onto a patio on the lower level and deck on the second level. The second level bedroom hallway lies open to the family room below through a stub wall and 3 x 3 openings, certainly a wise step toward good air circulation. All upstairs bedrooms feature walk-in closets. A wetbar is shared by the family and living rooms and lies conveniently close to a covered patio and kitchen.

First floor — 2,445 sq. ft.
Second floor — 898 sq. ft.
Garage — 687 sq. ft.
Covered patios — 244 sq. ft.

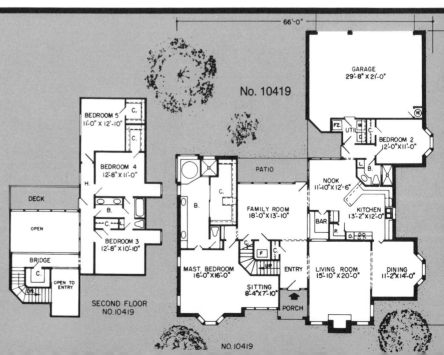

No. 10419

134

Eating Options Offered

No. 10421

The kitchen's location next to the nook and dining room, and only steps away from the covered patio, offers numerous options for both formal and informal dining. The kitchen is well-planned to save steps during food preparation, yet roomy enough for someone who likes to spread out. The dining area, which can be shut off from the kitchen by way of wood folding doors, is sunken 6 inches and lit with natural light from six 6 ft. windows. Glass variations across the front exterior also include arched gameroom windows, three arched windows in the master suite which form a box type bay, three 7'-6" living room leaded windows and leaded sidelight and transom at entry.

First floor-1,605 sq. ft.
Second floor-732 sq. ft.
Garage-525 sq. ft.
Patio-395 sq. ft.

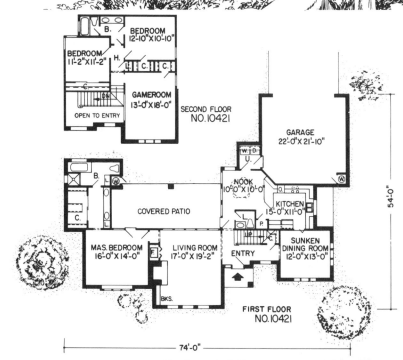

Bridge Over Foyer Introduces Unique Features Of Four-bedroom

No. 10535

The dramatic, two-story foyer opens into a cathedral-ceilinged great room, complete with a cozy fireplace that is framed with built-in bookcases. On either side of the foyer are the parlor and the formal dining room. The spacious kitchen is completely equipped and even has an octagonal breakfast nook tucked into a bank of windows. The first-floor master bedroom boasts a quaint, but roomy sitting room. Three more bedrooms, two baths and a loft with a view of both the great room and the foyer are located on the second floor.

First floor—2,335 sq. ft.
Second floor—1,157 sq. ft.
Basement—2,281 sq. ft.
Garage—862 sq. ft.

Plan Boasts Accommodating Kitchen

No. 1008

Handy to patio, family room and living room, the kitchen in this home offers a snack bar and a garage entrance. Convenience marks the entire plan, which supplies a closeted entrance foyer to channel traffic. Warm and cozy, the family room is furnished with wood-burning fireplace. Three ample bedrooms share two full baths.

First floor—1,510 sq. ft.
Storage room—108 sq. ft.
Carport—417 sq. ft.

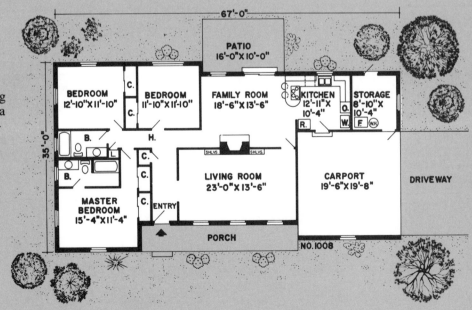

67'-0"

PATIO 16'-0" X 10'-0"

BEDROOM 12'-10" X 11'-10"

BEDROOM 11'-10" X 11'-10"

FAMILY ROOM 18'-6" X 13'-6"

KITCHEN 12'-11" X 10'-4"

STORAGE 8'-10" X 10'-4"

35'-0"

B.

H.

C.

B.

SHLVS. SHLVS.

LIVING ROOM 23'-0" X 13'-6"

CARPORT 19'-6" X 19'-8"

DRIVEWAY

MASTER BEDROOM 15'-4" X 11'-4"

ENTRY

PORCH

NO. 1008

Master Retreat Crowns Contemporary Plan

No. 10625

The dramatic roof lines of this three-bedroom gem only hint at the wonderful angles that lie inside. From a sheltered porch, the foyer leads to a two-story great room with sloping ceilings and a huge fireplace. For outdoor lovers, the open plan unites the kitchen, dining, and living areas with a rear deck. Upstairs, dramatic angles are repeated in the master suite, tucked away from other parts of the house on its own landing. A few steps up, two more bedrooms share the upper reaches of this intriguing contemporary.

First floor — 990 sq. ft.
Second floor — 980 sq. ft.
Garage — 450 sq. ft.

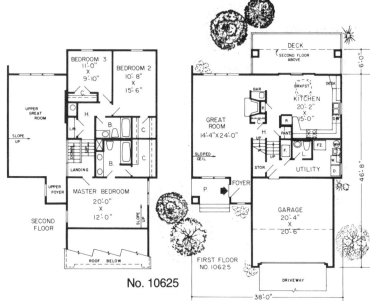

Two Fireplaces Provide Warm Appeal

No. 10601

Imagine how impressive this stone exterior and tile roof looks in the morning light. Inside, treat yourself to lavish living. This home is something special with rare features like a parlor and thoughtful touches like the double coat closet in the foyer. The master suite is a knockout with its generous dimensions, walk-in closet, dressing area, deluxe bath, and private door to the patio. This home can accommodate entertaining on any scale thanks to roomy, well-defined spaces for the parlor, dining room, living room, den, and family room with wet-bar. You'll find all the little extras that make life relaxing.

First floor — 3,025 sq. ft.
Garage — 722 sq. ft.
Patio — 403 sq. ft.

At Home on a Hillside

No. 10644

You'll just love the excitement of living in this 4 bedroom, 3 1/2 bath beauty; every room has an interesting shape! From the foyer, view the recessed ceilings of the dining room, the bump-out windows of the parlor, and the fireplaced family room with patio. Beyond the central stairwell lies the angular kitchen with a skylit breakfast nook. The master bedroom suite is right down a short hall. Each of the upstairs bedrooms has direct access to a full bath. And, don't worry about carrying a heavy laundry basket down the stairs. A centrally located chute delivers dirty clothes to the laundry room.

First floor — 1,593 sq. ft.
Second floor — 818 sq. ft.
Basement — 863 sq. ft.
Garage — 720 sq. ft.

A Karl Kreeger Design

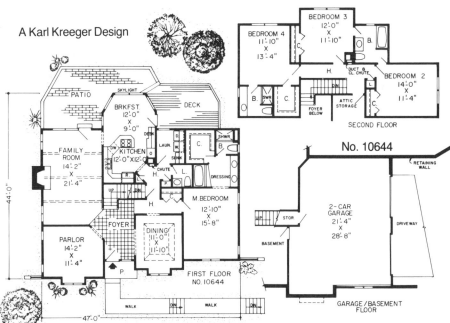

Attractive Entry Created By Plant Ledge

No. 10438

Dormers, decorative gable vents and bay windows balance on either side of the front entrance to give the exterior facade a look of symmetry. Inside, a planter ledge is found above the entry, lit by the two dormers and accessed through a bedroom for plant care. Raised hearth fireplaces, found in both the master bedroom and living room, share a chimney. Two skylights illumine the master bath and all area on the second floor.

First floor – 1,454 sq. ft.
Second floor – 1,270 sq. ft.

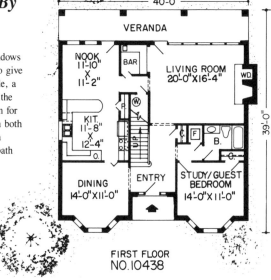

SECOND FLOOR

FIRST FLOOR
NO.10438

Interesting Sunken Areas

No. 10441

The exterior of this design is as impressive as the interior is livable. Just inside the double front doors, a brick column corner and exposed beams visually separate the entry and hall from the dining room. Straight ahead and to the left, floors of the living room and master bedroom drop 6 inches with the rear of the master bedroom dropping another 6 inches to create a cozy sitting area with a corner fireplace. Two-story windows, brick fireplace, built-in bookcases, exposed ceiling beams and a wet bar grace the living room. A second wet bar and bookcases are also found in the second floor loft which is open to the living room below.

First floor – 2,721 sq. ft.
Second floor – 732 sq. ft.
Garage – 681 sq. ft.

FIRST FLOOR
NO. 10441

SECOND FLOOR

Two-story Tile Foyer Welcomes Guests And Family Alike

No. 10501

Make a wonderful first impression or return home to this massive, welcoming foyer and step right into the great room of this tastefully appointed design. The great room is enlarged by a wrap-around deck and highlighted by a fireplace, built-in bookcases and wet-bar. The first floor master suite is equally inviting with its spacious dressing area and separate bath. Adjacent to the central great room, the kitchen area has its own built-in desk, octagonal morning room and central island. The second floor includes three bedrooms linked by a balcony which overlooks the great room and the open foyer.

First floor-2419 sq. ft.
Second floor-926 sq. ft.
Garage-615 sq. ft.
Basement-2419 sq. ft.

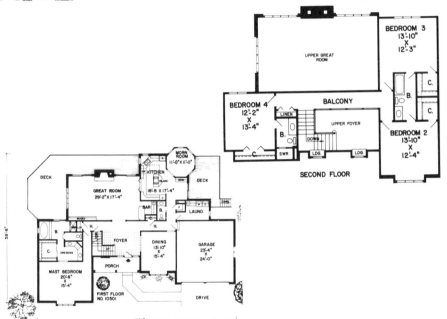

SECOND FLOOR

BEDROOM 3
13'-10" X 12'-3"

BEDROOM 4
12'-2" X 13'-4"

BALCONY

UPPER GREAT ROOM

UPPER FOYER

BEDROOM 2
13'-10" X 12'-4"

LINEN

DOWN

LDG   LDG

SWR.

FIRST FLOOR
No. 10501

DECK

GREAT ROOM
29'-2" X 17'-4"

MORN ROOM
11'-0" X 11'-0"

KITCHEN
18'-8" X 17'-4"

DECK

LAUND.

BAR

FOYER

DINING
13'-10" X 15'-4"

GARAGE
23'-4" X 24'-0"

MAST. BEDROOM
20'-8" X 15'-4"

PORCH

DRIVE

80'-8"

58'-6"

Rough Cedar and Stucco Accent Facade

No. 10447

A built-in planter separates the living and dining areas of this elegant home to add a feeling of spaciousness. And, imagine the decorating options. A central kitchen is just a few steps away from the formal dining room and a large breakfast nook whose window-wall offers a magnificent view of the patio and backyard. Four bedrooms are well situated for privacy, with the 4th useful as a study or sewing room. Note other nice touches such as large windows everywhere, a wetbar in the family room, and a fireplace in the living room.

First floor — 2,630 sq. ft.
Garage — 522 sq. ft.

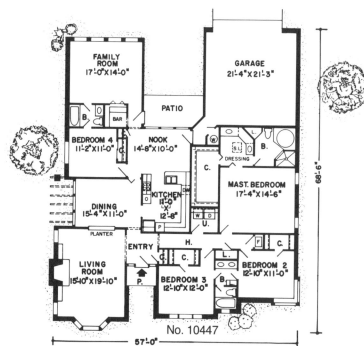

No. 10447

Three Fireplaces Provide Warm Feeling

No. 10670

Vaulted ceilings, a gently curving staircase, and high, arched windows make the entry to this spacious, five-bedroom home an airy celebration of light and space. A short hall leads from the formal dining room to the cozy family room, island kitchen, and sunny breakfast nook with adjoining brick patio. Warmed by its own fireplace, the master bedroom shares a private wing on the first floor with a bedroom that could double as a study. The second floor deck off the library is a great place to enjoy a sunny afternoon. And, don't worry about storage. Two pantries, a room-sized wetbar, and walk-in closets in every bedroom mean you'll never have to worry about clutter.

First floor — 2,959 sq. ft.
Second floor — 1,076 sq. ft.
Garage — 764 sq. ft.

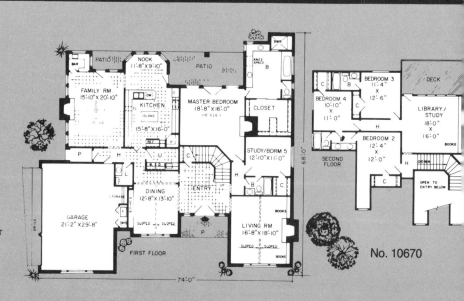

No. 10670

Secluded and Spectacular Bedroom

No. 10451

Create a secluded sanctuary for your master bedroom: a generous space with charming fireplace,
individual dressing rooms, and skylit bathing area.
Relax away from the clutter and noise of the children's rooms, especially if you create a study or
sewing room from bedroom two. You'll love the
courtyard effect created by glassed-in living spaces
overlooking the central covered patio with skylights. The sprawling charm of this house creates a
sense of privacy everywhere you go. Extra touches,
such as the wetbar and dual fireplaces for family
and living room set this home apart.

First floor — 2,864 sq. ft.
Garage — 607 sq. ft.

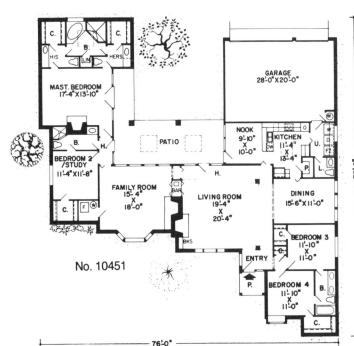

No. 10451

Design Features Six Sides

No. 1074

Simple lines flow from this six-sided design, affordably scaled, but sizable enough for a growing family, Active living areas are snuggled centrally between two quieter bedroom and bath areas in the floor plan. A small hallway, accessing two bedrooms and a full bath on the right side, may be completely shut off from the living room, providing seclusion. Another bath lies behind a third bedroom on the left side, complete with washer/dryer facilities and close enough to a stoop and rear entrance to serve as a mud room.

First floor-1,040 sq. ft.
Storage-44 sq. ft.
Deck-258 sq. ft.
Carport-230 sq. ft.

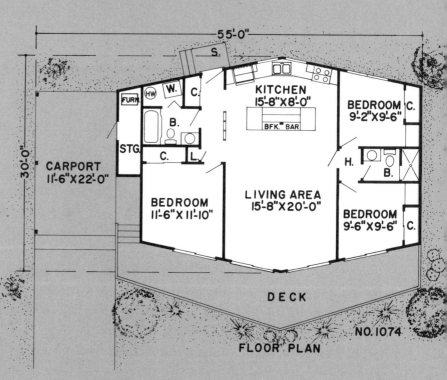

CARPORT 11'-6"X22'-0"

KITCHEN 15'-8"X8'-0"

BFK. BAR

BEDROOM 9'-2"X9'-6"

STG.

BEDROOM 11'-6"X 11'-10"

LIVING AREA 15'-8"X20'-0"

BEDROOM 9'-6"X9'-6"

55'-0"

30'-0"

DECK

NO. 1074

FLOOR PLAN

Vacation retreat or year round living

No. 1078

A long central hallway divides formal from informal areas, assuring privacy for the two bedrooms located in the rear. Also located along the central portion of the design are a utility room and neighboring bath. The furnace, water heater and washer dryer units are housed in the utility room. An open living/dining room area with exposed beams, sloping ceilings and optional fireplace occupies the design's front. Two pairs of sliding glass doors access the 411 feet of deck from this area. The house may also be entered from the carport on the right or the deck on the left.

First floor-1,024 sq. ft.
Carport & Storage-387 sq. ft.
Deck-411 sq. ft.

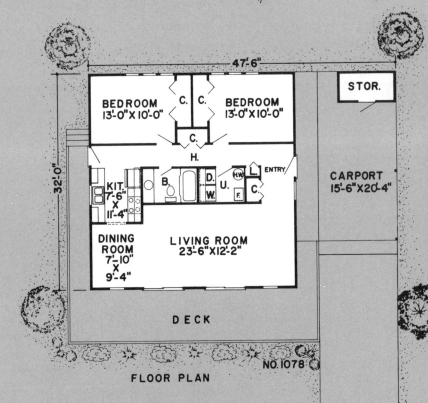

FLOOR PLAN   NO.1078

A Plan with Lofty Ideas

No. 21120

An attractive beginning for this home is found in the centrally located foyer. Down several steps lies a sunken family room, accentuated by two stories of glass at its rear, cathedral ceiling and a fireplace. The family room shares openness of design with the adjacent kitchen and dining room. Stairs spiral from the foyer to a second level loft which overlooks the family room below from a full length balcony and accesses a private exterior deck through glass doors on the other side. A master bedroom with its own bath lies secluded to the left of the foyer. An additional bath and washer/dryer facilities are located off the hall to the master suite. A carport, 49 square feet of storage at its rear and a covered terrace, accessed from the kitchen and family room, complete the plan.

First floor — 947 sq. ft.
Second floor — 232 sq. ft.
Carport — 346 sq. ft.
Storage — 49 sq. ft.

No materials list available

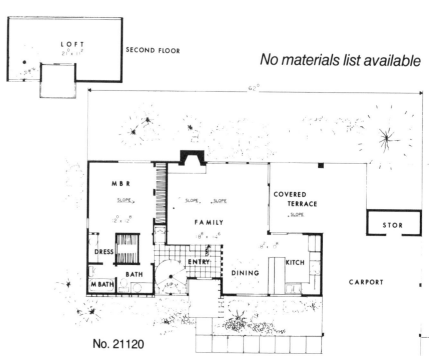

No. 21120

Octagon Sitting Room

No. 10418

Imagine relaxing in your sitting room in front of a hearty fire after a leisure shower or bath, then snuggling into bed for a long night's rest, all without ever leaving your master bedroom suite and its comforts. Lines from the sitting room's octagon shape position the fireplace at an angle and carry over into the bath and hallway to add angled diversity to these areas. Windows here, as well as in the living center and dining room, are a full 8 feet. A raised-hearth fireplace, exposed beams, built-in bookshelves, and patio access are features of the 18 x 23 living center, open opposite the fireplace to the entry way. Ceilings of the entry rise two stories and watch over a short bridgeway linking stairs to the second level rooms.

First floor — 2,600 sq. ft.
Second floor — 854 sq. ft.
Garage — 638 sq. ft.
Patio & porch — 354 sq. ft.

No. 1041

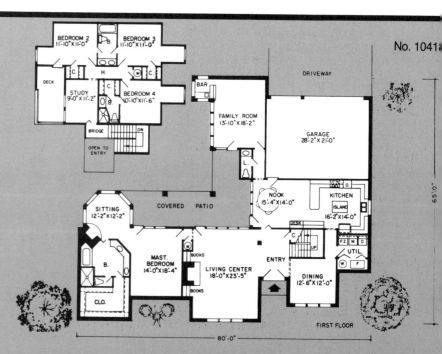

Designed for Entertaining

No. 10587

The double doors of the vaulted entry are just a hint of the graceful touches in this three-bedroom home. Curves soften the stairway, deck, and the huge bar that runs between the formal and informal dining areas. Skylights, bay, and bump-out windows flood every room with light. And when the sun goes down, you can keep things cozy with fireplaces in the family and sunken living rooms. For a quiet retreat, sneak upstairs to deck off the master bedroom suite.

First floor — 2,036 sq. ft.
Second floor — 1,554 sq. ft.
Garage — 533 sq. ft.

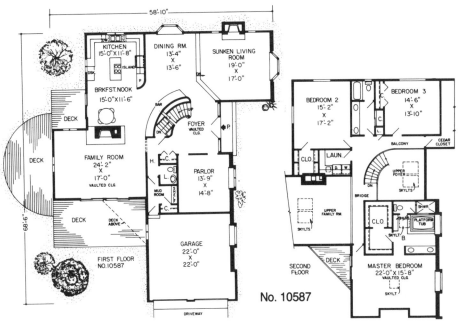

Airy Lattice Work Lends Charm to Central Core Design

No. 10453

The central traffic pattern for this unique design is the tiled foyer and hallway which link the dining room, living room, and family room around a wet-bar that is accessible to all three rooms. Located at the far corner of the tiled hall are the kitchen, laundry, and informal dining area. The step-saving arrangement of the kitchen is enhanced by the peninsula which links the area to the octagonal dining nook. The rear patio extends the open plan as it is visible through the many windows located along the rear walls of the dining nook, the family room and the master bedroom.

Main living area — 2,115 sq. ft.
Garage — 569 sq. ft.

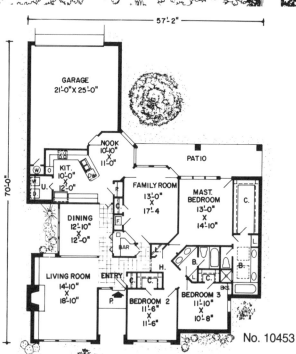

No. 10453

Ideal for a Narrow Lot

No. 10774

With its appealing, L-shaped exterior and compact design, this two-bedroom beauty is the perfect home for the small family on a budget. A half wall and streetside garage insure your privacy, presenting an attractive face to passers-by. You'll appreciate the convenience of the kitchen with its adjoining breakfast bar, storage pantry, and laundry nook. And the handy wetbar just off the fireplaced living room makes entertaining easy. Step out to the rear patio through sliders in the living room or master suite. Both the front and master bedrooms feature adjoining baths.

Main living area — 1,290 sq. ft.
Garage — one-car

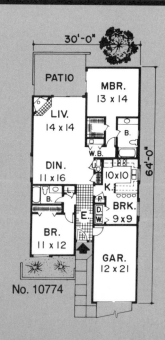

No. 10774

Deck Doubles Outdoor Living Space

No. 10619

This one-level contemporary is a one-of-a-kind design just made for the sun lover. With a huge front deck featuring pass-through convenience from the kitchen, a rear patio, and an abundance of windows, you're guaranteed a cheerful atmosphere, even on the coldest day. The central focus of this contemporary charmer is the sunken living room, with its three window walls and massive fireplace. Open to the kitchen, foyer, and handy bar area, this elegant room seems even larger because of its soaring ceiling. And, just behind the fireplace, an indoor hot tub turns the skylit sunspace into a private spa. The foyer separates active areas from the front bedroom and vaulted master suite. Another bedroom shares a quiet spot behind the garage with a full bath and utility area.

First floor — 2,352 sq. ft.
Basement — 2,352 sq. ft.
Garage — 696 sq. ft.

A Karl Kreeger Design

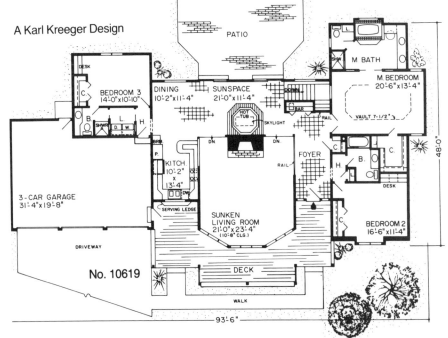

No. 10619

Rural Farmhouse Profile

No. 26001

A varied gabled roof, a large railed front porch and wood create a picturesque rural farmhouse profile in this plan. On the lower level a central hallway channels traffic easily to all rooms — a spacious formal living room and family-dining area with a bay window and fireplace in the front, and a bedroom suite, utility area, and kitchen at the back. A mudroom is suitably located adjacent to the utility area. A sheltered outside entrance to the utility room and the double garage is given by a breeze-way-porch. On the second level three bedrooms nearly encircle a center bath.

First floor — 1,184 sq. ft.
Second floor — 821 sq. ft.
Basement — 821 sq. ft.
Garage — 576 sq. ft.
Front porch — 176 sq. ft.
Side porch — 69 sq. ft.

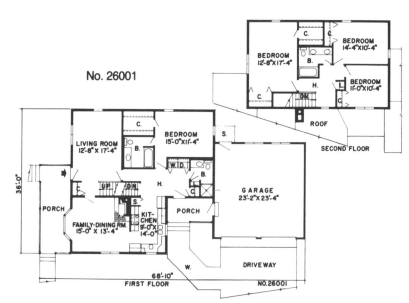

No. 26001

Multi-Level Excitement

No. 20102

With abundant windows, a skylit breakfast room with sliders to a rear deck, and an open plan over-looking the sunken living room below, the foyer level of this distinctive home is a celebration of open space. You'll appreciate the step-saving design of the island kitchen that easily serves both dining rooms. And, you'll enjoy the warmth of the living room fireplace throughout the lower levels of the house. A stairway leads from the foyer to the bedroom level that houses the spacious master suite with a private bath, and two additional bedrooms served by a full bath. The lucky inhabitant of the fourth bedroom, tucked away at the top of the house, will love this private retreat overlooking the two floors below.

First level — 1,003 sq. ft.
Second level — 808 sq. ft.
Third level — 241 sq. ft.
Basement — 573 sq. ft.
Garage — 493 sq. ft.

A Karl Kreeger Design

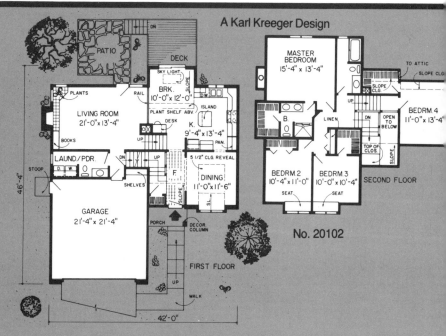

No. 20102

Bedroom Tower Creates Interesting Roof Line

No. 10618

Sloping ceilings and lofty open spaces are dominant features in this four-bedroom family home. Leading from the stairs to a full bath and two bedrooms, the upstairs hall is a bridge over the foyer and rustic living room. The dining room lies just off the foyer, adjacent to the island kitchen and breakfast room. The vaulted master suite with attached deck, a family bath, and bedroom with walk-in closet occupy a private wing.

First floor — 1,492 sq. ft.
Second floor — 475 sq. ft.
Garage — 413 sq. ft.

No. 10618

A Karl Kreeger Design

You Deserve This Classic Beauty

No. 20094

Sturdy stucco, fieldstone, and rough-hewn timbers lend a distinguished air to this updated Tudor classic. And inside, modern and traditional elements unite to create a masterpiece your family will never outgrow. Look at the soaring foyer, the elegant recessed ceilings in the dining room and master suite, and the book-lined library off the fireplaced living room. Imagine the convenience of an island kitchen with wetbar service to the living room, and an adjoining, skylit breakfast room. And, think about how the three-and-a-half baths that serve the first-floor master suite and three upstairs bedrooms will make the morning rush a thing of the past.

First floor — 2,047 sq. ft.
Second floor — 789 sq. ft.
Basement — 2,047 sq. ft.
Garage — 524 sq. ft.

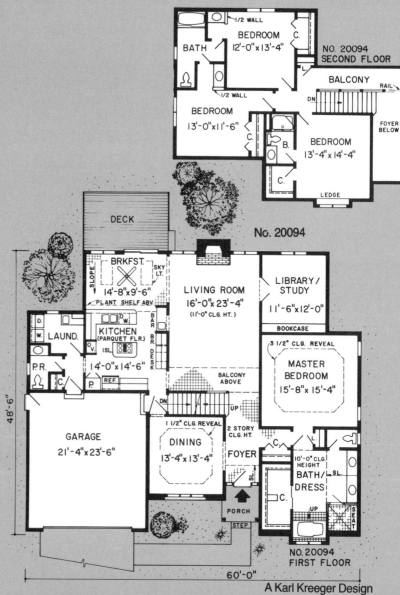

A Karl Kreeger Design

Covered Porch Offered in Farm-type Traditional

No. 20064

This pleasant traditional design has a farmhouse flavor exterior that incorporates a covered porch and features a circle wood louver on its garage, giving this design a feeling of sturdiness. Inside on the first level from the foyer and to the right is a formal dining room complete with a bay window and an elevated ceiling and a corner china cabinet. To the left of the foyer is the living room with a wood-burning fireplace. The kitchen is connected to the breakfast room and there is a room for the laundry facilities. A half bath is also featured on the first floor. The second floor has three bedrooms. The master bedroom, on the second floor, has its own private bath and walk-in closet. The other two bedrooms share a full bath. A two-car garage is also added into this design.

First floor — 892 sq. ft.
Second floor — 836 sq. ft.
Basement — 892 sq. ft.
Garage — 491 sq. ft.

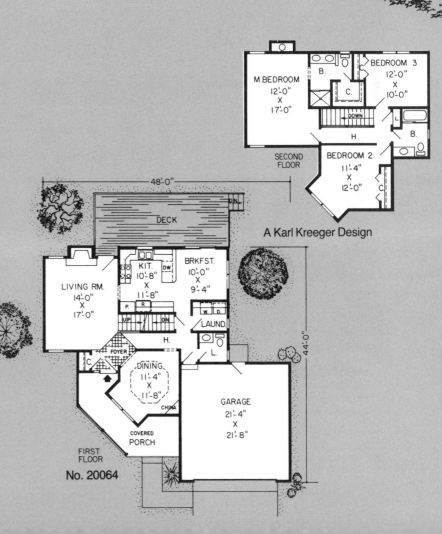

A Karl Kreeger Design

No. 20064

Sunlight Will Stream Into This Many-windowed Design

No. 10456

Twelve-foot beamed ceilings grace the expansive living room which is further extended by the patio-facing window wall. The adjoining dining room is defined by a lower ceiling and enhanced by an over-sized bay window of leaded glass. The spacious kitchen features many cabinets, a walk-in pantry, center work island, and a nook which also looks onto the patio. The master bedroom has a five-piece bath with a skylight plus an extra large walk-in closet. The two smaller bedrooms share a full bath, and a third bedroom, located between the kitchen and dining room, might find use as a guest bedroom or a study.

First floor — 2,511 sq. ft.
Garage — 517 sq. ft.

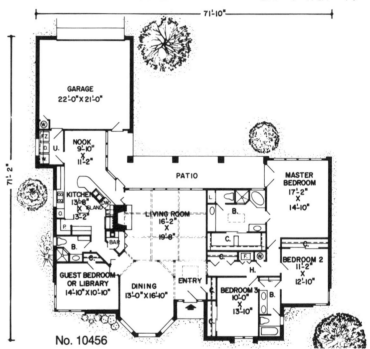

No. 10456

Perfect for Parties

No. 10663

Does your family enjoy entertaining? Here's your home! This handsome, rambling beauty can handle a crowd of any size. Greet your guests in a beautiful foyer that opens to the cozy, bayed living room and elegant dining room with floor-to-ceiling windows. Show them the impressive two-story gallery and book-lined study, flooded with sunlight from atrium doors and clerestory windows. Or, gather around the fire in the vaulted family room. The bar connects to the efficient kitchen, just steps away from both nook and formal dining room. And, when the guests go home, you'll appreciate your luxurious first-floor master suite and the cozy upstairs bedroom suites with adjoining sitting room.

First floor — 2,446 sq. ft.
Second floor — 844 sq. ft.
Garage — 660 sq. ft.

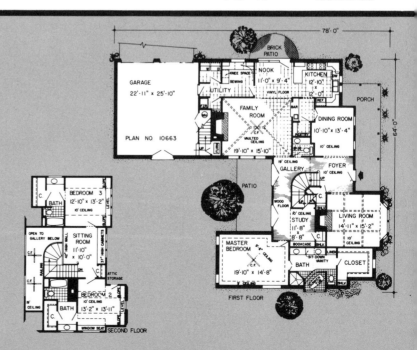

Compact Home Has Open Design

No. 10455

The airlock entry saves energy and opens onto the raised foyer which extends inward toward the adjacent dining and living rooms. The living room has a window wall which overlooks the lawn, a fireplace with hearth, built-in bookcases, a wetbar and direct access to the patio. The dining room has direct access to the step-saver kitchen with its plentiful storage and convenient peninsula. Along the opposite side of the house are the three bedrooms. Individual dressing areas within the master suite include separate vanities and walk-in closets.

First floor — 1,643 sq. ft.
Garage — 500 sq. ft.

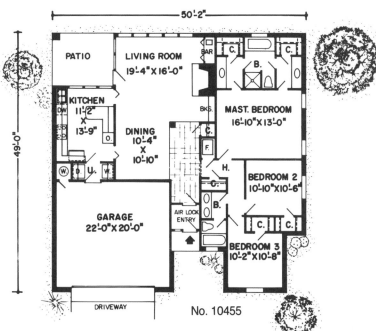

First floor plan No. 10455, 50'-2" × 49'-0"

PATIO — LIVING ROOM 19'-4" X 16'-0" — BAR
KITCHEN 11'-2" X 13'-9" — DINING 10'-4" X 10'-10" — MAST. BEDROOM 16'-10" X 13'-0"
BEDROOM 2 10'-10" X 10'-6"
GARAGE 22'-0" X 20'-0" — AIR LOCK ENTRY — BEDROOM 3 10'-2" X 10'-8"
DRIVEWAY — No. 10455

Three Bedroom Ranch Makes Good Use of Space

No. 10483

Lots of living is packed into this well designed home which features a combined kitchen and dining room. The highly functional U-shaped kitchen includes a corner sink under double windows. Opening onto the dining room is the living room which is illuminated by both a front picture window and a skylight. Its lovely fireplace makes this an inviting place to gather. The sleeping area of this home contains three bedrooms and two full baths; one of which is a private bath accessed only from the master bedroom.

First floor - 1,025 sq. ft.
Garage - 403 sq. ft.

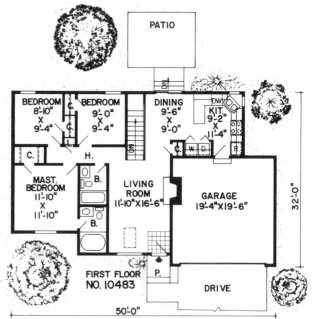

Greenhouse Adds Charm and Warmth to Multi-level Plan

No. 10468

The well-placed solar greenhouse is located on the lower level of this inviting design. Sliding glass doors open into the greenhouse from the family room while casement windows over the kitchen sink open into the space above. The master bedroom also has access to the outdoors through sliding glass doors onto an elevated deck. Two additional bedrooms are located across the hall along which is a conveniently placed area. The living room is warmed by a hearthed fireplace and adjoins the combined kitchen and dining areas.

Upper level - 1,294 sq. ft.
Family room level - 292 sq. ft.
Garage - 608 sq. ft.
Greenhouse - 164 sq. ft.

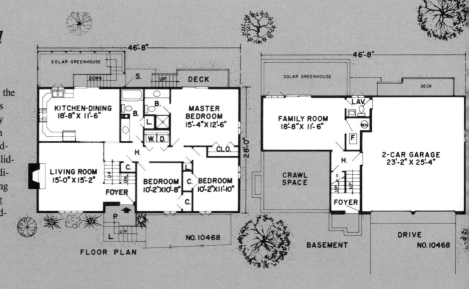

Two-way Fireplace Warms Living Areas

No. 10652

Stucco, fieldstone, and rough-hewn timbers grace the elegant exterior of this three-bedroom family home. But with abundant windows, high ceilings, and an open plan, this cheerful abode is a far cry from the chilly Tudor castle of long ago. Flanked by a vaulted formal dining room and a stairway to the upstairs bedrooms, full bath, and built-in cedar closet, the central foyer leads to a spacious living room, kept comfortable in any season by a ceiling fan. Nearby, the first-floor master suite is loaded with amenities: a walk-in closet, skylit double vanities, and a sunken tub. Notice the cooktop island convenience in the kitchen, the built-in bar adjacent to the living room, and the rear deck accessible through French doors in the breakfast room.

First floor — 1,789 sq. ft.
Second floor — 568 sq. ft.
Basement — 1,789 sq. ft.
Garage — 529 sq. ft.

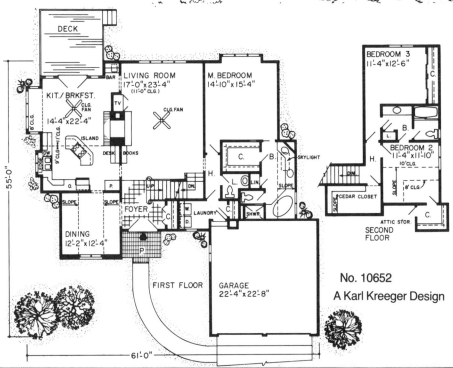

No. 10652

A Karl Kreeger Design

Simple Yet Elegant Lines Enclose Livable Plan

No. 10484

This two-story home offers integrated living spaces for an active family. The front breakfast room is just across the counter from the efficiently organized kitchen which is highlighted by a bumped-out window over the double sink. Neatly tucked between the kitchen and breakfast room is the laundry center. Adjacent to the kitchen is the dining room which flows into the living room and the warmth of its hearthed fireplace. Upstairs are three bedrooms including a generous master suite.

First floor — 869 sq. ft.
Second floor — 840 sq. ft.
Garage — 440 sq. ft.

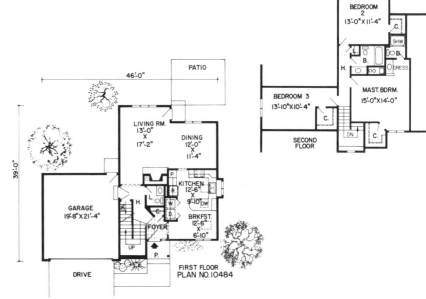

Contemporary Design Features Four Bedrooms and Three-car Garage

No. 10488

An ideal home for a family with teenagers, this striking design is enhanced by the interesting window treatment in both the kitchen and dining rooms. The first floor includes formal living and dining rooms as well as a large family room complete with a fireplace and a wet bar. The first floor bedroom with its private entrance to the bath would be ideal for guests. Highlighting the second floor is the spacious master bedroom which adjoins a luxurious dressing room with an extra large walk-in closet. Two more bedrooms flank an additional bath. The second floor balcony yields a commanding view of the first floor living and dining rooms.

First floor — 1,540 sq. ft.
Second floor — 1,122 sq. ft.
Garage — 626 sq. ft.

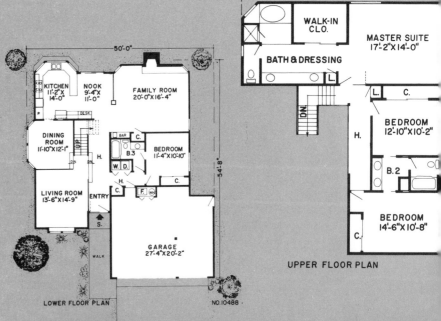

Simple Lines Enhanced By Elegant Window Treatment

No. 10503

The arched window highlights the front den and provides a homey spot for reading or an excellent location for a home office. The sloped ceiling of the living room enhances the feeling of spaciousness provided by the wall of windows which look out onto the rear deck. The dining room, adjacent to the living room, features a planning desk and opens directly onto the efficiently arranged kitchen. The bedrooms are gathered on the opposite side of this home. The master suite has a separate dressing area, complete with walk-in closet and double vanities plus a bath which includes both a tiled tub and a shower.

First floor-1,486 sq. ft.
Garage-462 sq. ft.

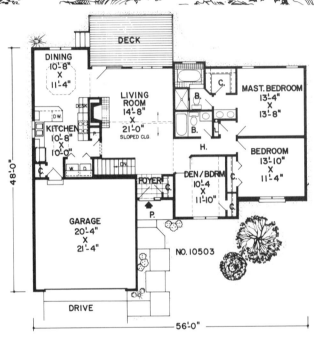

DECK

DINING
10'-8" X 11'-4"

LIVING ROOM
14'-8" X 21'-0"
SLOPED CLG.

KITCHEN
10'-8" X 10'-0"

MAST. BEDROOM
13'-4" X 13'-8"

BEDROOM
13'-10" X 11'-4"

DEN/BDRM
10'-4" X 11'-10"

FOYER

GARAGE
20'-4" X 21'-4"

NO. 10503

DRIVE

48'-0"

56'-0"

Front Bedroom Features Corner Window Seat

No. 10758

You won't find any wasted space in this sunny, contemporary beauty. This ingenious plan eliminates unnecessary walls, adding soaring ceilings to create an airy atmosphere. Open railings and single steps separate the fireplaced family and living rooms from the entry and dining areas. To complete the outdoor feeling, sliders in the family room and both dining rooms open to a rear deck and patio. You'll find a bedroom, complete with an adjoining full bath tucked behind the garage. Notice the bar across the hall, tucked under the stairs that lead to three more bedrooms. You'll love the private master suite, with its own private deck and skylit spa area.

First floor — 2,027 sq. ft.
Second floor — 1,476 sq. ft.
Garage — 650 sq. ft.

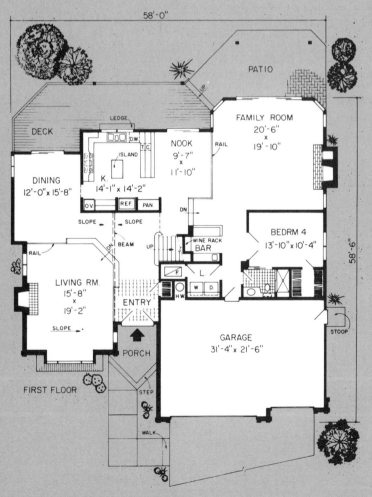

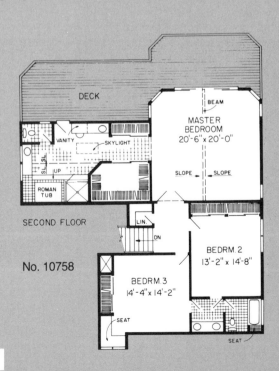

Window-Studded Brick Facade Communicates Success

No. 20353

Stepping into the soaring, skylit foyer of this gracious, brick beauty, with the balcony above and vaulted dining room to the left, you'll know you've found your dream home. And, this gem combines sun-filled ambience with convenient features: a spacious island kitchen with adjoining pantry that serves the rounded glass-walled breakfast room, rear patio, formal dining room, and family room with ease; a built-in bar in the family room just steps away from the elegant parlor; a bath off every bedroom upstairs. With its double-vanitied bath complete with a circular spa, two-way access to a private deck, and cozy fireplace, the master suite alone is reason to choose this elegant home.

First floor — 1,807 sq. ft.

Second floor — 1,359 sq. ft.

Basement — 1,807 sq. ft.

Garage — 840 sq. ft.

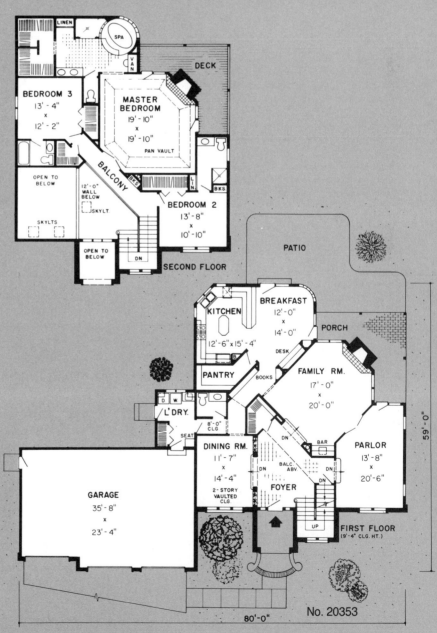

Upstairs Gables Provide Cozy Sitting Nooks

No. 20117

Here's an attractive home loaded with amenities and plenty of room for your growing family. Formal and family areas are well separated in this distinctive home, with an expansive living and dining room arrangement tucked right off the central foyer. The kitchen and breakfast room overlook a rear deck, the perfect spot for a summer barbecue. Just steps away, you'll find the elegant master suite with its huge, walk-in closet and double vanities. Upstairs, let your imagination wander through two bedrooms adjoining a full, skylit bath, a handy cedar closet for winter storage, and the intriguing loft tucked above the rest of the house.

First floor — 1,766 sq. ft.
Second floor — 999 sq. ft.
Basement — 1,730 sq. ft.
Garage — 504 sq. ft.

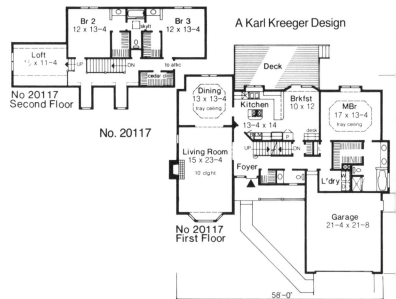

A Karl Kreeger Design

No 20117 Second Floor

No. 20117

No 20117 First Floor

Corner Fireplace Warms Living Room

No. 10581

Bring the great outdoors inside in this luxurious 4 bedroom, 3 bath home. Enter the dramatic 2-story foyer from the 3-car garage or the double front doors. The living area is perfect for entertaining. Parlor, formal dining room, kitchen, breakfast room and living room revolve around a central staircase. You can spend your outdoor hours on the deck off the breakfast room, or screened porch off the living room. Two bedrooms, including the master suite with walk-in closet, two baths and a laundry room complete the first floor. Upstairs, the balcony overlooks the foyer and leads to two more bedrooms and a full bath.

First floor — 1,916 sq. ft.
Second floor — 740 sq. ft.
Basement — 1,916 sq. ft.
Screened porch — 192 sq. ft.
Garage — 814 sq. ft.

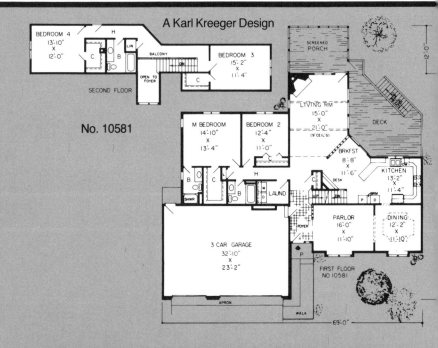

A Karl Kreeger Design

No. 10581

SECOND FLOOR

FIRST FLOOR NO 10581

162

Dignified Design Opens to Family Style Floor Plan

No. 10496

Four spacious bedrooms are arranged on the upper level of this plan so that privacy is maintained without any wasted space. Two of the bedrooms share a bath while the other two large bedrooms each have a private bath and a walk-in closet. The living space on the lower level is highlighted by a spacious family room with beamed ceiling, fireplace, bookcases, wetbar and direct access to both the patio and informal dining nook. The more formal dining room and living room are located on the other side of the well-designed U-shaped kitchen. The double garage even has plenty of room for a workshop and extra bicycles.

Lower level — 1,330 sq. ft.
Upper level — 1,301 sq. ft.
Garage — 610 sq. ft.
Basement — 765 sq. ft.

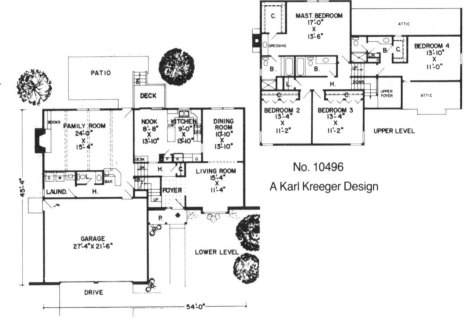

No. 10496

A Karl Kreeger Design

Special Purpose Rooms Highlight Distinctive Design

No. 10492

With a special television room plus a family room and an upstairs sitting room, there's plenty of opportunity for everyone in the family to enjoy personal activities and pursuits. The well designed kitchen adjoins the formal dining room and also has its own dining nook with lots of windows for sunny family breakfasts and lunches. Both the living room and family room open onto patios for indoor/outdoor entertaining. The second floor sitting room, complete with fireplace and warm hearth, adjoins the spacious master suite with its six-piece bath complete with Roman tub and oversized, walk-in closet. Two smaller bedrooms flank a walk-through bath to complete the second floor of this roomy, family home.

First floor — 2,409 sq. ft.
Second floor — 2,032 sq. ft.
Garage — 690 sq. ft.

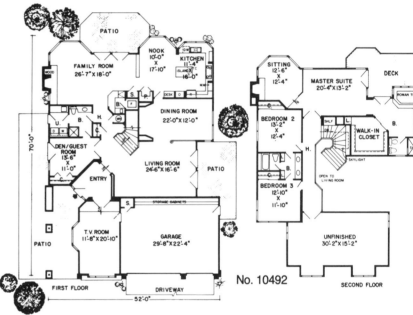

No. 10492

FIRST FLOOR
SECOND FLOOR

A Home for Your Growing Family

No. 10692

Walking into this gracious family home, you can see it's designed for convenient living. Formal living and dining rooms flank the two-story entry. Look up and discover the sunny study that links the four upstairs bedrooms and adjoining baths. From the central hallway with handy powder room, you can reach the master suite or the family living suite that features a roomy, angular kitchen, utility room, breakfast nook, and fireplaced family room.

First floor — 2,313 sq. ft.
Second floor — 1,256 sq. ft.
Garage — 662 sq. ft.

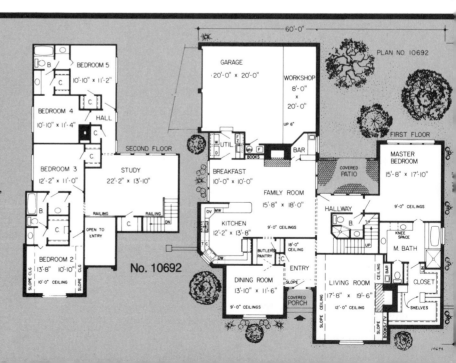

No. 10692

PLAN NO. 10692

SECOND FLOOR
FIRST FLOOR

Arches Grace Classic Facade

No. 10677

Do you have a small lot, but love open space? Here's your answer! This compact beauty uses built-in planters and half-walls to define rooms without closing them in. Look at the first floor plan. The living room features a cozy sitting area dominated by a half-round window, then rises to nearly two stories for a wide-open feeling. At the rear of the house, the family room and kitchen, divided only by a cooktop peninsula, share the airy atmosphere. Sliders unite this sunny area with an outdoor patio that mirrors the shape of the dining bay. Peer down at the living room from your vantage point on the balcony that connects the three bedrooms upstairs. And, be sure to notice the double sinks and built-in vanity in the master bath, a plus when you're rushed in the morning.

First floor — 932 sq. ft.
Second floor — 764 sq. ft.
Garage — 430 sq. ft.
Basement — 920 sq. ft.

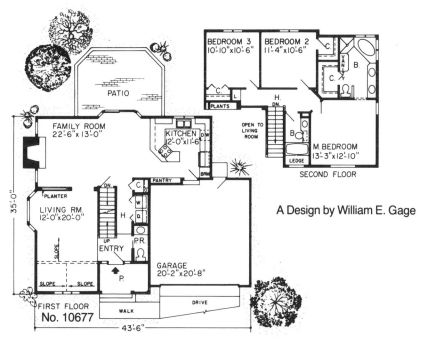

A Design by William E. Gage

Two-story Window Flanked by Stone Dominates Facade

No. 10494

This handsome, stone-trimmed home has many amenities which are sure to please the most discriminating tastes. The tiled foyer leads either to the upper two bedrooms, the master bedroom or the central living room. A corner, built-in bookcase plus a fireplace and a window wall complete this gracious room. The front dining room is convenient to the unusually workable kitchen with its cooking penninsula and adjacent breakfast nook. With floors of tile and three walls of windows this warm room is bathed in light.

First floor - 1,584 sq. ft.
Second floor - 599 sq. ft.
Garage - 514 sq. ft.
Basement - 1,584 sq. ft.

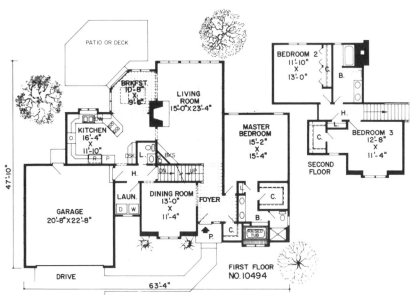

Sun Space Warms To Entertaining

No. 10495

Tile is used to soak up solar warmth in the sun space and also adds tailored accent to the total home arrangement. Leading from the air-lock entry toward the living spaces of this marvelous home, the tile separates the activity areas from the sleeping quarters. With two bedrooms on the second story, the lower area includes the master bedroom suite with its divided bath and walk-in closet. The utilitarian areas of the home are also enhanced by direct access to the sun space plus a space-stretching central island.

First floor - 1,691 sq. ft.
Second floor - 512 sq. ft.
Garage - 484 sq. ft.
Sun Space - 108 sq. ft.
Basement - 1,691 sq. ft.

Beamed Ceiling Accents Family Room of Liveable Home

No. 10465

The beamed ceiling plus the fireplace and built-in bookcase of the comfortable family room in this design make it an ideal plan for casual elegance. The family room also shares a wet bar with the adjacent living room. Across the entry from the living room, the dining room is easily reached from the efficient kitchen. Three bedrooms are aligned along one side of the home with two full baths within a few steps of each. The master suite is located along the opposite side with its own bath, complete with skylight, and spacious walk-in closet.

First floor - 2,144 sq. ft.
Garage - 483 sq. ft.

GARAGE
20'-0" X 20'-0"

BEDROOM 4
9'-10"
X
11'-0"

NOOK
11'-0"
X
10'-4"

PATIO

FAMILY ROOM
14'-0"
X
16'-8"

MASTER BEDROOM
13'-10"
X
14'-0"

KITCHEN
10'-0"
X
12'-2"

BEDROOM 3
9'-10"
X
10'-8"

DINING
11'-4"
X
14'-0"

ENTRY

LIVING ROOM
12'-10"
X
16'-10"

BAR

BEDROOM 2
11'-0"
X
9'-10"

65'-0"

57'-4"

NO. 10465

Charming Traditional Design

No. 10572

Warm features abound in this attractive traditional design. The exterior has a stucco and brick frontage with a wood shake shingle roof and wood veneer siding on its side and rear elevations. Excellent traffic patterns exist on the first floor. Three bedrooms are located to the left of the foyer. Additionally on the first floor, the master bedroom has a walk-in closet and its own full bath. Two other bedrooms share a full bath. Straight ahead of the foyer is a spacious great room with a beautiful open-beamed ceiling and at the end of the great room is a large wood-burning fireplace with built-in bookshelves located on both sides of the fireplace. To the right of the foyer is the dining room with an elevated ceiling and a bay window.

First floor — 2,022 sq. ft.
Dormer plan — 354 sq. ft.
Basement — 1,980 sq. ft.
Garage — 526 sq. ft.

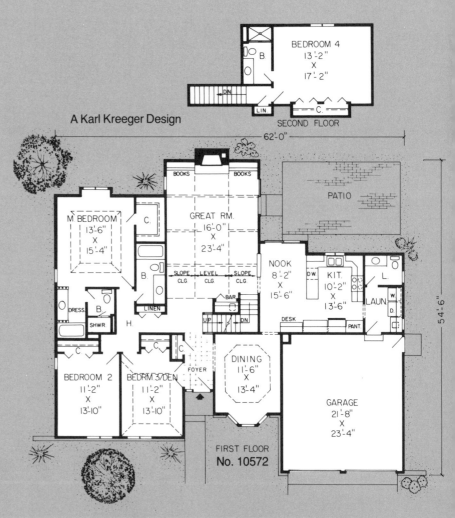

A Karl Kreeger Design

SECOND FLOOR

FIRST FLOOR
No. 10572

Intelligent Plan Separates Formal, Family Areas

No. 20359

Here's an elegant home where you can entertain in style without dislocating the kids. A sunken study, living room, and dining room surround the central foyer, which features a breathtaking view of an open, curving staircase and wide-open balcony loft. Reach informal areas at the rear of the house through the spacious laundry room, or step past the pantry to the island kitchen that easily serves all active areas. You'll love the adjoining, skylit breakfast room, separated from the vaulted family room by built-in planters. An enclosed porch gives the kids a place to play even when the weather's bad. And, you'll appreciate the privacy of an elegant master suite that shares the second floor with three other bedrooms, each with adjoining baths.

First floor — 2,516 sq. ft.
Second floor — 1,602 sq. ft.
Basement — 2,516 sq. ft.
Garage — 822 sq. ft.

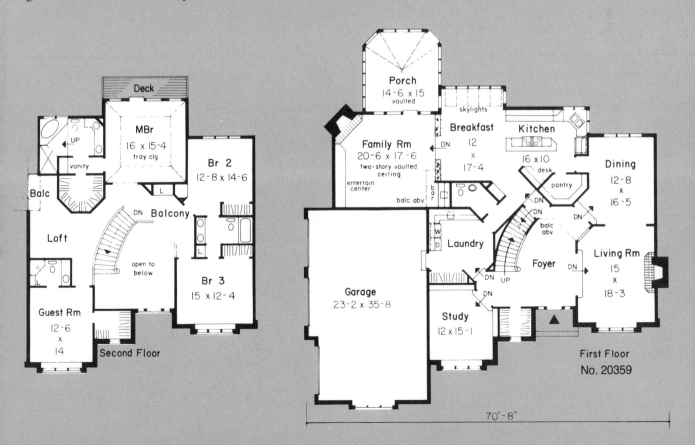

Elegant Design Is Perfect
For A Hillside Setting

No. 10497

Nestled on a hillside this elegant design opens its lower level recreation room with lots of windows and sliding-door access to the patio. Also located on the lower level are two large bedrooms, each with its own walk-in closet, plus a special study area or television room. The main floor is organized around the central great room which boasts a garden area and large fireplace. The spacious kitchen provides plenty of storage and an island plus room for informal dining. The kitchen's roominess is enhanced by the adjacent sunporch; the perfect place for breakfast or lunch. Also located on the main floor are two more bedrooms including the master suite with its four-piece bath and walk-in closet.

Main floor-1883 sq. ft.
Lower level-1395 sq. ft.
Sunporch-131 sq. ft.
Basement-619 sq. ft.
Garage-722 sq. ft.

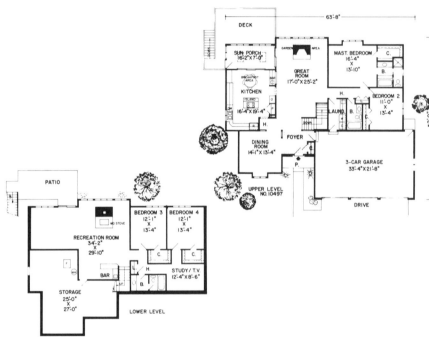

No Wasted Space in This
Two-story Traditional

No. 10489

On the second floor of this home are three bedrooms and two baths, including the roomy master bedroom. The master bedroom features double closets and a spacious five-piece bath. The open plan of the first floor features large rooms plus plenty of built-in features. The inviting family room is enhanced by fireplace, wet bar, sliding glass doors and direct access to the well designed kitchen. Special touches in the kitchen include a pantry and a bump-out window above the sink. A raised living room and a formal dining room with its own built-in china cabinet complete this compact plan.

First floor — 1,156 sq. ft.
Second floor — 937 sq. ft.
Garage — 440 sq. ft.

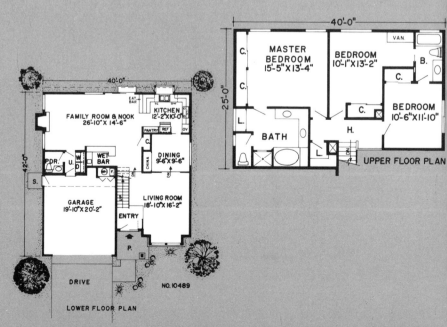

Four-Bedroom Split-Level Packed with Features

No. 10499

The handsome exterior of this home only hints at the multiple conveniences it encloses. The lower level family room is enhanced by its wet bar, built-in bookcase, and sliding door exit to the large covered patio. Also secluded on this level is an ideal bedroom for guests with its own bath and roomy walk-in closet. The entry level opens to the living room which features a fireplace and two skylights. Overlooking the living room are the kitchen and dining areas. The L-shaped kitchen shares an eating bar with the dining room which opens on to the screened porch. Just down the hall from these living areas are the fully appointed master suite and two additional bedrooms.

Upper levels — 1493 sq. ft.
Lower levels — 717 sq. ft.
Basement — 396 sq. ft.
Garage — 560 sq. ft.

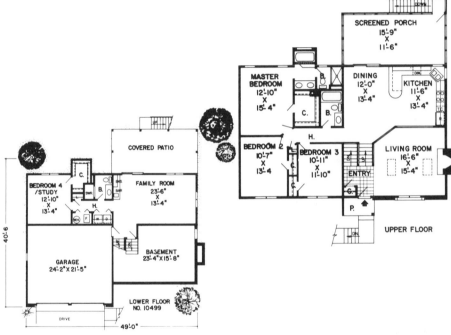

Easy-living Plan

No. 10574

Don't worry about storage problems in this sprawling traditional. Every inch of space is put to good use. The well designed floor plan revolves around a two-story central foyer. You'll find utility and dining areas grouped together. The screened porch off the breakfast room is a lovely mealtime spot on a summer day. Right down the hall, family and living rooms insure a cozy atmosphere day and night with expansive windows and fireplaces. You'll find the master suite, with its double vanities and room-size closet, tucked away at the end of the hall. The kids won't have much trouble keeping their rooms clean with extra-large closets, window seat storage, and their own bath upstairs.

First floor — 2,215 sq. ft.
Second floor — 1,025 sq. ft.
Basement — 2,215 sq. ft.
Garage and storage — 618 sq. ft.

Music Room Enhances Special Design

No. 10584

If music is the love of your life, consider this special home. A remarkable chamber with cathedral ceiling and built-in cabinets is devoted to the pleasures of sound. The rest of the home is stylish as well. The handsome kitchen serves an eating bar as well as a breakfast room and large dining area with vaulted ceiling. The master bedroom enjoys a bath with a walk-in closet. Large bedrooms inhabit the 2nd floor with a loft area that overlooks the foyer below. Gracious touches like the breezeway, screened porch, and courtyards complete a magnificent home.

First floor — 1,860 sq. ft.
Second floor — 901 sq. ft.
Basement — 1,823 sq. ft.
Screened porch — 168 sq. ft.
Breezeway — 112 sq. ft.
Garage — 677 sq. ft.

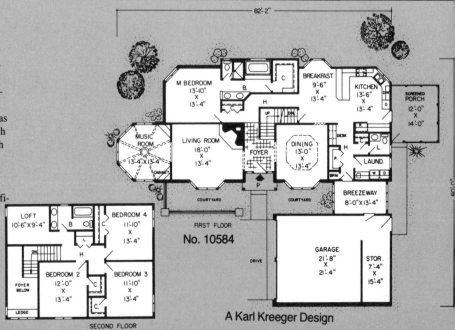

A Karl Kreeger Design

Trim Plan Designed For Handicapped

No. 10360

Attractive and accessible, this three-bedroom home has been carefully detailed to provide both comfort and self-sufficiency for the handicapped individual. Ramps allow entry to garage, patio and porch. Doors and windows are located so that they can be opened with ease, and both baths feature wall-hung toilets at a special 16-18'' height. Spacious rooms, wide halls, and the over-sized double garage allow a wheelchair to be maneuvered with minimal effort, and the sink and cooktop are also located with this in mind. Besides these functional aspects, the design also boasts a great room, inviting and open to the living areas and patio.

First floor-1,882 sq. ft.
Garage-728 sq. ft.

PATIO

GREAT ROOM
33'-3" X 15'-2"

DINING
13'-4"X14'-0"

BATH   BATH   BEDROOM
11'-7"X9'-10"   C.

F.

DINETTE   KITCHEN
14'-0"X14'-0"

MASTER
BEDROOM
12'-6"X17'-4"

H.   S.   RAMP

LIN.   ENTRY

C.   BEDROOM
11'-10"X10'-0"   C.   PORCH

RAMP   UTIL.
W.D.

DOUBLE GARAGE
27'-8" X 25'-4"

RAMP

86'-7"

62'-0"

NO.10360

FLOOR PLAN

W.

DRIVEWAY

Create a Dramatic Impression

No. 20122

The two-story bay of this magnificent Tudor masterpiece is certain to impress entering guests. And, the well-designed interior will ease the chores of entertaining. Notice the ideal location of the parlor and formal dining room just off the foyer. The well-appointed kitchen will make even the most elegant dinner party a breeze. Window walls link informal family areas at the rear of the house with the outdoor deck and backyard. And, the first-floor master suite, with its garden tub, room-size closet, and step-in shower is another convenience you'll surely appreciate. Two full baths serve the four upstairs bedrooms, which feature intriguing shapes, loads of windows, and walk-in closets.

First floor — 1,779 sq. ft.
Second floor — 1,298 sq. ft.
Basement — 1,757 sq. ft.
Garage — 568 sq. ft.

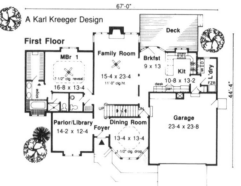

No. 20122

Excellent First Home

No. 28015

Solar storage cells on the south side contribute to the energy-saving effectiveness of this well-designed beginning family home. Three bedrooms and two baths occupy the east wing. The master bedroom features a large walk-in closet and private bath. The great room opens out onto a patio while the kitchen gives access to the large double garage. A breakfast bar separates the kitchen from the living area while giving the feeling of spacious and open living. An air-lock entry adds to the energy-saving features.

First floor — 1,296 sq. ft.
Garage — 484 sq. ft.

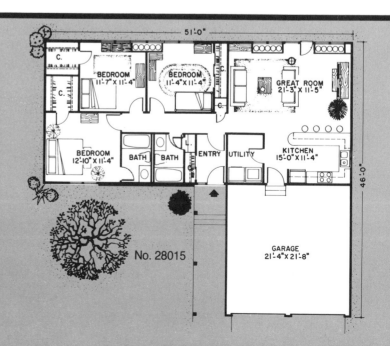

No. 28015

No. 20081

Contemporary Classic on Three Levels

No. 20081

You'll find wonderfully shaped rooms, soaring ceilings, and an abundance of windows in this cheery contemporary home. Sharing the first level with the foyer, the master suite features a towering half-round window and private bath with double sinks. Up a few stairs, active areas are arranged for convenience. Notice the location of the kitchen, just steps away from formal and informal dining rooms. The living room is warmed by a fireplace, and boasts easy access to an outdoor deck. Two more bedrooms, tucked upstairs in a quiet spot, are connected by a balcony that overlooks the foyer.

First floor — 1,374 sq. ft.
Second floor — 489 sq. ft.
Basement — 845 sq. ft.
Garage — 484 sq. ft.

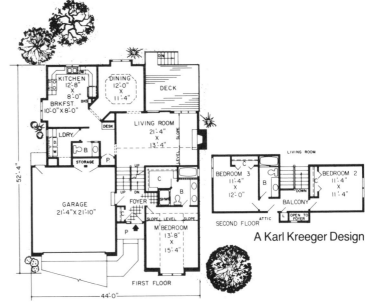

A Karl Kreeger Design

Hip Roof Design, Family-centered Space

No. 22008

Inside this trim hip roof plan, space is alloted for a variety of family activities. Spotlighted is the sizable beamed family room with fireplace and access to porch. The bordering gameroom edges a handy half bath, and the dining nook connects to, and visually enlarges, the kitchen. Four bedrooms and two full baths are planned.

House-2,074 sq. ft.
Garage-544 sq. ft.

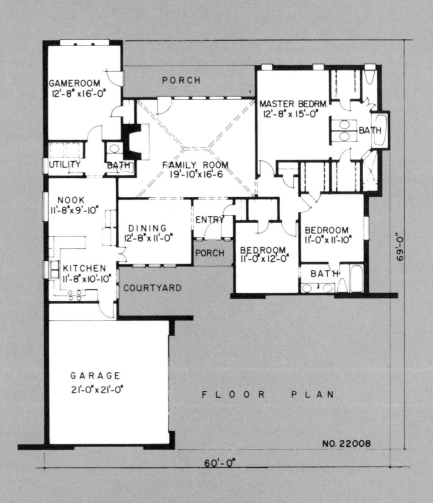

GAMEROOM 12'-8" x 16'-0"

PORCH

MASTER BEDRM. 12'-8" x 15'-0"

BATH

UTILITY

BATH

FAMILY ROOM 19'-10" x 16-6

NOOK 11'-8" x 9'-10"

DINING 12'-8" x 11'-0"

ENTRY

BEDROOM 11'-0" x 11'-10"

PORCH

KITCHEN 11'-8" x 10'-10"

BEDROOM 11'-0" x 12'-0"

COURTYARD

BATH

GARAGE 21'-0" x 21'-0"

FLOOR PLAN

69'-0"

NO. 22008

60'-0"

Brick-layered Home Plans 4 Bedrooms

No. 22004

Four roomy bedrooms, featuring a master bedroom with extra large bath, equip this plan for a large family or overnight guests. The centrally located family room merits a fireplace, wet bar, and access to the patio, and a dining room is provided for formal entertaining. An interesting kitchen and nook, as well as two and one half baths, are featured.

House-2,070 sq. ft.
Garage-474 sq. ft.

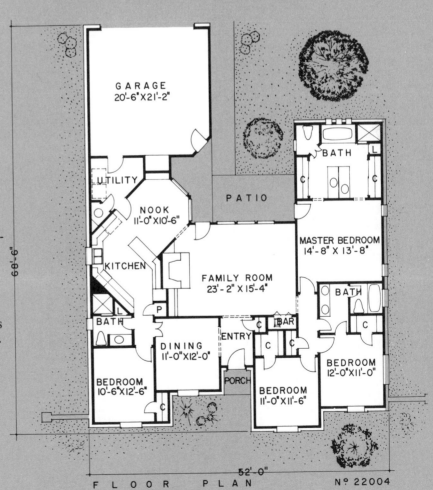

GARAGE
20'-6" X 21'-2"

UTILITY

NOOK
11'-0" X 10'-6"

KITCHEN

PATIO

BATH

MASTER BEDROOM
14'-8" X 13'-8"

FAMILY ROOM
23'-2" X 15'-4"

BATH

BATH

DINING
11'-0" X 12'-0"

ENTRY

BAR

BEDROOM
10'-6" X 12'-6"

PORCH

BEDROOM
11'-0" X 11'-6"

BEDROOM
12'-0" X 11'-0"

68'-6"

52'-0"

FLOOR PLAN

No. 22004

Lavish Plan Exercise In Luxury

No. 20006

From its impressive facade to its smallest details, this cut stone two story home expresses luxury. Four bedrooms include a first floor master bedroom suite indulged with two private baths, two walk-in closets, and adjoining 27-foot library. Firelit living room rises two stories for a dramatic effect and, with the cozy den with built-in bar, opens to the long balcony. Patio, deck and pool are outlined for the rear yard, and useful half bath, dressing rooms and sauna complete the basement level. The breakfast room opens to a screened porch, and utility room and triple garage are featured.

First floor — 3,975 sq. ft.
Second floor — 2,205 sq. ft.
Basement — 3,975 sq. ft.
Garage — 753 sq. ft.

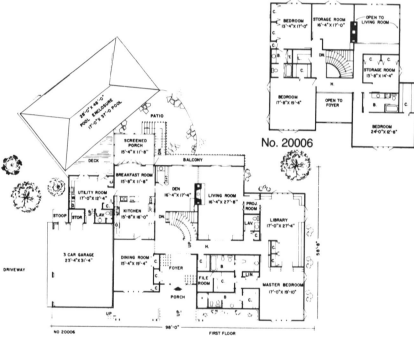

No. 20006

Roomy Ranch Design

No. 10594

This delightful ranch design utilizes space with great efficiency. Enter a tiled foyer and be greeted by an excellent floor plan designed to handle traffic. Off the foyer to the right, the great room has a sloping open-beamed ceiling and a wood-burning fireplace. A den-bedroom lies to the left of the foyer. Connected to the great room is the dining room and the kitchen. Sliding glass doors lead from the dining room out onto a large wooden deck. Other features in this plan include a laundry room and two other bedrooms that have their own full baths. A two-car garage is also added for convenience.

First — 1,565 sq. ft.
Basement — 1,576 sq. ft.
Garage — 430 sq. ft.

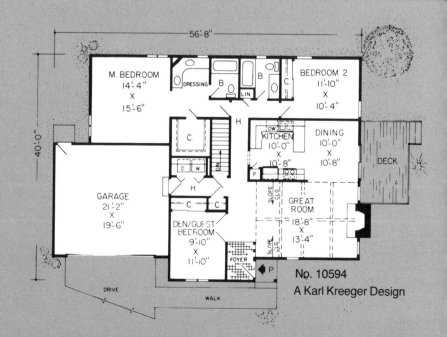

No. 10594
A Karl Kreeger Design

Compact Design for a Small Lot

No. 10597

Sloping ceilings and a corner fireplace distinguish the living room of this cozy three bedroom home. Eat in the formal dining room with recessed ceiling or in the roomy kitchen, which features sliding glass doors to the patio. Walk by the laundry and pantry to the master bedroom suite. Upstairs, two bedrooms share a bath with double sinks.

First floor — 1,162 sq. ft.
Second floor — 464 sq. ft.
Basement — 1,118 sq. ft.
Garage — 450 sq. ft.

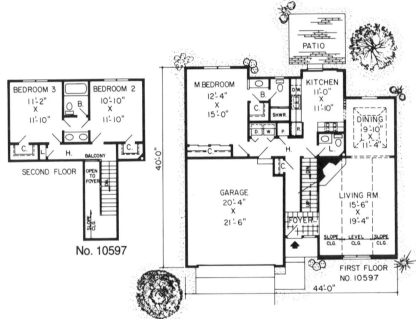

SECOND FLOOR
No. 10597

FIRST FLOOR
No. 10597

Tasteful Elegance Aim Of Design

No. 22020

With an exterior that expresses French Provincial charm, this single level design emphasizes elegance and offers a semi-circular dining area overlooking the patio. To pamper parents, the master bedroom annexes a long dressing area and private bath, while another bath serves the second and third bedrooms. A wood-burning fireplace furnishes the family room.

House proper — 1,772 sq. ft.
Garage — 469 sq. ft.

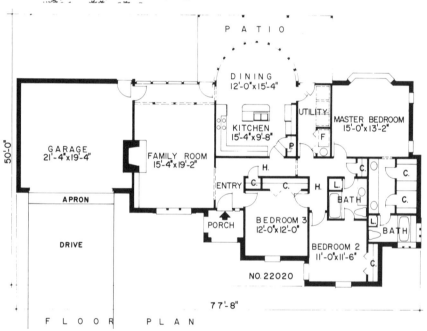

Old Fashioned Charm

No. 21124

An old fashioned, homespun flavor has been created using lattice work, horizontal and vertical placement of wood siding, and full length front and rear porches with turned wood columns and wood railings. The floor plan features an open living room, dining room and kitchen. A master suite finishes the first level. An additional bedroom and full bath are located upstairs. Here, also, is found a large bonus room which could serve a variety of family needs. Or it can be deleted altogether by adding a second floor balcony overlooking the living room below and allowing the living room ceilings to spaciously rise two full stories. Wood floors throughout the design add a final bit of country to the plan.

First floor-835 sq. ft.
Second floor-817 sq. ft.

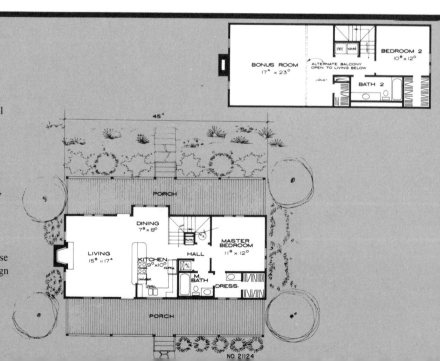

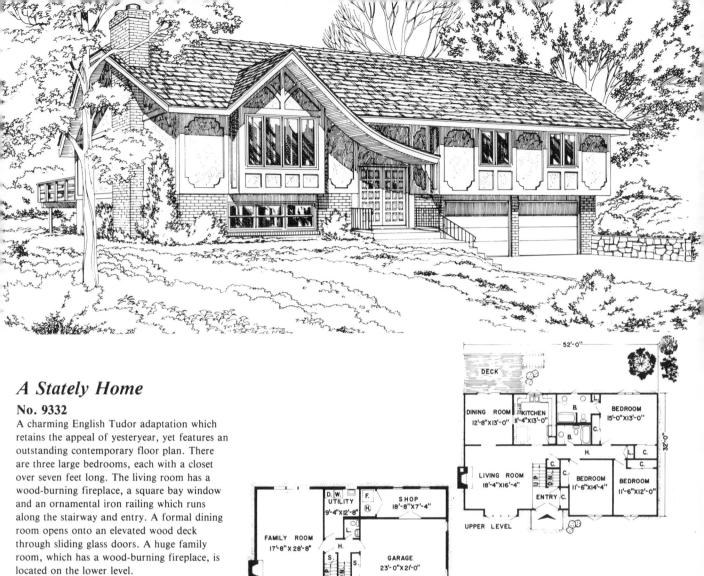

A Stately Home

No. 9332

A charming English Tudor adaptation which retains the appeal of yesteryear, yet features an outstanding contemporary floor plan. There are three large bedrooms, each with a closet over seven feet long. The living room has a wood-burning fireplace, a square bay window and an ornamental iron railing which runs along the stairway and entry. A formal dining room opens onto an elevated wood deck through sliding glass doors. A huge family room, which has a wood-burning fireplace, is located on the lower level.

Upper level-1,633 sq. ft.
Lower level-858 sq. ft.
Garage & shop-718 sq. ft.

LOWER LEVEL
NO. 9332

FAMILY ROOM
17'-8" X 28'-8"

D.W.
UTILITY
9'-4" X 12'-8"

SHOP
18'-8" X 7'-4"

GARAGE
23'-0" X 21'-0"

ENTRY

WALK

DRIVEWAY

UPPER LEVEL

DECK

DINING ROOM
12'-8" X 13'-0"

KITCHEN
11'-4" X 13'-0"

BEDROOM
15'-0" X 13'-0"

LIVING ROOM
18'-4" X 16'-4"

ENTRY

BEDROOM
11'-6" X 14'-4"

BEDROOM
11'-6" X 12'-0"

52'-0"

32'-0"

Bedrooms Flank Active Areas for Privacy

No. 20104

Hate to climb stairs? This one-level gem will accommodate your family in style, and keep your housework to a minimum. Recessed ceilings add an elegant touch to the dining room and master suite. And, with half walls, skylights, and a handy rear deck off the sunny breakfast room, there's an airy feeling throughout the centrally-located active areas. You'll appreciate the convenience of built-in storage in the kitchen and fireplaced living room, and the huge bedroom closets that keep the clutter down. Look at the private master bath with its twin vanities, raised tub and walk-in shower. Don't you deserve a little luxury?

Main living area — 1,686 sq. ft.
Basement — 1,677 sq. ft.
Garage — 475 sq. ft.

A Karl Kreeger Design

No. 20104

Entry Hints at Appealing Interior

No. 10678

Interesting angles give every room in this three-bedroom home a distinctive shape. Stand in the foyer and look up. Soaring ceilings in the window-walled living room rise to dizzying heights. Step past the powder room to find a fireplaced family room, wide open to the convenient kitchen with built-in desk and pantry. Just outside, there's lots of warm weather living space on the deck surrounding the dining room. Walk upstairs to the vaulted den that links the bedrooms and provides a comfortable spot for enjoying a good book. And, look at the adjoining deck! Can't you imagine perching up there on a sunny day, watching the world go by?

First floor — 1,375 sq. ft.
Second floor — 1,206 sq. ft.

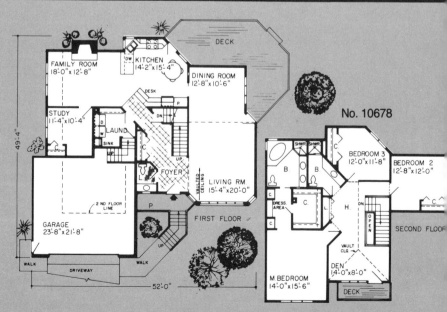

No. 10678

Courtyard Adds Interest

No. 22010

Well-defined contemporary lines are softened by a semi-enclosed courtyard visible from the dining area of this striking design. The 30-foot family room is dominated by a fireplace, resulting in a spacious but cozy area for entertaining. The island kitchen merges with dining nook, and bedrooms are large, featuring the master bedroom and its luxurious bath.

Living area — 2,174 sq. ft.
Garage — 506 sq. ft.

FLOOR PLAN   NO. 22010

Put the Sun to Work

No. 20007

Soaring peaks and gentle curves distinguish the facade of this appealing family home. Inside, every room benefits from the warmth of the sunken sunroom. Built-ins add convenient touches to every room: a window seat and bookshelves in the beamed living room, a display case for your collectibles in the foyer hall, and a handy wetbar in the fireplaced family room. Eat in the dining room, the breakfast bay off the island kitchen, or have a barbecue on the deck. You'll enjoy the view of the sunroom from the cozy office at the top of the stairs, which shares a full bath with the two rear bedrooms. Cathedral ceilings and twin palladium windows give the expansive master suite an even greater sense of space.

First floor — 1,212 sq. ft.
Second floor — 1,253 sq. ft.
Basement — 1,212 sq. ft.
Garage — 400 sq. ft.

NO. 20007
SECOND FLOOR

No. 20007

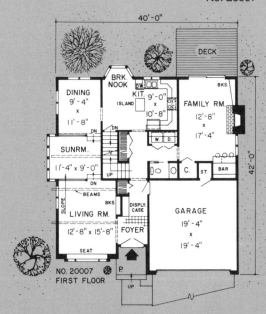

NO. 20007
FIRST FLOOR

SOLAR HOME

Passive Solar and Contemporary Features

No. 26110

Numerous southern glass doors and windows, skylights and a greenhouse clue the exterior viewer of the passive solarness of this contemporary design. For minimum heat loss, 2 × 6 studs for R-19 insulation are shown in exterior walls and R-33 insulation is shown in all sloping ceilings. The living room employs a concrete slab floor for solar gain. Basement space is located under the kitchen, dining room, lower bedroom and den. A northern entrance through a vestibule and French doors channels you upward to the first floor living area. A unique feature on this level is the skylit living room ceiling which slants two stories. Second story rooms are lit by clerestory windows. Two balconies are on this level, and exterior one off the bedroom and an interior one overlooking the living room.

First floor — 902 sq. ft.
Second floor — 567 sq. ft.

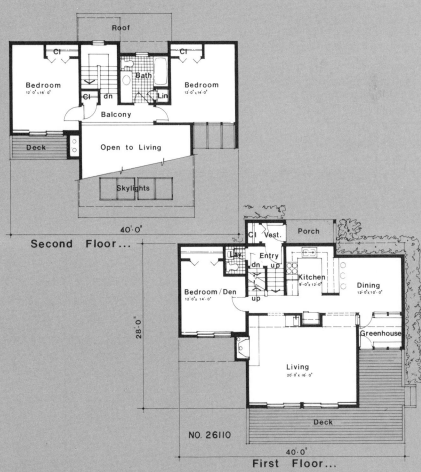

Second Floor...

First Floor...

Fireplace Adds a Cozy Touch

No. 10760

Here's a handsome split-entry home that separates active and quiet areas. Step down to the garage level that includes a basement recreation and work-shop area perfect for the household hobbyist. A short staircase leads up to the soaring living room, where the open feeling is accentuated by a huge bow window and a wide opening to the formal din-ing room. The kitchen lies behind swinging double doors, and features access to a raised rear deck. A few steps up, you'll find two full baths and three bedrooms with extra-large closets. Sloping ceilings add dramatic appeal to the private bedroom wing.

First floor — 1,676 sq. ft.
Basement recreation area — 592 sq. ft.
Workshop — 144 sq. ft.
Garage — 697 sq. ft.

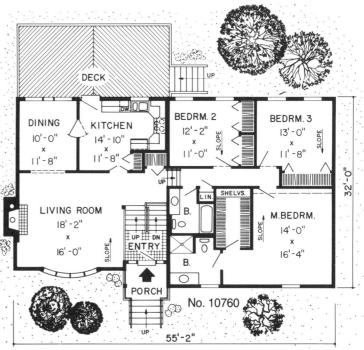

No. 10760

Multiple Peaks Add Interesting Angles

No. 10600

This Tudor style 3-bedroom home is unusually attractive with its stone accents and impressive win-dows. Its sizeable rooms appear larger thanks to sloped ceilings and a tasteful floor plan. A quaint breakfast nook with bow window provides a buffer between the no-nonsense kitchen and elegant, airy dining room. Comfort comes naturally in the living room which features a large fireplace with stone hearth. An outside patio is easily accessible through sliding doors and enjoys private access to the mas-ter bedroom.

First floor — 1,219 sq. ft.
Garage — 410 sq. ft.

FLOOR PLAN

No. 10600

Inviting Porch Enlarges Compact Home

No. 10646

This modified Cape with attached two-car garage can house a growing family for a bargain price. Double doors in the cozy living room open to the bay-windowed family room with fireplace and patio access. Eat in the family-size kitchen or formal dining room. Up the central stairway, the vaulted ceiling in the master suite creates a spacious feeling. Three other bedrooms and a bath share the second floor.

First floor — 930 sq. ft.
Second floor — 980 sq. ft.
Basement — 900 sq. ft.
Garage — 484 sq. ft.

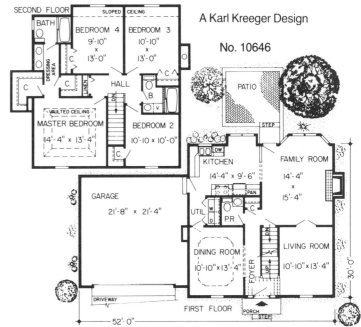

A Karl Kreeger Design

No. 10646

SECOND FLOOR

BATH

BEDROOM 4
9'-10" x 13'-0"

BEDROOM 3
10'-10" x 13'-0"

SLOPED CEILING

DRESSING AREA

C.

LINEN

HALL

C.

B

MASTER BEDROOM
VAULTED CEILING
14'-4" x 13'-4"

BEDROOM 2
10'-10 x 10'-0"

C.

FIRST FLOOR

PATIO

STEP

KITCHEN
14'-4" x 9'-6"

FAMILY ROOM
14'-4" x 15'-4"

PAN.

UTIL

W D

P.R.

GARAGE
21'-8" x 21'-4"

DINING ROOM
10'-10" x 13'-4"

LIVING ROOM
10'-10" x 13'-4"

FOYER

UP

DN

DRIVEWAY

PORCH
STEP

52'-0"

30'-0"

Multi-level Contemporary

No. 26111

The features of this multi-level contemporary home lend character to both the exterior and interior. A wooden deck skirts most of three sides. Great variety in the size and shape of doors and windows is apparent. Inside the living room forms a unique living center. It can be reached from sliding glass doors from the deck or down several steps from the main living level inside. It is overlooked by a low balcony from the entryway and dining room on the lower level and from the second floor landing. Large windows on both the right and left keep it well lit. A fireplace here is optional. Ceilings slope upward two stories. A partial basement is located below the design.

First floor-769 sq. ft.
Second floor-572 sq. ft.

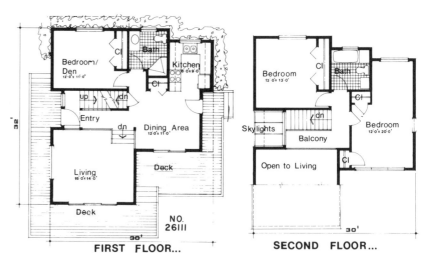

Sunken Living Areas In Compact Floor Plan

No. 26114

Step down from the entry level to the sunken living, dining, kitchen areas of this floor plan. The fireplaced living room looks out through double sliding glass doors to a wrap around deck which ends in outside storage. Ceilings slope up above a balcony which also shares the second level with two bedrooms and a bath. An optional third bedroom/den lies on the lower level.

First floor – 696 sq. ft.
Second floor – 416 sq. ft.
Basement – 696 sq. ft.
Storage – 32 sq. ft.
Deck – 232 sq. ft.

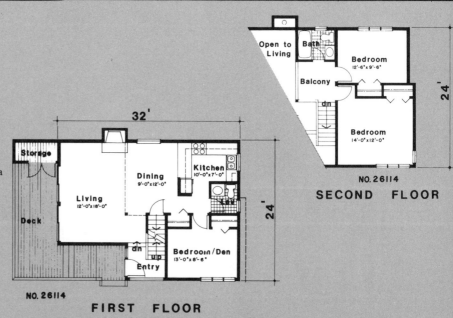

Family Room Highlights Popular Design

No. 10504

The inviting family room of this home contains its own wetbar and fireplace and opens onto the patio through sliding glass doors. Entertaining will be easy because of the location of the extra large kitchen. The L-shaped kitchen features an island snack bar plus additional space for eat-in convenience. The formal dining and living rooms are joined for a more spacious design and are accented by plenty of windows. The three large bedrooms include large wall closets. One bedroom features mirrored closet doors and separate vanity and shower.

First floor — 1,922 sq. ft.
Garage — 422 sq. ft.

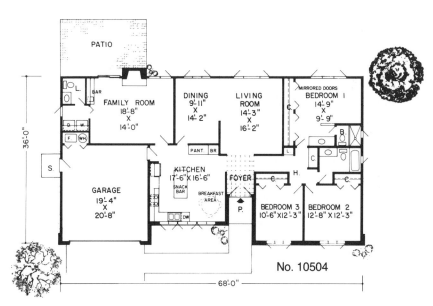

SOLAR HOME

Contemporary Ranch Design

No. 26740

Sloping cathedral ceilings are found throughout the entirety of this home. A kitchen holds the central spot in the floor plan. It is partially open to a great hall with firebox and deck access on one side, daylight room lit by ceiling glass and full length windows on another, and entryway hallway on a third. The daylight room leads out onto a unique double deck. Bedrooms lie to the outside of the plan. Two smaller bedrooms at the rear share a full bath. The more secluded master bedroom at the front has its own full bath and access to a private deck.

Living area-1,512 sq. ft.
Garage-478 sq. ft.

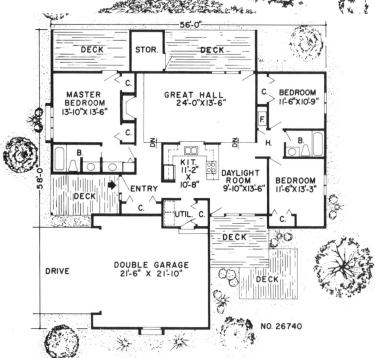

Enticing Angles

No. 26500

From every angle this two-story house has a special allure. Thrusting rooflines echoed in the siding pattern creates an exciting exterior. Entrance to this unique home is gained through an air-lock-garden assuring privacy and comfort. Interior pleasures include a magnificent great room and sunken conversation area with a fireplace. Sliding glass doors from the great room open onto a large patio. Slightly elevated are the kitchen, dining room and breakfast room with bay windows. The master bedroom upstairs has a private deck.

First floor-1,818 sq. ft.
Second floor-484 sq. ft.
Basement-530 sq. ft.
Garage-797 sq. ft.

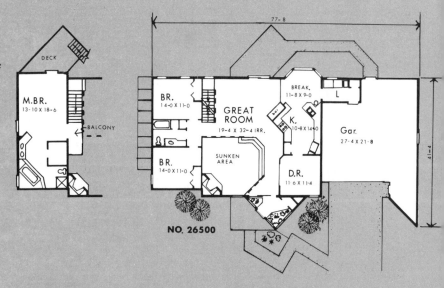

A Library in Every Room

No. 10686

Spectacular is one word you could use to describe the remarkable quality of light and space in this four-bedroom family home. Well-placed skylights and abundant windows bathe every room in sunlight. The huge, two-story foyer features an angular, open staircase that leads to the bedrooms, and divides the space between the vaulted living and dining rooms. At the rear of the house, the wide-open family area includes the kitchen, dinette, and fireplaced family room complete with built-in bar and bookcases. Vaulted ceilings in the screened porch are mirrored upstairs in the master suite, which features two walk-in closets, double vanities, and a luxurious jacuzzi.

First floor — 1,786 sq. ft.
Second floor — 1,490 sq. ft.
Basement — 1,773 sq. ft.
Garage — 579 sq. ft.

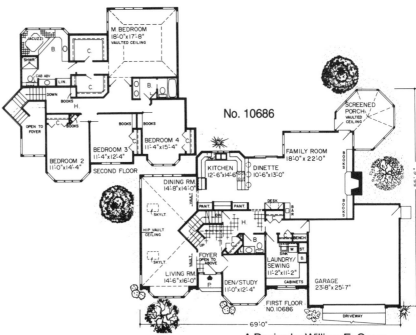

No. 10686

A Design by William E. Gage

Gingerbread Charm

No. 20084

Victorian touches combine with a modern floor plan to make this four-bedroom masterpiece a special home you'll never want to leave. Brightened by a towering bump-out window, the sloping living room is just across the foyer from formal dining. Walk up the stairs, and you'll find four roomy bedrooms, including a luxurious master suite with twin vanities. Or, go straight ahead into the enormous, fireplaced family room. The adjoining breakfast room is just across the counter from a convenient U-shaped kitchen. Thanks to a two-sided view from the sink, dishwashing duties may just become a little more pleasant.

First floor — 1,330 sq. ft.
Second floor — 1,339 sq. ft.
Garage — 477 sq. ft.

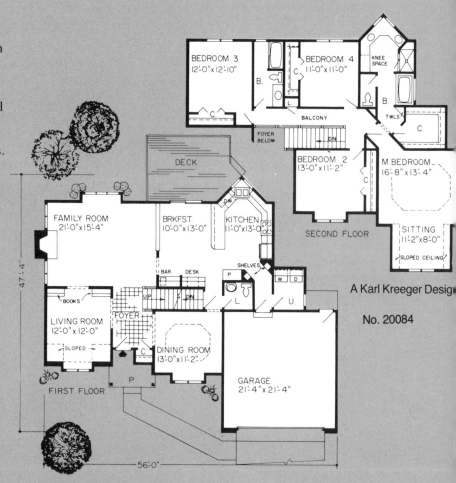

A Karl Kreeger Design

No. 20084

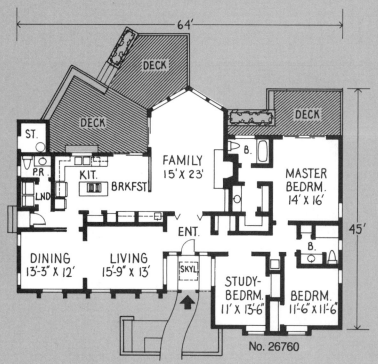

Unusual Design Creates Comfortable Living

No. 26760

The central focus of this highly pleasing 3 bedroom ranch is the family room, its largest most architecturally interesting space. The first room seen upon entering, this room features a prow shape, a beamed ceiling and a fireplace. Sliding glass doors give access to the multi-leveled deck. The well designed kitchen has a center work island and a large breakfast area overlooking the deck. The dining room and the living room are conveniently placed for ease of entertaining. The master bedroom has a private bath and dressing room. Also included are plenty of closets and a private deck. Two smaller bedrooms share a spacious bath.

Living area — 2,023 sq. ft.
Decks — 589 sq. ft.
Outdoor storage — 36 sq. ft.

Facade Features Vertical Columns

No. 10645

This two-story home is perfect for the family that wants to keep sleeping quarters quiet. Closets and a hallway muffle sound from the foyer. Upstairs, the location of two additional bedrooms and full skylit bath over the garage and sleeping areas below insures a restful atmosphere. The dining room is located directly off the foyer. With an angular ceiling and massive fireplace, the great room opens to the kitchen and breakfast nook, which features sliding glass doors to an outdoor patio.

First floor — 1,628 sq. ft.
Second floor — 609 sq. ft.
Basement — 1,616 sq. ft.
Garage — 450 sq. ft.

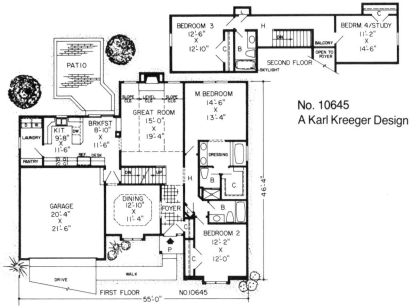

No. 10645
A Karl Kreeger Design

Sunken Living Room Highlights Unusual Floor Plan

No. 10508

The semi-circular arrangement of this home accents an open floor plan which uses an elevated hall to separate the living areas. The sunken living room has its own wetbar, built-in bench seat and planters. The family room features a fireplace, built-in bookcases and shares a bar with the adjacent kitchen. The patio area is open to the dining room, kitchen and family room for easy entertaining. The master bedroom also overlooks the patio. Its large bath is divided into compartments and has a large walk-in closet. The other two bedrooms each have their own baths and spacious closets.

First floor — 2,251 sq. ft.
Garage — 533 sq. ft.

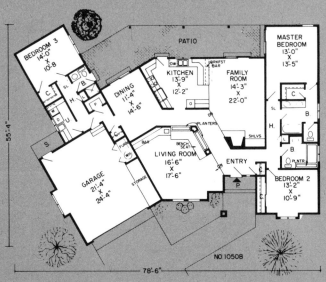

No. 10508

Vaulted Ceilings Make
Every Room Special

No. 10698

This gracious five-bedroom family home offers spectacular views, both inside and out. Survey the two-story morning room and yard beyond from a vantage point upstairs. Two bedrooms adjoining a full bath and covered deck share the upper level with the loft. Enjoy the same view from the island kitchen, separated from the morning room only by a counter. Delight in pool vistas from a covered patio, or from living and family rooms. Both have beamed, ten-foot ceilings, massive fireplaces, and share a wetbar and access to the patio. Gaze at the stars through the skylight over the bath in the master suite. Down a hallway behind double doors, the suite features a raised tub, built-in dressing tables, and fireplaced sitting room with vaulted ceiling.

First floor — 4,014 sq. ft.
Second floor — 727 sq. ft.
Garage — 657 sq. ft.

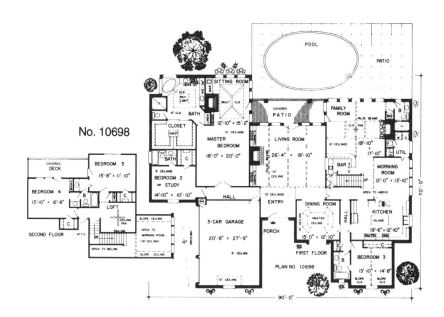

No. 10698

New England Classic

No. 26850

This updated 18th century traditional home offers a practical as well as an attractive choice for today's homeowner. The wood exterior and cedar shingle roofing help make the house energy-efficient. Wood is also used extensively throughout the interior to continue the traditional mood. On the first floor, the living room and dining room flank a large foyer offering an immediate air of hospitality. A family room with a brick hearth, a kitchen with a center work island, and a bedroom suite are also featured. Upstairs there are three additional bedrooms and a laundry room. The master suite has a fireplace and a private bath.

First floor — 1,297 sq. ft.
Second floor — 1,091 sq. ft.

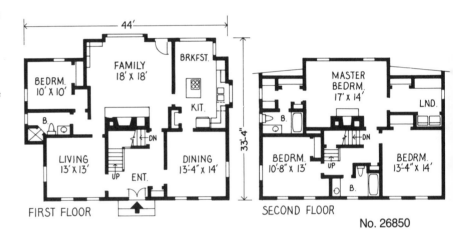

No. 26850

Loft Overlooks Opulent Foyer

No. 10583

This hillside home, characterized by enormous rooms and two garages, is built on two levels. From the foyer, travel down one hall to a cozy bedroom, full bath, island kitchen, laundry and garage. Or, walk straight into the sun-filled great and dining rooms with wrap-around deck. One room features a massive fireplace, built-in bookshelves, and access to the lofty study; the other contains a window greenhouse. For ultimate privacy, the master bedroom suite possesses a lavish skylit tub. On the lower level are two additional bedrooms, a bath, and a rec room with bar that opens onto an outdoor patio.

First floor — 2,367 sq. ft.
Basement (unfinished) — 372 sq. ft.
Basement (finished) — 1,241 sq. ft.
Loft — 295 sq. ft.
Garage (lower level) — 660 sq. ft.
Garage (upper level) — 636 sq. ft.

No. 10583
A Karl Kreeger Design

First-Time Owner's Delight

No. 20063

A distinctive exterior of wood veneer siding with a large, picture window combines with just a touch of brick to set this simple one and a half story design into a class of its own. On the first level, the foyer leads directly into the living room which has a fireplace and is open to the dining room. The kitchen lies just to the left of the dining room. A laundry room is conveniently placed between the kitchen and the garage. The master bedroom lies on the first floor and has a full bath and walk-in closet. On the second floor two more bedrooms exist and share a full bath. There is also a loft area open to the living room below.

First floor — 1,161 sq. ft.
Second floor — 631 sq. ft.

A Karl Kreeger Design

No. 20063

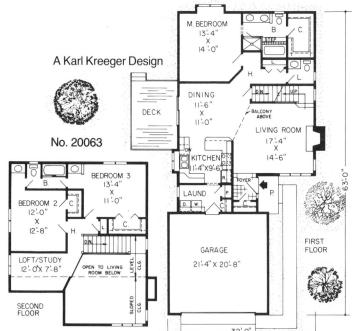

M. BEDROOM
13'-4" X 14'-0"

DINING
11'-6" X 11'-0"

DECK

LIVING ROOM
17'-4" X 14'-6"

BALCONY ABOVE

KITCHEN
11'-4" X 9'-6"

LAUND.

FOYER

FIRST FLOOR

GARAGE
21'-4" X 20'-8"

63'-0"

32'-0"

BEDROOM 3
13'-4" X 11'-0"

BEDROOM 2
12'-0" X 12'-8"

LOFT/STUDY
12'-0" X 7'-8"

OPEN TO LIVING ROOM BELOW

SECOND FLOOR

SLOPED CLG.

Step Down to the Living Room

No. 26880

This all-wood dramatic home features a large living room that is one step down from the dining room and entry way. Two bedrooms share a bath, while the master bedroom shows a fireplace, sitting room and private bath. The large deck is accessible from both the master suite and the breakfast room. The upper level houses the game room with its own deck. Thick cedar shingles add interest to the roof, and the cedar siding requires little maintenance. This home would be an asset wherever it was built.

First floor — 2,357 sq. ft.
Second floor — 271 sq. ft.

No. 26880

Designed for Privacy

No. 10657

From the three-car garage to the sunroom with hot tub, this house is equipped for gracious living. The skylit foyer leads three ways: up to 2 bedrooms, a full bath, and dramatic loft with balcony; into the formal dining room with bump-out window and recessed ceiling; or into the ample living room, flooded with light and featuring a fireplace. The island kitchen is convenient to both living and morning rooms. Approach the deck or sunroom from the morning room. The master bedroom suite, which features a room-sized closet, double vanity, and skylit tub with separate shower, is tucked away into its own corner for maximum privacy.

First floor — 1,831 sq. ft.
Second floor — 814 sq. ft.
Basement — 1,831 sq. ft.
Garage — 828 sq. ft.

A Karl Kreeger Design
No. 10657

A Touch of Classic Elegance

No. 20079

There's no wasted space in this compact home that combines the best of classic design and modern convenience. If you're a traditionalist, you'll love the half-round windows, clapboard and brick facade, and cozy fireplace. But, from the moment you walk past the portico, you'll find exciting contemporary touches: soaring ceilings, a dramatic balcony, a U-shaped kitchen, and wide-open living areas. Laundry facilities are conveniently adjacent to downstairs bedrooms. You'll enjoy retreating upstairs to your very private master suite.

First floor — 1,200 sq. ft.
Second floor — 461 sq. ft.
Garage — 475 sq. ft.
Basement — 1,200 sq. ft.

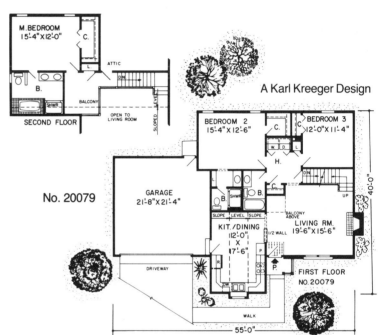

A Karl Kreeger Design

M. BEDROOM 15'-4" X 12'-0"

ATTIC

SECOND FLOOR

BALCONY

OPEN TO LIVING ROOM

SLOPED LEVEL

No. 20079

BEDROOM 2 15'-4" X 12'-6"

BEDROOM 3 12'-0" X 11'-4"

GARAGE 21'-8" X 21'-4"

BALCONY ABOVE

LIVING RM. 19'-6" X 15'-6"

KIT./DINING 12'-0" X 17'-6"

DRIVEWAY

FIRST FLOOR NO. 20079

WALK

55'-0"

40'-0"

Classic Warmth

No. 10684

This compact traditional with clapboard exterior and inviting, sheltered entry boasts loads of features that make it a special home. Look at the built-in seat by the garage entry, the handy breakfast bar that separates the kitchen and family room, and the convenient powder room just off the foyer. Cathedral ceilings lend an airy quality to the living and dining rooms. A single step down keeps the two rooms separate without compromising the open feeling that's so enjoyable. Sliders lead from both dining and family rooms to the rear patio, making it an excellent location for an outdoor party. Tucked upstairs, the three bedrooms include your own, private master suite.

First floor — 940 sq. ft.
Second floor — 720 sq. ft.
Walk-out basement — 554 sq. ft.
Crawl space — 312 sq. ft.
Garage — 418 sq. ft.

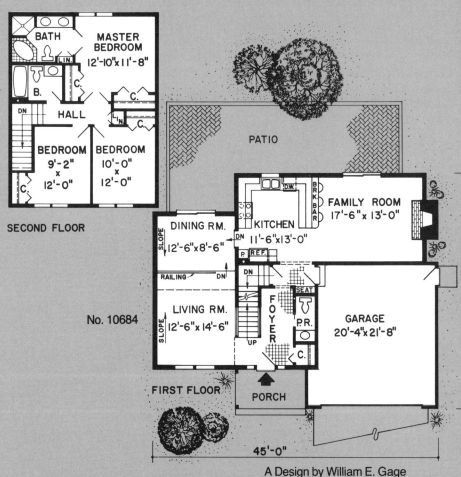

A Design by William E. Gage

200

Victorian Details Enhance Facade

No. 10593

A charming porch shelters the entrance of this four bedroom home with country kitchen. In colder climates, the closed vestibule cuts heat loss. Off the central foyer, the cozy living room shares a fireplace with the family room, which contains a bar and access to the patio and screened porch for entertaining. The bay windowed breakfast room is handy for quick meals. Or, use the formal dining room with octagonal recessed ceiling. All the bedrooms, located on the second floor, have walk-in closets.

First floor — 1,450 sq. ft.
Second floor — 1,341 sq. ft.
Basement — 1,450 sq. ft.
Garage — 629 sq. ft.
Covered porch — 144 sq. ft.

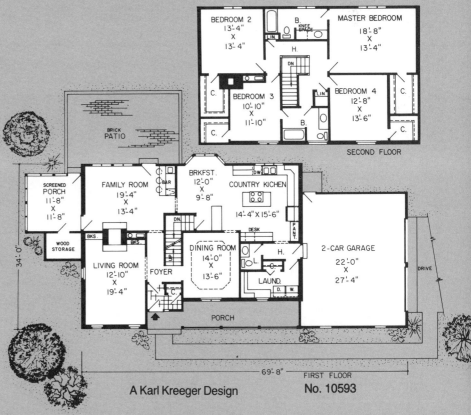

A Karl Kreeger Design   No. 10593

Circular Kitchen Is Center of Family Activities

No. 10514

The unusual design of this kitchen provides the centerpiece for this thoroughly delightful floor plan. The kitchen is further enhanced by the tiled hallways which surround it and delineate the adjacent living areas. The dining room, which opens onto the patio with large glass doors, includes both a built-in hutch and a display case. The large family room has a fireplace with its own wood storage and provides direct access to the sunspace. The master bedroom suite has a private patio, a bay window, five-piece bath, separate vanity and a large, walk-in closet.

First floor — 1,954 sq. ft.
Garage — 448 sq. ft.
Sunroom — 144 sq. ft.

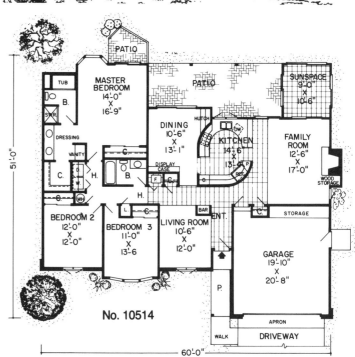

No. 10514

One-Level Living is a Breeze

No. 10656

Zoned for privacy and convenience, this contemporary ranch is a perfect home for people who like to entertain. The central foyer divides quiet and active areas. Sound deadening closets and a full bath with double vanities keep the noise to a minimum in the bedroom wing. The deck off the master suite is a nice, private retreat for sunbathing or stargazing. Look at the recessed ceilings and bay windows in the dining room off the foyer. What a beautiful room for a candlelit dinner. Living areas at the rear of the house surround a brick patio so guests can enjoy the outdoors in nice weather. And, the open plan of the kitchen, nook, and vaulted great room keep traffic flowing smoothly, even when there's a crowd.

First floor — 1,899 sq. ft.
Basement — 1,890 sq. ft.
Garage — 530 sq. ft.

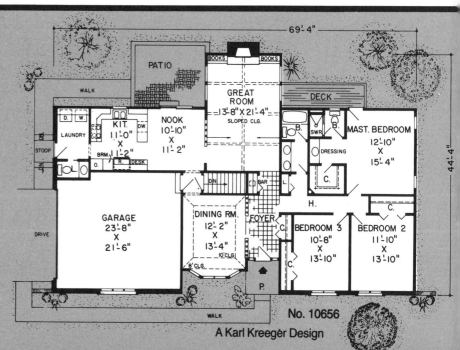

No. 10656

A Karl Kreeger Design

Elegant and Inviting

No. 10689

Traditional and modern elements unite to create an outstanding plan for the family that enjoys outdoor entertaining. Wrap-around verandas and a three-season porch insure the party will stay dry, rain or shine. You may want to keep guests inside, in the elegant parlor and formal dining room, separated by a half wall. The adjoining kitchen can be closed off to keep meal preparation convenient, but removed from the bustle. The family will enjoy informal meals at the island bar, or in the adjoining breakfast nook. Even the fireplaced gathering room, with its soaring ceilings and access to the porch, is right nearby. You'll appreciate the first-floor master suite, and the upstairs laundry location.

First floor — 1,580 sq. ft.
Second floor — 1,164 sq. ft.
Basement — 1,329 sq. ft.
Garage — 576 sq. ft.

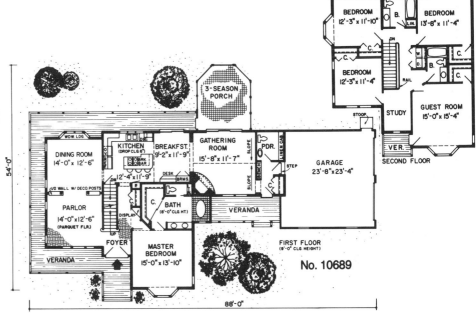

A Design by William E. Gage

Garden Room Dominates Plan

No. 28018

This is a 2-story passive solar home designed for the outdoor enthusiast. The upper levels shows two bedrooms and a bath on the east side and a studio and storage area on the west. A balcony overlooks the garden room on the main floor which also shows a large master bedroom with private bath and large walk-in closet, living room, formal dining area, kitchen and pantry. A guest bath and a den complete the floor plan. Direct solar gain through the south facing garden room windows provides much of the heating requirements for this home.

First floor — 2,527 sq. ft.
Second floor — 1,115 sq. ft.
**Garage, lavatory, workshop —
884 sq. ft.**

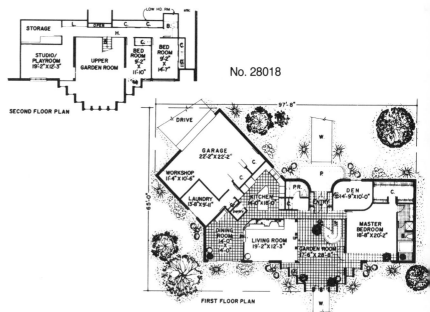

No. 28018

Lakeshore Home Spells Livable

No. 10138

Take the luxurious features of a second floor sun-deck, ground level patio, and spacious living and family rooms; combine with four full-size bed-rooms; add to this two and one-half baths in a unique and practical arrangement, a ground-floor utility room and a well-grouped kitchen, and you've got a home that's both livable and dazzling.

**Upper level — 1,196 sq. ft.
Lower level — 1,196 sq. ft.**

No. 10138

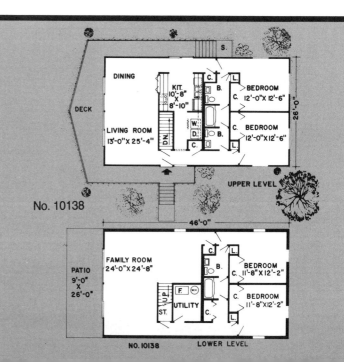

Foyer Isolates Bedroom Wing

No. 20087

Don't worry about waking up the kids. They'll sleep soundly in a quiet atmosphere away from main living areas, on a hallway off the foyer of this charming one-level. Sunny and open, the living room features a window-wall flanking a massive fireplace, and access to a deck at the rear of the house. The adjoining dining room boasts recessed ceilings, and pass-through convenience to the kitchen and breakfast room. You'll find the master suite, tucked behind the two-car garage for maximum quiet, a pleasant retreat that includes double vanities, a walk-in closet, and both shower and tub.

First floor — 1,568 sq. ft.
Basement — 1,568 sq. ft.
Garage — 484 sq. ft.

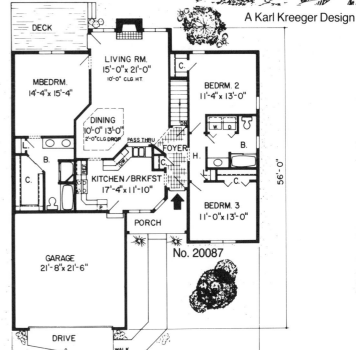

A Karl Kreeger Design

DECK

LIVING RM.
15'-0"x 21'-0"
10'-0" CLG. HT.

MBEDRM.
14'-4"x 15'-4"

BEDRM. 2
11'-4"x 13'-0"

DINING
10'-0"x 13'-0"
2'-0" CLG DROP

PASS THRU

FOYER

KITCHEN/BRKFST
17'-4"x 11'-10"

BEDRM. 3
11'-0"x 13'-0"

PORCH

GARAGE
21'-8"x 21'-6"

No. 20087

56'-0"

DRIVE

WALK

Greenhouse Brightens Compact Three-bedroom

No. 20053

The L-shaped living and dining room features a cozy fireplace for wintertime and opens onto the deck for summertime fun. Adjoining the deck is the greenhouse which will be enjoyed year round. The kitchen features breakfast space, a built-in desk, pantry and a compact laundry area. Also on the first floor is the master bedroom with its private, five-piece bath. Both the entry foyer and the living room are open to the second floor creating a bridge between the two second floor bedrooms. In addition to the second floor's two bedrooms, full bath and linen closet, there is access to a large storage area under the eaves.

First floor–1,088 sq. ft.
Second floor–541 sq. ft.
Greenhouse–72 sq. ft.
Garage–473 sq. ft.

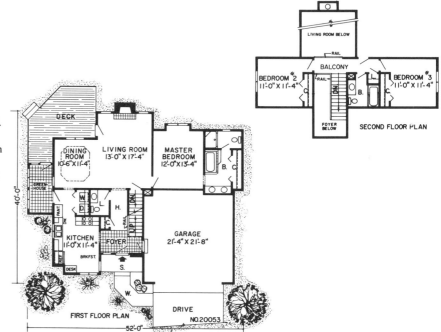

Master Bedroom At Entry Level

No. 20060

Angulation best describes this contemporary design. At the front entrance, an attractive half-circle window transom is built above the door. Through the foyer, the kitchen is centered perfectly between the breakfast area and a more formal dining area. The breakfast room leads onto a very large wooden deck through sliding glass doors. From the breakfast room, the living room comes complete with a wood-burning fireplace, plus the extra feature of a sloping, open beamed ceiling. This design offers the master bedroom on the entry level, and it has a dressing area, a walk-in closet and a full bath. The second level offers two bedrooms with a full bath and a convenient cedar closet.

First floor–1,279 sq. ft.
Second floor–502 sq. ft.
Basement–729 sq. ft.
Garage–470 sq. ft.

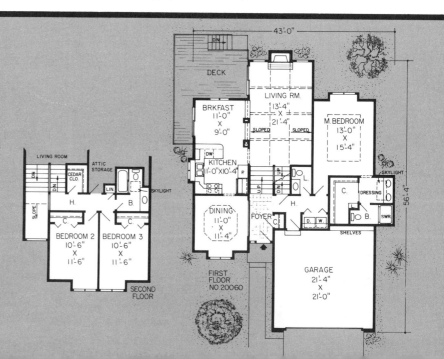

Bridge Adds Interior Drama

No. 20059

An upstairs bridge overlooks the dynamic foyer and living room of this well-planned home. Both the living room and the dining room have access to a large backyard deck. The conveniently located kitchen has an adjoining breakfast area, a large pantry and washer/dryer located close by. The master bedroom, on the first floor, is a treat with its unusual window treatment and spacious bath and walk-in closet. Two bedrooms on the second level are separated by the balcony. Another bath, as well as plenty of closet space, is upstairs. In addition, the second floor is mostly built into the existing roof structure for lower construction costs.

First floor-1,234 sq. ft.
Second floor-520 sq. ft.
Basement-1,234 sq. ft.
Garage-477 sq. ft.

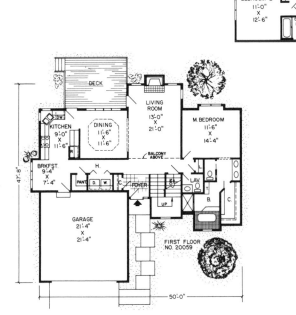

Master Suite On A Private Level

No. 26810

Its four floors staggered at half-level intervals, this house is both architecturally fascinating and effectively planned. Entering on the third level, one sees dining and sunken living rooms ahead on a space-expanded diagonal. The corridor kitchen extends into a traffic-free space open to living areas on one side, and a deck makes the outdoors a natural part of all social areas. One half-level higher, the master bedroom connects to a study and deck plus a luxurious compartmented bathroom. On the second level, two smaller bedrooms have a landing with a bath and convenient laundry. The lowest level of the house is a recreation basement. Framing of this house uses large studs and rafters spaced at wide intervals to cut construction time, reduce the need for lumber and open deeper gaps for thicker insulating batts.

Upper level—1,423 sq. ft.
Lower level—1,420 sq. ft.
Garage—478 sq. ft.

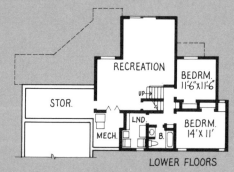

Country Living

No. 26860

The design of this comfortable home says country living at its best. Constructed of energy-efficient wood for beauty and warmth, this home offers room for a growing family at an affordable price. The master bedroom and bath are on the second floor with a small deck. Two bedrooms and a bath are separated from the living area on the main level by the foyer. The living room and family room both have their own deck. A large eat-in kitchen and separate dining room complete this energy conscious design.

First floor-1,434 sq. ft.
Second floor-369 sq. ft.

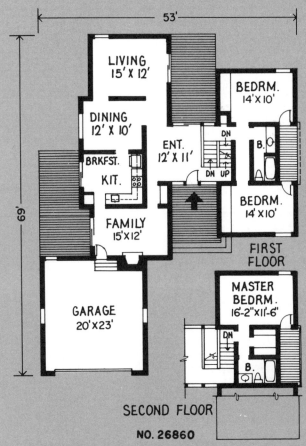

LIVING 15' X 12'

BEDRM. 14' 10'

DINING 12' X 10'

ENT. 12' X 11'

DN

B.

BRKFST.

KIT.

DN UP

BEDRM. 14' 10'

FAMILY 15'X12'

FIRST FLOOR

53'

69'

GARAGE 20'x23'

MASTER BEDRM. 16'-2"x11'-6"

DN

B.

SECOND FLOOR

NO. 26860

Striking Entryway

No. 20054

An expansive entrance with a cathedral ceiling in the living room offers a view of the entire house. The washer and dryer are located in the bedroom area, and even with small square footage, this home has a large master bedroom area and separate dining room and breakfast area. The deck is partially under the roof. The roof framing on this plan is simple, but the exterior is still interesting with its large window and the farmhouse porch.

First floor — 1,461 sq. ft.
Basement — 1,435 sq. ft.
Garage — 528 sq. ft.

Beamed Ceiling and Corner Fireplace Add Unusual Accents

No. 10506

This home's spacious living room will be enjoyed by guests and family alike. In addition to the beamed ceiling and corner fireplace, it opens onto a large, angled deck and has its own wetbar. The living room also adjoins the dining room and shares an eating bar with the kitchen. This well designed kitchen provides plenty of work space and storage plus room for extra cooks. The three bedrooms complete the floor plan. The master bedroom has a full-wall closet, five-piece bath plus direct access to the deck through sliding glass doors.

First floor — 1,893 sq. ft.
Garage — 494 sq. ft.

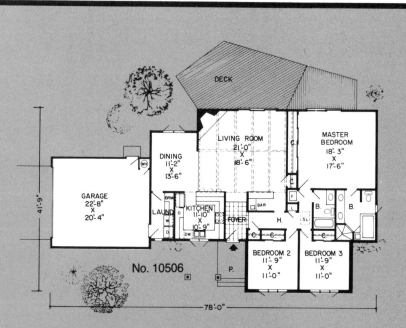

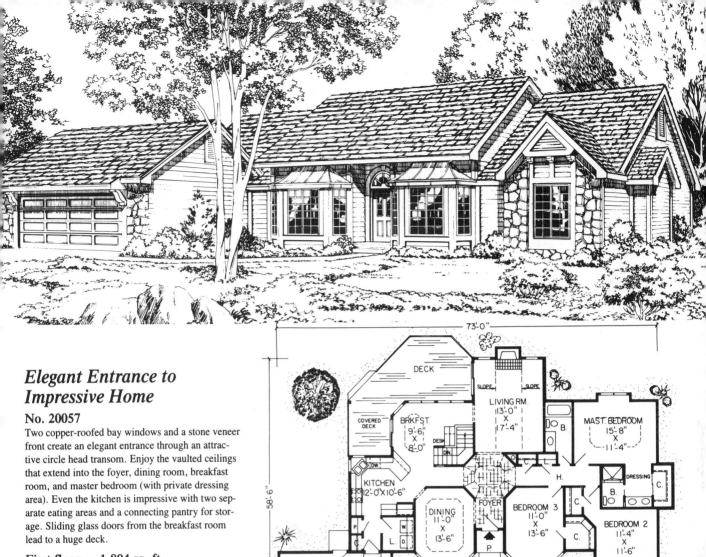

Elegant Entrance to Impressive Home

No. 20057

Two copper-roofed bay windows and a stone veneer front create an elegant entrance through an attractive circle head transom. Enjoy the vaulted ceilings that extend into the foyer, dining room, breakfast room, and master bedroom (with private dressing area). Even the kitchen is impressive with two separate eating areas and a connecting pantry for storage. Sliding glass doors from the breakfast room lead to a huge deck.

First floor — 1,804 sq. ft.
Basement — 1,804 sq. ft.
Garage & workshop — 499 sq. ft.

73'-0"

58'-6"

DECK

SLOPE   SLOPE

LIVING RM.
13'-0"
X
17'-4"

MAST. BEDROOM
15'-8"
X
11'-4"

COVERED
DECK

BRKFST.
9'-6"
X
8'-0"

B.

DRESSING

KITCHEN
12'-0" X 10'-6"

H.

B.

C.

FOYER

BEDROOM 3
11'-0"
X
13'-6"

C.

C.

DINING
11'-0"
X
13'-6"

BEDROOM 2
11'-4"
X
11'-6"

C.

P.

No. 20057

A Karl Kreeger Design

GARAGE
21'-8"
X
22'-0"

Ranch Incorporates Victorian Features

No. 20058

This wonderful Victorian-featured ranch design incorporates many luxury conveniences normally offered in larger designs. The master bedroom is expansive in size, with an oversized full bath complete with a walk-in closet, an individual shower, a full tub, and two-sink wash basin. A large kitchen area is offered with a built-in island for working convenience. The kitchen also has its own breakfast area. Located next to the kitchen is a half-bath. The living area is separated from the dining room by a half-partitioned wall. Two large bedrooms complete the interior of the house. They have large closets and share a full bath. A two-car garage and a wood deck complete the options listed in this design.

First floor-1,787 sq. ft.
Basement-1,787 sq. ft.
Garage-484 sq. ft.

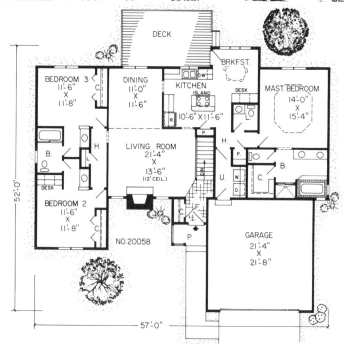

Three Bedroom Features Open Plan And Cathedral Ceilings

No. 20051

The tiled foyer of this charming home rises to the second floor balcony and is lighted by a circular window. To the right of the foyer are the powder room, the compact laundry area and the entrance to the well-designed kitchen. The efficiency of the kitchen with its central island, built-in desk and pantry is augmented by the bump-out window over the sink and the adjacent breakfast area with its sloped ceiling and sliding-door access to the deck. The combined living and dining room features a fireplace, built-in bookcase and sloped ceiling.

First floor-1,285 sq. ft.
Second floor-490 sq. ft.
Basement-1,285 sq. ft.
Garage-495 sq. ft.

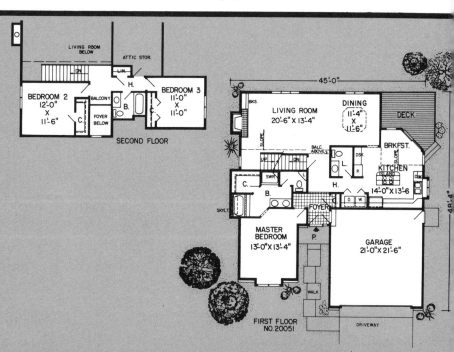

Attractive Floor Plan Enhances Traditional Design

No. 20056

This three-bedroom, two-bath home offers comfort and style. The master bedroom is complete with its own bath with a skylight. A beamed ceiling and fireplace in the living area add charm to the more traditional family room. A spacious laundry room adjoins the kitchen and breakfast area. The country-style front porch and large front windows in the breakfast and dining rooms lend a cozy atmosphere to this eye-catcher.

First floor-1,669 sq. ft.
Basement-1,669 sq. ft.
Garage-482 sq. ft.

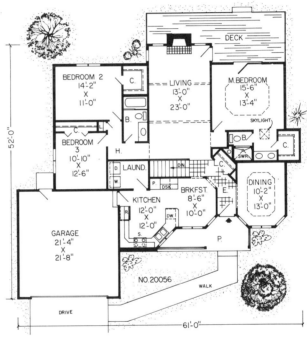

Inexpensive Ranch Design

No. 20062

This simple but inexpensive ranch design has a brick and vertical siding exterior. The interior has a well set-up kitchen area with its own breakfast area by a large picture window. A formal dining room is located near the kitchen. The living room has one open beam across a sloping ceiling. A large hearth is in front of a wood-burning fireplace. Inside the front entrance a tiled foyer incorporates closet space and has many different room entrances through which an individual can walk. Three bedrooms are offered in this design. The master bedroom has an extremely large bath area with its own walk-in closet. Two other bedrooms share a full bath. There is also a linen closet and a closet for the washer and dryer area. A two-car garage is offered in this plan.

Main floor-1,500 sq. ft.
Basement-1,500 sq. ft.
Garage-482 sq. ft.

Options Abound In Traditional Design

No. 20061

A lot can be said about this unique design. Its exterior is vertical siding, shake shingle and rock and the large round picture window sets this design off from all others. The interior is delightfully planned beginning with the kitchen that has a built-in pantry, refrigerator, dishwasher and range. Additionally the kitchen has a breakfast bar, an open-beamed ceiling with a skylight plus a breakfast area with lots of windows. A very formal dining room is partitioned from the living room. The living room has two open beams running down a sloping ceiling, and a wood-burning fireplace. There is a laundry closet and the foyer area also has a closet. Three bedrooms share a full bath. The master bedroom has an open-beamed, sloping ceiling with a spacious bath area and a walk-in closet.

First floor-1,667 sq. ft.
Basement-1,657 sq. ft.
Garage-472 sq. ft.

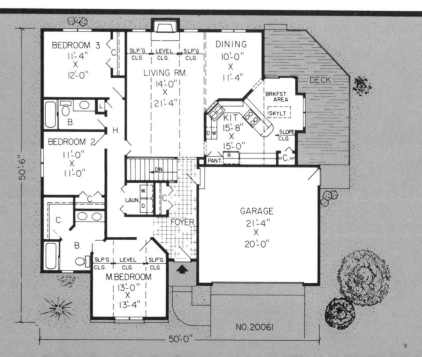

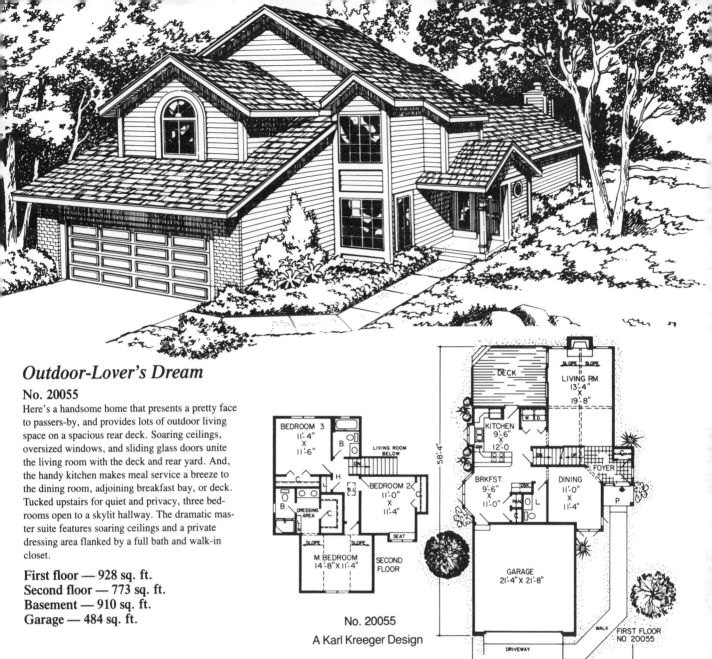

Outdoor-Lover's Dream

No. 20055

Here's a handsome home that presents a pretty face to passers-by, and provides lots of outdoor living space on a spacious rear deck. Soaring ceilings, oversized windows, and sliding glass doors unite the living room with the deck and rear yard. And, the handy kitchen makes meal service a breeze to the dining room, adjoining breakfast bay, or deck. Tucked upstairs for quiet and privacy, three bedrooms open to a skylit hallway. The dramatic master suite features soaring ceilings and a private dressing area flanked by a full bath and walk-in closet.

First floor — 928 sq. ft.
Second floor — 773 sq. ft.
Basement — 910 sq. ft.
Garage — 484 sq. ft.

No. 20055

A Karl Kreeger Design

A Heat-Gathering Garden Room

No. 26820

One of the smallest rooms in this house, the garden room, might turn out to be the most important. Oriented south or southwest, its skylight and insulating glass wall gather sunlight that will not only make plants thrive but will also help heat the house. Sliding glass doors can be opened to draw this heat into the living areas to supplement the conventional mechanical system. The design guarantees many pleasures for outdoor enthusiasts: two decks, skylighting, year-around green views of the garden room, even a potting room by the back door. The core of the plan is a "keeping room" combining kitchen, breakfast area and family area by a fireplace. Each living area has three exposures for exhilerating light and summer comfort.

First level – 1,618 sq. ft.
Second level – 907 sq. ft.
Basement – 1,621 sq. ft.
Garage – 552 sq. ft.
Garden room – 98 sq. ft.

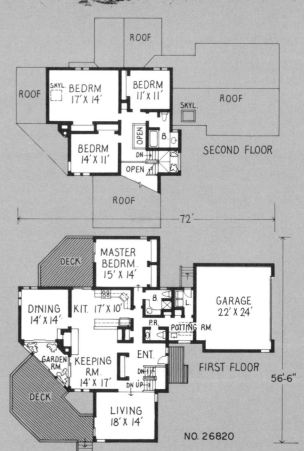

SECOND FLOOR

ROOF		
SKYL. BEDRM 17' X 14'	BEDRM 11' X 11'	
ROOF		
BEDRM 14' X 11'	OPEN B. DN OPEN	
ROOF		

72'

FIRST FLOOR

DECK
MASTER BEDRM. 15' X 14'
GARAGE 22' X 24'
DINING 14' X 14'
KIT. 17' X 10'
B.
POTTING RM.
P.R.
GARDEN RM.
KEEPING RM. 14' X 17'
ENT.
DN UP
DECK
LIVING 18' X 14'

56'-6"

NO. 26820

Three Bedrooms And A Loft

No. 26890

Words alone cannot adequately describe this marvelous three bedroom home. The main floor is on three levels with kitchen, breakfast nook, dining area and conversation pit on the lower level. Upon entering this home, you are treated to a view of the well designed atrium and then to your left is a family room. The third level shows two large bedrooms sharing a bath and a centrally located laundry room. The master bedroom is also on this level and is lavishly complimented with a private bath which includes it's own whirlpool and large dressing room. Completing the picture is a spiral stair leading to the loft which overlooks the atrium. Earth berming contributes to the energy efficient qualities of this fine home.

First floor - 2431 sq. ft.
Loft - 312 sq. ft.
Garage - 701 sq. ft.

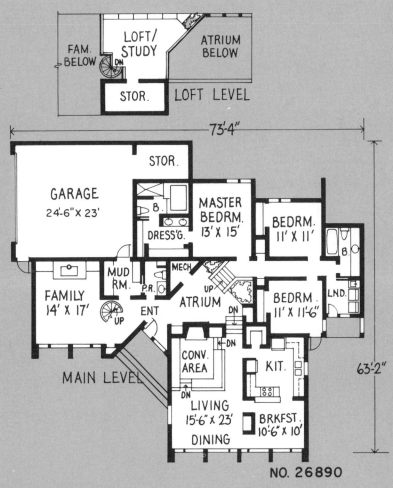

LOFT LEVEL

MAIN LEVEL

NO. 26890

Rear Deck Adds Outdoor Living Space

No. 10746

This three-bedroom beauty boasts an updated wood and brick exterior, over-sized windows, and a sheltered entry you'll appreciate on a rainy day. If you do get caught in a downpour, step down the entry hall past the formal dining room to the two-story great room, and dry off by the fire. The handy kitchen, just across the counter from a cozy breakfast nook, features a built-in pantry and planning desk, just steps away from the garage entry. And, the first-floor master suite with its own private bath is an added convenience you're sure to enjoy. Two upstairs bedrooms share a full bath and a balcony vantage of the great room below.

**First floor — 1,753 sq. ft.
Second floor — 549 sq. ft.
Garage — 513 sq. ft.**

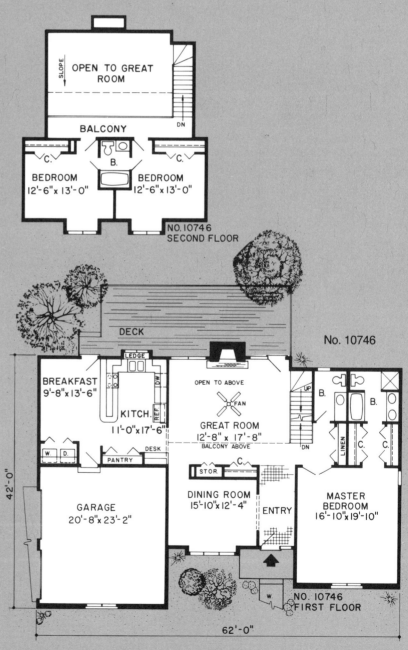

Family Living on Two Levels

No. 20090

Stacked window towers grace the facade of this spacious, four-bedroom classic with attached garage. The formal parlor and dining room right off the foyer feature decorative ceilings. Family areas at the rear of the house are arranged for convenient access to the island kitchen. You'll love the skylit breakfast room with its surrounding outdoor deck. And, when there's a chill in the air, you'll appreciate the coziness of a fireplace in the family room. Send the kids upstairs at bedtime, where three bedrooms share a roomy, skylit bath with double vanities. You can enjoy your first-floor master suite that includes double vanities, a huge, walk-in closet, and an elegant recessed ceiling.

First floor — 1,888 sq. ft.
Second floor — 833 sq. ft.
Basement — 1,888 sq. ft.

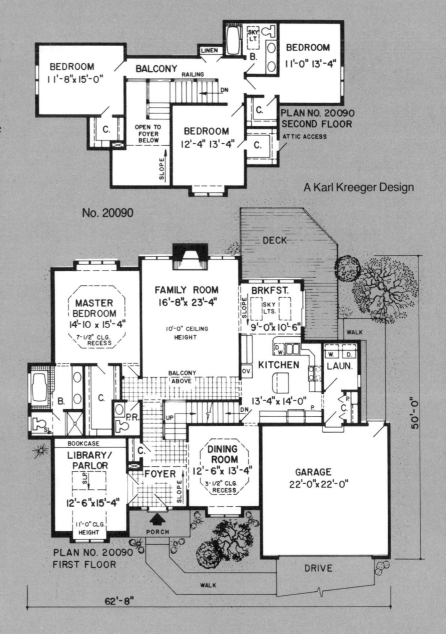

A Karl Kreeger Design

Order Your Blueprints Now!

How Many Sets of Plans Will You Need?

Experience shows that the **Standard 8-Set Construction Package** is best. You'll speed every step of construction and avoid costly building errors by ordering enough sets to go around. And, usually everyone wants their own set. Consider your lending institution, general contractor and all of his subcontractors; foundation; framing; electrical; plumbing; heating/air conditioning; drywall; and finish carpenters – as well as a set for you.

Minimum 5-Set Construction Package gives an efficient planner a choice. Although eight sets relieves you of worry about sets being lost or ruined on the job, you can carefully hand sets down as work progresses and might have enough copies to go around with the five set package.

One Complete Set of Blueprints lets you study the blueprints, so you can plan your dream home. But, keep in mind . . . One set is never enough for actually building your home.

Here's What You Get!

Our accurate and complete blueprints contain everything you need to begin building your dream home:

- Front, rear, and both side views of the house (elevations)
- Floor plans for all levels
- Roof plan
- Foundation plan
- Universal Plot plan
- Typical wall sections (sectional slices throughout the home)
- Kitchen and bathroom cabinet details
- Fireplace details (where applicable)
- Stair details (where applicable)
- Locations of electrical fixtures and components
- Specifications and contract form
- Energy Conservation Specifications Guide

Please note: All plans are drawn to conform with one or more of the industry's major national building standards. However, local building codes may differ from national standards. We recommend that you check with your local building officials.

Remember to Order a Materials List!

Our materials list for your home plan will help you save money! This helpful list is available at a small additional charge and gives the quantity, dimensions and specifications for all major materials needed to build your home (small hardware like nails, screws, etc. are omitted). With this valuable list, you'll get faster and more accurate bids from your contractors and building suppliers. In addition, you'll avoid paying for unnecessary materials and waste. Materials lists are available for all home plans except where otherwise indicated, but can only be ordered along with a set of home plans. **Please Note:** Due to differences in local building codes, regional requirements and builder preferences . . . electrical, plumbing, and heating/air conditioning equipment requirements are not provided as part of the material list.

(handwritten note) You'll get results fast -- and save money, too!! -- with our complete, accurate professional blueprints. I know you'll love your new home. Sincerely, Whitney Garlinghouse

Discover Reverse Plans at no extra charge!

You may find that a particular house would suit your taste or fit your lot better if it were "reversed." A reverse plan turns the design end-for-end. That is, if the garage is shown on the left side and the bedrooms on the right, the reverse plan will place the garage on the right side and the bedrooms on the left. To see quickly how a design will look in reverse, hold your book up to a mirror.

If you want to build your Garlinghouse Home in reverse, then order your plans reversed. You'll receive one mirror-image, reversed set of plans (with "backwards" lettering and dimensions) as a master guide for you and your builder. The remaining sets in your order are then sent as shown in our publication for ease in reading the lettering and dimensions. These "as shown" sets will all be marked "REVERSED" with a special stamp to eliminate confusion on the job site. **Reverse plans are available only on multiple set orders.**

Modify Your Garlinghouse Home Plan!

Your custom dream home can be as wonderful as you want. Easy modifications, such as minor non-structural changes and simple building material substitutions, can be made by any competent builder without the need for blueprint revisions.

However, if you are considering making major changes to your design, we strongly recommend that you seek the services of an architect or professional designer. Even these expensive professional services will cost less with our complete, detailed blueprints as a starting point.

Reproducible Mylars Make Plan Modifications Easier!

Ask about our Reproducible Mylars for your home design. They're inexpensive and provide a design professional with a way to make custom changes directly to our home plans and then print as many copies as you need of the modified design. It's a perfect way to create a truly custom home! Prices range from $340 to $415 plus mailing charges. **Call 1-800-235-5700 to find out more about our Reproducible Mylars.** Please Note: Reproducible mylars are not available for plans numbered 90,000 and above, or for plans numbered 19,000 through 19,999.

PRICE SCHEDULE

One Complete Set of Blueprints	$125.00
Minimum Construction Package (5 Sets)	$170.00
Standard Construction Package (8 Sets)	$200.00
Each Additional Set Ordered With One of the Above Packages	$20.00
Materials List (with plan order only)	$15.00

Prices are subject to change without notice

Important Shipping Information

Your order receives our immediate attention! However, please allow 10 working days from our receipt of your order for normal UPS delivery. You can call in your credit card order TOLL FREE and avoid the additional mail delay for your order to reach us.

Note that UPS will deliver **only** to street addresses and rural route delivery boxes and **not** to Post Office Box Numbers. Please print your complete street address. If no one is home during the day, you may use your work address to insure prompt delivery.

We **MUST** ship First Class Mail to Alaska or Hawaii, APO, FPO, or a Post Office Box. Please note the higher cost for First Class Mail.

Domestic Shipping

UPS Ground Service	$5.75
First Class Mail	$7.75
Express Delivery Service	Call for details 1-800-235-5700

International Orders & Shipping

If you are ordering from outside the United States, please note that your check, money order, or international money transfer **must be payable in U.S. currency.**

We ship all international orders via Air Parcel Post for delivery (surface mail is extremely slow). Please refer to the schedule below for the mailing charge on your order and substitute this amount for the usual mailing charges for domestic orders.

International Shipping

	One Set	Multiple Sets
Canada	$5.75	$9.75
Mexico & Caribbean Nations	$16.50	$39.50
All other Nations	$18.50	$50.00

Canadian orders are now duty free.

For Fastest Service...
ORDER TOLL FREE
1-800-235-5700

Connecticut, Alaska, Hawaii, & all foreign residents call 1-203-632-0500. Please have your credit card and order code number ready when you call.

FAX: 1-203-632-0712

BLUEPRINT ORDER FORM

GARLINGHOUSE

Send your Check, Money Order or **Credit Card information** to:
The Garlinghouse Company
34 Industrial Park Place, P.O. Box 1717
Middletown, CT 06457

Order Code No.

H90B4

PLAN NO._____

QTY. ☐ as shown ☐ reversed

_____ 1 Set Pkg. **($125.00)** . . . . . . = $_____

_____ 5 Set Pkg. **($170.00)** . . . . . . = $_____

_____ 8 Set Pkg. **($200.00)** . . . . . . = $_____

_____ Additional Sets **($20.00 ea.)** . = $_____

_____ Materials List **($15.00)** . . . . . = $_____

Shipping Charges (see charts) . . . . . = $_____

Subtotal . . . . = $_____

Sales Tax* . . . . = $_____
  *Kansas residents add 5.25% sales tax
  Connecticut residents add 8% sales tax

TOTAL AMOUNT ENCLOSED $ [   ]

Thank You for Your Order!

BILL TO:

Name_____
Please Print

Address_____

City & State_____ Zip_____

Phone (_____)_____

SHIP TO:

Name_____
Please Print

Address_____

City & State_____ Zip_____

Phone (_____)_____

METHOD OF PAYMENT: ☐ Check ☐ Money Order

Charge to: ☐ Visa ☐ MasterCard

[| | | | | | | | | | | | | | |]

Signature_____ Exp. Date_____ /____

Builder's Library

The books on this page were written with the professional home builder in mind. They are all comprehensive information sources for contractors or for those beginners who wish to build like contractors.

▶ **2600. Building Underground** This has been compiled on earth sheltered homes, built all over North America— homes that are spacious, attractive and comfortable in every way. These homes are more energy efficient than above ground houses. Physical security, low operating costs, and noise reduction further enhance their attractiveness. 304 pp.; 85 photos; 112 illus.; Rodale Press (paperback) **$14.95**

◀ **2518. Build Your Own Home** An authoritative guide on how to be your own general contractor. This book goes through the step-by-step process of building a house with special emphasis on the business aspects such as financing, scheduling, permits, insurance, and more. Furthermore, it gives you an understanding of what to expect out of your various subcontractors so that you can properly orchestrate their work. 112 pp.; Holland House (paperback) **$12.95**

◀ **2596. How To Get It Built** No matter how small or how large your construction project is, building will be easier with this informative guidebook. This text was prepared for people involved in building on a non-professional basis. Guidelines have been carefully prepared to follow step-by-step construction-cost savings methods. Written by an architect/contractor, this book offers home construction owners the planning, construction and cost saving solutions to his own building needs. 238 pp.; over 300 illus.; (paperback) Hashagen **$18.00**

from the Leading Publishers in the Do-It-Yourself Industry!!!

▶ **2508. Modern Plumbing** All aspects of plumbing installation, service, and repair are presented here in illustrated, easy-to-follow text. This book contains all the information needed for vocational competence, including the most up-to-date tools, materials, and practices. 300 pp.; over 700 illus.; Goodheart-Willcox (hardcover) **$19.96**

▲ **2607. Radon: The Invisible Threat** This book will help you become more aware of this potentially harmful situation, with easy, step-by-step instructions, to help you detect the presence of Radon Gas in your home. Also included is a simple test that could prevent your home from becoming a victim of this environmental hazard. 224 pp.; Rodale (paperback) **$12.95**

▲ **2546. Blueprint Reading for Construction** This combination text and workbook shows and tells how to read residential, commercial, and light industrial prints. With an abundance of actual drawings from industry, you learn step by step about each component of a set of blueprints, including even cost estimating. 336 pp.; Goodheart-Willcox (spiral bound) **$21.28**

▲ **2570. Modern Masonry** Everything you will ever need to know about concrete, masonry, and brick, is included in this book. Forms construction, concrete reinforcement, proper foundation construction, and bricklaying are among the topics covered in step-by-step detail. An excellent all-round reference and guide. 256 pp.; 700 illus.; Goodheart-Willcox (hardcover) **$19.96**

▼ **2514. The Underground House Book** For anyone seriously interested in building and living in an underground home, this book tells it all. Aesthetic considerations, building codes, site planning, financing, insurance, planning and decorating considerations, maintenance costs, soil, excavation, landscaping, water considerations, humidity control, and specific case histories are among the many facets of underground living dealt with in this publication. 208 pp.; 140 illus.; Garden Way (paperback) **$10.95**

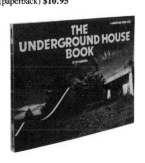

▼ **2504. Architecture, Residential Drawing and Design** An excellent text that explains all the fundamentals on how to create a complete set of construction drawings. Specific areas covered include proper design and planning considerations, foundation plans, floor plans, elevations, stairway details, electrical plans, plumbing plans, etc. 492 pp.; over 800 illus.; Goodheart-Willcox (hardcover) **$26.60**

▲ **2510. Modern Carpentry** A complete guide to the "nuts and bolts" of building a home. This book explains all about building materials, framing, trim work, insulation, foundations, and much more. A valuable text and reference guide. 492 pp.; over 1400 illus.; Goodheart-Willcox (hardcover) **$25.20**

▲ **2506. House Wiring Simplified** This book teaches all the fundamentals of modern house wiring; shows how it's done with easy-to-understand drawings. A thorough guide to the materials and practices for safe, efficient installation of home electrical systems. 176 pp.; 384 illus.; Goodheart-Willcox (hardcover) **$10.00**

▼ **2544. Solar Houses** An examination of solar homes from the standpoint of lifestyle. This publication shows you through photographs, interviews, and practical information, what a solar lifestyle involves, how owners react to it, and what the bottom-line economics are. Included are 130 floor plans and diagrams which give you a clear idea of how various "active" and "passive" solar systems work. 160 pp.; 370 illus. Pantheon (paperback) **$9.95**

▼ **2592. How to Design & Build Decks & Patios** Learn how to create decks and patios to suit every type of lot and lifestyle. This fully illustrated source book includes detailed information on design and construction as well as special charts on building and paving materials. Full color, 112 pp.; Ortho (paperback) **$7.95**

2586. How to Design & Remodel Kitchens — This book takes you through steps beginning with evaluating your present kitchen and designing a new one to hiring a contractor or doing the work yourself. It offers solid information on the things you need to know to create the kitchen that best fits your needs. Full color charts and illustrations. 96 pp.; Successful (paperback) **$6.95**

▲ **2612. Baths** With charts and illustrations provided, BATHS gives tips on new storage ideas, suggestions on whirlpools and saunas, and a tour of 30 of the best-designed baths in the United States. Assistance is provided in the form of addresses of leading manufacturers and helpful organizations, to aid you in the remodeling of your bath. 154 pp.; Rodale (paperback) **$12.95**

▼ **2611. Tile It Up! Plumb It Up!** Using the many illustrations and the easy steps included in this valuable book, you will be able to work just like the professionals. This book provides step-by-step instructions on plumbing and tiling, enabling the do-it-yourselfer to complete these projects with a minimum of time providing maximum results. 43 pp.; XS Books (paperback) **$6.95**

▼ **2516. Building Consultant** The new home buyer's bible to home construction. This encyclopedia of home building explains in comprehensive detail about all the various elements that go into a completed house. It enables you to deal with the construction of your new home in a meaningful way that will avoid costly errors, whether you use a contractor or build it yourself. 188 pp.; Holland House (paperback) **$12.95**

Builder's Library order form

Yes! send me the following books:

book order no.		price
_____	$	_____
_____	$	_____
_____	$	_____
_____	$	_____
_____	$	_____
_____	$	_____

Postage & handling (one book only)	$	1.75
Add 50¢ postage & handling for each additional book	$	_____
Canada add $1.50 per book	$	_____
Resident sales tax: Kansas (5.25%)	$	_____
Connecticut (8%)	$	_____
TOTAL ENCLOSED	$	_____

No C.O.D. orders accepted; U.S. funds only.
prices subject to change without notice

My Shipping Address is:
(please print)

Name _____

Address _____

City _____

State _____ Zip _____

Send your order to:
(With check or money order enclosed)

The Garlinghouse Company
34 Industrial Park Place
P.O. Box 1717
Middletown, Connecticut 06457

For Faster Service . . .
CHARGE IT! (203) 632-0500

☐ MasterCard ☐ Visa

Card # |_|_|_|_|_|_|_|_|_|_|_|_|_|_|_|

Exp. Date _____

Signature _____

▼ **2604. The Low Maintenance House** At last, an idea-packed book that will save you thousands of hours on home maintenance. It's an essential planning guide for anyone building a home. Discover new as well as time-tested techniques and products for cutting down the time, and slashing the money you spend to clean and repair your home . . . from roof to basement, from front yard to backyard garden. This book will earn its price, and your thanks, over and over again. 314 pp.; Rodale (hardback) **$19.95**

▲ **2605. Contracting Your Home** With over 150 illustrations, this guide offers many suggestions and ideas on contracting your own home. Many forms you can copy and re-use are provided, giving checklists and a glossary of terms used by the professionals, as well as all the necessary estimating forms. 279 pp.; Betterway Publications (paperback) **$18.95**

▼ **2608. Cut Your Electric Bill in Half** With assistance from this book, you may be able to cut your future electric bills by up to 80%! With tables outlining the effective use of all your home appliances and recommendations for money-saving appliances, this book is a MUST for the budget-conscious household. 160 pp.; Rodale (paperback) **$9.95**

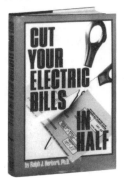

▲ **2542. Designing and Building a Solar House** Written by one of America's foremost authorities on solar architecture. It is a practical "how-to" guide that clearly demonstrates the most sensible ways to marry good house design with contemporary solar technology. Included is a thorough discussion of both "active" and "passive" solar systems, and even a listing of today's leading solar homes. 288 pp.; 400 illus.; Garden Way (paperback) **$15.95**

▼ **2610. The Backyard Builder** Here is a step-by-step guide for over 150 projects for the gardener and homeowner, accompanied by over 100 photos, 400 illustrations, materials lists and shopping guides. You are sure to find many useful, attractive projects that the entire family can help with. 656 pp.; Rodale (hardcover) **$21.95**

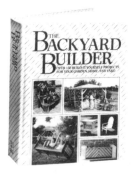

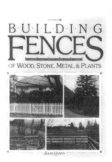

▲ **2606. Building Fences** With emphasis on function and style, this guide to a wide variety of fence-building is a solid how-to book. With easy-to-read instructions, and plenty of illustrations, this book is a must for the professional and the do-it-yourselfer. 188 pp.; Williamson Publishing (paperback) **$13.95**